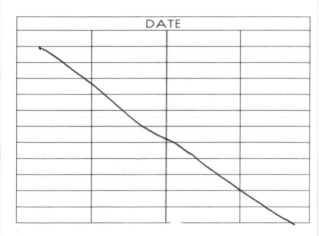

DATE			

The Allegory of Adventure

Also by Tom Artin:

Earth Talk: Independent Voices on the Environment

The Allegory of Adventure

Reading Chrétien's
Erec and *Yvain*

Tom Artin

Lewisburg

Bucknell University Press
London: Associated University Presses

Associated University Presses, Inc.
Cranbury, New Jersey 08512

Associated University Presses
108 New Bond Street
London W1Y OQX, England

Library of Congress Cataloging in Publication Data

Artin, Tom.
    The allegory of adventure: reading Chrétien's *Erec* and *Yvain*.

    Bibliography: p.
    1. Chrestien de Troyes, 12th cent. Erec et Enide.
2. Chrestien de Troyes, 12th cent. Chevalier au lyon.
I. Title.
PQ1445.E7A8   841'.1   73-687
ISBN 0-8387-1257-6

The author thanks Princeton University Press for permission to quote selections from Erich Auerbach, *Mimesis: The Representation of Reality in Western Literature,* translated by Willard R. Trask (copyright 1953 by Princeton University Press; Princeton Paperback, 1968), pp. 73–139. Reprinted by permission of Princeton University Press.

PRINTED IN THE UNITED STATES OF AMERICA

for

E. Harris Harbison

in memory

Contents

Preface

This book has its genesis in the enthusiasm for medieval art kindled in me by D. W. Robertson, Jr., in his undergraduate course in Chaucer at Princeton in the fifties. It was especially in the small weekly discussion sections, where there was the chance to question, challenge, and sometimes grapple with the lecturer, that one got the feel of this strange medieval world, the "Dark Ages," established on a system of thought and value one rejected almost out of hand, yet fascinating, seductive even, for its crystal logic, its trenchant sense for the reality of life, its utterly shimmering ideals transforming the commonest events. Robbie had a miraculous way of revealing in the driest doctrine a surprising illumination of the human condition—of removing an encrustation of age which had made brilliant, humane men and women of the Middle Ages appear dour, awkward, and silly. Paradoxically, it was by insisting on the distinction between their historical and philosophical context and our own, by showing how the experience of life was essentially different in the Middle Ages, that he made the culture so vividly accessible. He had a raucous, often ribald laugh, which came from deep inside his body, but from deep inside his spirit too, which taught as well as anything about the wholeness of medieval life.

I wasn't a good student in those days. I had frivolous interests outside my studies, one of which was playing jazz trombone, another of which was reading books that hadn't been assigned instead of those that had. Nevertheless, I had some pretty strong opinions regarding Chaucer, and Robbie (in violation of the rule that only graduate students were worth talking to) always took them seriously, even though I was only an undergraduate. It is true that his way of taking one's opinion seriously was often disputatious, sometimes downright sarcastic. I was reading a lot of Hawthorne at the time, and Robbie, who is comically intolerant of anything that strikes him as falsely sentimental, needled me every chance he got about this particular aberration of taste and judgment. I remember the heavy-handed irony, and then the infectious guffaw with which he conceded that Chaucer and Hawthorne had after all much in common . . . in that they had both run customs houses. I went on reading Hawthorne undaunted, but it was Chaucer I came back to in graduate school, once more under Robbie's tutelage.

Whenever a man's work is as seminal as Robbie's has been for medieval literary studies, the acknowledgments of indebtedness prefaced to books that follow to gather the fruit and glean the leavings come to seem hackneyed and perfunctory. The true acknowledgment is of course in the work itself, in which whatever debt is real shines through in any case. But let it be said that whatever new ground is glimpsed in this book is seen from the vantage of Robbie's broad shoulders—his guidance as teacher, and as writer, most notably of the remarkable *Preface to Chaucer* (Princeton, 1964). It serves as one more lesson in the love of learning to know that no one is more conscious than Robbie, in his turn, of how we all must stand on each other's shoulders to see the little we are able.

Two others deserve special mention and profound thanks for their encouragement and help in seeing this work through to publication. Thomas Roche of Princeton read and advised me on portions of the manuscript. Howard Helsinger read it all, and offered in long hours of discussion (when Beth would simply give him up and go to bed) astute criticism, good brandy, and much solace.

Acknowledgments

I would like to thank the following publishers for permission to quote from copyrighted material:

The Bobbs-Merrill Company, Inc., for selections from Saint Augustine: ON CHRISTIAN DOCTRINE, translated by D. W. Robertson, Jr., copyright © 1958, by the Liberal Arts ress, Inc., reprinted by permission of The Bobbs-Merrill Company, Inc.

University of Notre Dame Press, for selections from THE BIBLE AND THE LITURGY, copyright © 1956 by University of Notre Dame Press. Reprinted by permission.

Introduction

In his chapter on Yvain,[1] Erich Auerbach offers an illuminating description of the mystifying narrative style of Arthurian romance. The courtly ideal of the medieval aristocracy—that exclusive ethos of chivalry—was quite separate from and indeed served to conceal the real ruling function of the class, he notes. This ethos, itself a fantasy opposed to social and political reality, helps explain the appeal that the fantastical "matter of Britain" had for its courtly audience, in contradistinction to the style Auerbach identifies as more typically Christian; the *sermo humilis*, or new low style modeled on the immediacy of the Incarnation, a style in which simple reality, expressed in simple language, became the vehicle of transcendental meaning.

The courtly-chivalric ideal centered around personal election, over and above the distinction of birth. The aristocracy as a whole functioned as an exclusive social and political group, but within it "there were tendencies at

---

1. Erlich Auerbach, "The Knight Sets Forth," *Mimesis: The Representation of Reality in Western Literature*, trans. Willard Trask (Princeton, N. J., 1953), pp. 107–24. Reprinted by permission of Princeton University Press.

work which sought to base the solidarity of the group not on descent but on personal factors, on noble behavior and refined manners" (p. 121). The character of the true knight depended not on the accident of birth alone, nor on mere physical prowess, but on the development of inner values that led to personal election to knighthood. "But the most important point," Auerbach continues, "is that this emphasis on inner values by no means brought a closer approach to earthly realities. On the contrary: in part at least it was precisely the emphasis laid on the inner values of the knightly ideal which caused the connection with the real things of this earth to become ever more fictitious and devoid of practical purpose" (p. 122). The realities of social and political life had neither function nor importance in the courtly ideal; Auerbach shows how this generalization is borne out in the case of Yvain. "Calogrenant . . . has no political or historical task, nor has any other knight of Arthur's court. Here the feudal ethos serves no political function; it serves no practical reality at all; it has become absolute. It no longer has any purpose but that of self-realization" (pp. 116-17).

If the courtly audience had a taste for fantasy, we can easily understand why the stories revolving around the court of King Arthur, stories that derived in large part from bits and pieces of the mythology of the Celts, satisfied it. The reality of myth, namely, lies not in its outward fiction, but in the inner experience that the fiction expresses. Thus, fragments of a mythology that are divorced from its original structure of meaning and are reworked and rearranged, appear as the purest form of fantasy.

Yet this very appearance of meaninglessness paradoxically undoes itself. Precisely because the narrative of Arthurian romance typically gives so little sense of reality, of literal coherence, it betrays its mythological origins, and tantalizes us with intimations of hidden meanings. All the inconsistencies of plot and characterization, the curious anomalies that are apparently taken for granted by the poet, the casual tone with which marvels are narrated, rather more insistently raise questions than preclude them. Nevertheless, even when the romance gives us intimations of meaning, it is difficult to find a coherent thread on which to draw it out. Hence, although Auerbach accounts for the style of romance, he is frankly baffled by its meaning:

> The landscape is the enchanted landscape of fairy tale; we are surrounded by mystery, by secret murmurings and whispers. All the numerous castles and palaces, the battles and adventures . . . are things of fairyland: each time they appear before us as though sprung from the ground; their geographical relation to the known world, their sociological and economic foundations, remain unexplained. Even their ethical or symbolic significance can rarely be ascertained with anything approaching certainty. . . . It is sometimes possible to make out symbolic, mythological, or religious motifs . . . but it is rarely possible to define the meaning precisely, at least so long as the courtly romance remains true to type. (p. 114)

Interesting as it may be for its own sake, tracing the sources of the courtly romancers to occasionally identifiable origins in Celtic mythology and elsewhere is at best of incidental value in determining the medieval poet's meaning. Typically, source studies have ignored the problem of the poet's meaning altogether. For example, R. S. Loomis, comparing the texts of Chrétien's poems with their putative sources, apparently concludes that the poet had little interest in (not to say comprehension of) his materials; rather, he meant only to put together and dress up some good stories in terms of courtly and chivalric conventions. Coherent narrative was not his concern, only the evocation of quaint fantasy and the reflection of courtly sentiment. The casual attitude that Loomis ascribes to Chrétien suggests that the poet was a somewhat mindless link in a literary process essentially independent of him. Chrétien,

he writes, "displayed little originality . . . in the composition and shaping of his narratives, and deserves little
blame for certain strange oversights and incoherences."[2]
These "strange oversights and incoherences" are the consequence of reproducing "both the defects and the ex-
cellences of his originals. Thus only can one explain the
many mystifying characteristics of his work, the many od-
dities which suggest that he was drawing on a body of
inchoate and ultimately foreign tradition, and the exal-
tation of an alien king and court" (p. 24). Loomis correctly attributes the characteristic inconsistencies in the
Arthurian tradition to conflation of originally discrete narrative materials. But he implies that it was the poet's lack
of skill or literary sophistication that allowed these inconsistencies to remain. Loomis fails to see that because the
real coherence of meaning lies elsewhere than in the surface of his narrative, Chrétien had little interest in "recon-
ciling conflicting stories," as the scholar puts it. The ideal
of the courtly literary aesthetic was neither verisimilitude
nor narrative consistency.

Like Loomis, A. C. L. Brown leaves out of his study of
the sources of *Yvain*[3] a consideration of the kinds of literary concerns with which a twelfth-century poet would have
been likely to approach his work. As a result, he too concludes that Chrétien's attitude toward his art was rather
casual. Several of the episodes at the end of *Yvain* Brown
characterizes as "extensive insertions and additions" (p.
133), and he explains their presence by the hypothesis that
the poet "desired to bring his piece up to the length of his
Erec, Cligés and *Lancelot*" (p. 133). He may also have
wanted to throw in "a little of the knightly service to ladies
which was a convention of his time" (p. 133). Brown gives

2. Roger Sherman Loomis, *Arthurian Tradition and Chrétien de Troyes*
(New York, 1949), p. 38.
3. Arthur C. L. Brown, *Iwain: A Study in the Origins of Arthurian Romance,* Studies and Notes in Philology and Literature, vol. 8 (Boston, 1903).

us a picture not of a serious poet concerned with his art and its meaning, but of rather a hack, pandering to idle tastes. He does suggest that Chrétien deliberately "rationalized" the Celtic materials on which he drew, but he ignores the real intellectual and aesthetic context that served the poet as rational framework. He implies that he would naturally have been working toward realism, at least to the extent of reflecting real courtly life and presenting more believable situations than those of his sources. But judged on these criteria, Chrétien's work is crude. In any case, we know that the twelfth-century court artist was not striving for realism; if anything, as Auerbach shows, he was striving for the transcendance of it.

The weakness of the source studies is their tendency to focus on the sources to the neglect of the poems themselves. At the same time, interpretive criticism of the romances has proved equally inadequate because it has usually proceeded along lines of psychological analyses of character and action. But Chrétien treats character and action in a stylized and often ironic manner that cannot reveal psychological nuance. The medieval poet did not have our sense of the complex psychology of the individual. Mental processes were thought of in terms of generalized moral and emotional abstractions, which were not personal but had rather an independent, as it were Platonic reality. Although he shows characters passing through various emotional states, Chrétien is not interested in the emotions for their own sake, or in the delineation of their subtle transformations, but in the spiritual states to which those emotions attach.

Gustave Cohen, for instance, praises the poet for his finesse in describing Laudine's acceptance of her husband's murderer's suit. "Chrétien est un remarquable peintre de la femme," he writes, "et il excelle à en montrer les revirements et les ruses."[4] After having shown her tearing

---

4. Gustave Cohen, *Un grand romancier d'amour et d'aventure au XIIe siècle, Chrétien de Troyes et son oeuvre* (Paris, 1948), p. 360.

her gown, and rending her face and throat with her nails in excessive grief over her husband's death, "il s'applique avec une rare finese à la montrer, sous l'adroite pression de la suivante, glissant de la douleur à la curiosité, et de la curiosité, à l'amour" (p. 360). When we look at the text of *Yvain*, however, we find not the scene that Cohen praises as psychologically subtle, but rather a highly stylized scene, in which the poet attempts rather to represent a typical action than to describe or evoke a unique one. In fact, Cohen's praise is condescending, as though medieval poets were children, in whose works we are occasionally amazed to find first, awkward gropings toward the real achievements of later authors.

The same modern biases that lead Cohen to discover in Chrétien's work the anticipation of future artistic modes lead him to criticize Chrétien for the incoherence of the overall structure of his romances. The works are marred, he argues, by a plethora of unconnected adventures, grafted onto the major story line, determined only by random fantasy, and not arising by necessity out of the character of the protagonist. "Mais c'est là un petit défaut inhérent au genre" (p. 354), he graciously concedes. But surely it is odd to consider a characteristic which is inherent to a genre a fault. A "genre" is, after all, no more nor less than the sum of characteristics that are inherent to it. Cohen's judgment proceeds from anachronistic criteria. The historical critic's task, however, must be to discover in what terms characteristics that may jar modern sensibilities did make sense to Chrétien and his audience. Cohen properly suggests that Chrétien derived Yvain's lion from the Bestiary tradition, not from actual experience with lions, but he fails to follow up the implications of that connection. The Bestiary lion was nothing more than an overgrown poodle, he asserts, and Chrétien's lion thus has more of the faithful dog than *felis leo* in him. Cohen's mistake is to view the animal from a modern naturalist's perspective, while the medieval bestiarist (and, we may infer, Chrétien) views it from a moralist's.

Jean Frappier recognizes the currency of just such ideas of nature as the Bestiary represents. "Les pierres précieuses, les animaux, les couleurs, les nombres avaient un sens caché, une 'senefiance,' " he writes. "En face des textes, une disposition fréquente du clerc médiéval était qu'il fallait 'gloser la lettre,' comme dit Marie de France dans le prologue de ses *Lais*, ou encore 'moraliser,' découvrir une signification réligieuse, et cela jusque dans les fables du paganisme."[5] But Frappier does not apply this insight to his interpretation of the poems. Despite the fact that "la symbolique appartenait à l' 'outillage mental' du Moyen Age" (p. 21), the actual influence on Chrétien's work of this medieval way of seeing in visible things the vehicle of spiritual meaning, he concludes, was small. Chrétien's interest lay rather in psychology, in the painting of character. Frappier works out ingenious and complex psychological analyses of the characters' behavior, but they do not correspond to our actual experience of the poems. More important, the twelfth-century poet was precluded by precisely the *outillage mental* of which Frappier speaks, the intellectual framework in which he worked, from so much as the conception of "psychology," much less an overriding interest in it. Frappier's subtle analysis of Laudine's vacillation, for example, is impressive in the reading, but it does not correspond to the abrupt, psychologically coarse, and humorous treatment that we find when we return to the text. Again, he speaks of the character of Yvain as evolving. In fact, though, Chrétien shows us nothing like a continuous psychological evolution of character, but rather a series of static phases, each ushered in by an abrupt change in Yvain—his falling violently in love with Laudine at first sight, for example, or his plunge into desperate insanity, and the equally sudden cure miraculously effected by the damsels. Modern psychology sees character and

---

5. Jean Frappier, *Chrétien de Troyes, L'homme et l'oeuvre* (Paris, 1957), p. 21.

behavior in Hegelian terms, as the synthesis of internal tension. But the medieval view of psychic states and their alterations is typified in the *Psychomachia* of Prudentius, in which allegorized virtues struggle with, but ultimately triumph over the vices. In the medieval view, the tension between virtue and vice does not result in a third term, a synthesis, but in the unequivocal victory of one over the other.

As works of adaptation from pre-Christian sources, Chrétien's romances are rather typical of their time than otherwise. So many of the literary works of the Middle Ages have non-Christian sources—Classical, Germanic, and Celtic—that "Christianization" of alien materials might be considered the major characteristic of medieval literature. But it is a characteristic that is as misconstrued as it is pervasive. The question continually arises whether pagan sources have actually been assimilated into their new Christian context. Pious interpolators are conventionally suspected of having tampered with the pristine Urtext. Sometimes the poet himself is said to have introduced Christian elements merely to conform with necessary proprieties, even though he probably had little interest in serious religious ideas, which he must have found intrusive. Such efforts to distinguish and weed out newer from earlier literary material easily lead us away from a consideration of the work as it was actually received by its medieval audience.

Scholars who are disturbed by what they consider contamination of earlier sources overlook the empirical fact that real medieval audiences were willing to accept adulterated goods. One may legitimately pursue an interest in pre-Christian literature by extrapolation from surviving—and from that viewpoint genuinely contaminated—medieval texts. But if we wish to understand medieval literature on its own terms, our measure must be the actual values of medieval poets and their audiences. In this light, it is clearly irrelevant to ask whether a work of adaptation from pagan sources, the *Niebelungenlied*, for instanct, or Gottfried's *Tristan*, or *Beowulf*, has been fully "Christianized." Their audiences received these works in the context of Christian ideas so pervasive and so comprehensive that a poet did not need to evoke them explicitly to be understood in those terms. In fact, since medieval consciousness was Christian, not pagan, it could make sense of even explicitly pagan literature in no other terms. The question, then, is not whether the medieval poet and his audience understood a certain work to reflect Christian ideas and values, but rather *how* they understood it to do so.

As early as 1915, W. A. Nitze, in his important article "*Sans et matiere* dans les oeuvres de Chrétien de Troyes,"[6] argued that Chrétien's attitude toward the narrative materials on which he drew, the Celtic stories of adventure, was shaped by clerkly exegesis of Scripture and the Classics. "Quelle que soit la source de sa matière, son sans . . . est essentiellement le produit des écoles monastiques du XIIᵉ siècle, modifié toutefois pour satisfaire aux nouveaux et pressants besoins de la vie des cours françaises" (pp. 35 36). The very word *sans* as Chrétien employs it in *Lancelot* is adapted, according to Nitze, from the Latin exegetical term *sensus;* the poet worked quite consciously in the tradition of patristic exegesis, even though he was perhaps equally conscious of the novelty of applying such techniques to literature in the vulgar tongue.

Not surprisingly, Nitze cites as parallel Dante's explanation in the letter to Can Grande of the four senses of allegory in the *Paradiso* by analogy with patristic exegesis of Scripture. Dante's letter is a remarkable document, for it is not merely the judgment of some monkish commentator, but the statement of the poet himself, setting forth his own conscious intentions. The meaning of his work, Dante declares, is not simple but multiple; while there is a *literal* meaning, there are as well *allegorical* mean-

6. *Romania* 44 (1915–17) : 14–36.

ings indicated by the letter. He illustrates his method by analogy with the standard fourfold exegesis of Psalm 113:1. Dante apparently intended his own poem to be understood in terms of a similar fourfold scheme.

Patristic exegesis was based largely on the principle of typology, that is, the discovery of analogy among events of sacred history, all of which are connected in the central focus of Christian time, the Incarnation. Jean Daniélou points out that the typology of the New Testament has its foundations in the Old Testament prophecies of the greater works, analogous to the divine works of the past, which God would ordain in the future: there was to be a New Deluge, a New Exodus, A New Paradise, and so on.

> These prophecies constitute a primary typology that might be called eschatalogical, for the prophets saw these future events as happening at the end of time. The New Testament, therefore, did not invent typology, but simply showed that it was fulfilled in the person of Jesus of Nazareth. With Jesus, in fact, these events of the end, of the fullness of time, are now accomplished. He is the New Adam with whom the time of the Paradise of the future has begun. In Him is already realized that destruction of the sinful world of which the Flood was the figure. In Him is accomplished the true Exodus which delivers the people of God from the tyranny of the demon.[7]

Thus, the events of the Old Testament are connected eschatalogically with the end of time, and with the life of Christ. But they are connected by analogy with life of the Church too; there is a sacramental as well as a Christological typology. The Deluge and the Crossing of the Red Sea, for example, are both figures of Baptism; the manna with which the Israelites were fed in the wilderness is a figure of the Eucharist, and so on. "This means," Daniélou explains, "that the sacraments carry on in our midst

---

7. Jean Daniélou, *The Bible and the Liturgy* (Notre Dame, Ind., 1956), p. 5.

the *mirabilia*, the great works of God in the Old Testament and the New: for example, the Flood, the Passion and Baptism show us the same divine activity as carried out in three different eras of sacred history" (p. 5).

Its transcendence of time is the key to understanding typology. A scriptural figure relates to its allegorical meaning not simply as a sign to its referent. Rather, typology reveals the underlying equivalence among seemingly disparate events scattered throughout history. Consequently, it undermines the significance of time; historical or temporal distinctions are discovered to be superficial only, merely "literal." Time is carnal, but Scripture, in which letter and spirit are one, transcends it. As Auerbach writes:

> A connection is established between two events which are linked neither temporally nor causally—a connection which it is impossible to establish by reason in the horizontal dimension (if I may be permitted to use this term for a temporal extension). It can be established only if both occurrences are vertically linked to Divine Providence, which alone is able to devise such a plan of history and supply the key to its understanding. The horizontal, that is the temporal and causal, connection of occurrences is dissolved; the here and now is no longer a mere link in an earthly chain of events, it is simultaneously something which has always been, and which will be fulfilled in the future; and strictly, in the eyes of God, it is something eternal, something omni-temporal, something already consummated in the realm of fragmentary earthly event.[8]

We can explain the unreality of time in Arthurian romance in similar terms: events are related spiritually; time, although it has great symbolic significance, has no convincing reality as causal or sequential order among events.

The source studies show us that Chrétien's romances are not constructed whole out of the poet's imagination, but are made up in large part of pre-existing narrative materials,

---

8. *Mimesis*, pp. 64–65.

reordered and given new meaning. Similarly, their allegorical significance is not constructed with the schematic integrity of poems like the *Psychomachia* or the *Commedia*, and we must not expect to find a continuous and consistent allegorical relationship between the levels of narrative and meaning. In fact, whereas the delimiting characteristics of a conventional allegorical figure—the representation of a virtue or vice as a woman, for instance—keep it quite isolated in both abstractness and particularity, typology tends to view all things and persons and events as potentially equivalent. Thus, such allegorized material is likely to be considerably more complex and difficult to interpret. Characters are not simple allegorical figures, nor even necessarily consistent in their signification. Events are not linked one to another by a consistent logic, but by a shifting logic. No single detail provides the key to understanding the whole meaning of the poem; the meaning emerges rather from the accumulation of significant details—sacramental analogies, scriptural echoes and parodies, conventional symbols, and the like. By and large, the poet has been guided by the possibilities that have appeared to him in the given material, rather than by a deliberate and absolute principle independent of the fiction.

Rosemond Tuve refers to this characteristic of romance when she speaks of "intermittently significant" allegory. "The word 'intermittent' does not indicate the stop and go of some mechanical inner traffic light but rather the greater or less penetration of details of an incident with metaphorical meaning, the incident as a whole lending itself to a metaphorical as well as a literal reading."[9] The writer of this kind of allegory, she argues, is concerned with the creation of a total context of meaning, not with working out a consistent mechanism of equivalences. "I am not trying to show that symbolic meanings jerk about and reverse them-

9. Rosemond Tuve, *Allegorical Imagery: Some Medieval Books and Their Posterity* (Princeton, N. J., 1966), pp. 391–92.

selves irreponsibly," she writes, "but that the method of allegory forbids one to make rigid correspondences with objects; the writer is making a web of his connected meanings, not setting down notions in a picture-language of translatable signs" (p. 430). Miss Tuve explains the special character of allegorical figure in romance. As in the typology of Scripture on which it was patterned, a figure in romance is not simply a sign for something else; rather, the figure *shares* the meaning of some other thing or event. So, Yvain's experience at the fountain of storms, for instance, is imbued with the meaning of baptism. But we are not meant to understand this adventure in the enchanted forest actually to be an allegorical representation of the sacrament administered in church. The vision of the courtly romance is, on the contrary, of the chivalric life itself illuminated and filled with the meaning of the sacrament. Further, in her chapter "Imposed Allegory," Miss Tuve enunciates the principle according to which we must understand such figures. It is the large context of meaning that emerges through the course of a romance, what she calls "the principal drift," that controls the significance of details. "The principal drift *governs* the meanings attributable to the incidents borne upon the stream; the latter cannot take their own moral direction as they choose" (p. 235).

Approached in this light, the romances do reveal coherent patterns of meaning in the sequence of adventures that their protagonists undertake—adventures that are otherwise confusing in their appearance of whimsy. Presumably, the poet detected a "drift" of meaning in the stories he heard from the *conteurs* that he reinforced and drew together in reworking the narratives, and it is rather in the structure of this allegorical meaning than in the story-line that the coherence of his romances will be found.[10] The difficulty for

---

10. Some work along these general lines has been done. Most relevant to the present study is Maxwell Luria, "The Christian Tempest," Ph.D. dissertation (Princeton, 1965); Luria's chapter on *Yvain* has been revised and pub-

the modern reader is that much that was commonplace for Chrétien's twelfth-century audience is now obscure. The connection between narrative and meaning depends often on what has become for us arcane and unrelated information. Yet, the major equipment necessary to the interpretation of these romances is really quite basic: a knowledge of Scripture, and of common exegesis of important passages, such as is represented by the *Glossa Ordinaria;* a knowledge of the liturgy; an understanding of the sacraments and their administration; and access to such popular sources of symbolism as the Bestiary, lapidaries, and the like. Consultation of patristic writings may appear at times arcane, yet it is often the only way to retrieve what was common knowledge among sophisticated men of the Middle Ages.

The meaning of these adventures, we find, lies in their analogical relation to events of sacred history and to the sacraments, through whose agency those events are caused to be present in our daily lives. Love and adventure are, as we have always understood, the subject of romance, but the meaning of love and adventure does not remain in the realm of secular courtly ideals alone, but transcends those fictional ideals to partake of the meaning of their spiritual counterparts, grace and sacramental participation in the life of Christ. In *Erec* and *Yvain,* the road that leads to knightly adventure is the way also of spiritual perfection.

---

lished as "The Storm-making Spring and the Meaning of Chrétien's *Yvain,*" *Studies in Philology* 64 (July 1967), 564–85. D. W. Robertson, Jr., has outlined interpretations of *Cligés* and *Lancelot* in his *Preface to Chaucer* (Princeton, 1962), pp. 87–94, 448–57. Less persuasive is the work of Urban T. Holmes, Jr., and Sister M. Amelia Klenke on scriptural and liturgical parallels in *Perceval,* gathered in their *Chrétien, Troyes, and the Grail* (Chapel Hill, N. C., 1959). Also of considerable interest, although not concerned with the works of Chrétien, is Hans Schneider, *Sir Gawain and the Green Knight,* Cooper Monographs (Bern, 1961).

The Allegory of Adventure

1

Sowers of the Word

Remote as we are from the consciousness of the courtly society of twelfth-century France, we are lucky to have Chrétien's own indications of how he wished his poems to be received. Even the audience for which they were intended, he apparently feared, was likely to listen with only the fleshly ear, not the ear of the spirit, and so fail to hear their inner meaning. Modern readers must be all the more alert to the admonitions that even his contemporaries needed—an audience for whom romance-form and allegory were idiomatic, rather than quaint or stilted. That there is deeper significance than at once meets the eye in the fashionable Arthurian stories of adventure is covertly the principal theme of Chrétien's prologue to *Erec*:

> Li vilains dit an son respit
> Que tel chose a l'an an despit,
> Qui mout vaut miauz que l'an ne cuide,[1]

---

1. Kristian von Troyes, *Erec und Enide*, ed. Wendelin Foerster, 3rd ed. (Halle, 1934), p. 1, ll. 1-3. Quotations from *Erec et Enide* are from this edition throughout, and line references follow in the text. Quotations from *Yvain* are also from Foerster's critical text, Chrestien de Troyes, *Yvain* (*Le Chevalier au Lion*), The Critical Text of Wendelin Foerster, ed. T. B. W. Reid (Manchester, England, 1942); line references follow in the text.

the poem begins. The proverb expresses a general principle: things aren't always what they seem; outward form may deceptively conceal inner reality. But the proverbial statement is itself in the form of an example of the principle: proverbs, namely, are themselves precious bits of wisdom, spoken in the mouths of lowly peasants. The appearance of the peasant deceptively conceals the wisdom he carries within him, yet it paradoxically reveals it too. Unless you have a peasant to speak it, the wisdom of the proverb remains hidden. This paradox, that the revelation of truth depends on its concealment, that the relationship between outward form and inner reality is hidden, yet intimate, is the essential nature of parables and allegory. "Is a lamp brought in to be put under a bushel, or under a bed, and not on a stand? For there is nothing hid, except to be made manifest; nor is anything secret, except to come to light. If any man has ears to hear, let him hear."[2] In this passage from Mark, Jesus is expounding the nature of parables in response to his disciples' perplexity. Truth is only apparently hidden in parables, in order that it may be revealed. And this paradoxical relation between spirit and matter in parables does not arise from arbitrary literary convention, but from profound faith in the reality of the Incarnation, which is to say, in the immanence of God in his creation. C. H. Dodd explains that the style of realism of the parables of Jesus "arises from a conviction that there is no mere analogy, but an inward affinity, between the natural order and the spiritual order; or as we might put it in the language of the parables themselves, the Kingdom of God is intrinsically *like* the processes of nature and of the daily life of men."[3]

   This paradoxical nature of parables is the key to the ap-

----

2. Mark 4:21–23. The Bible that Chrétien knew was the Vulgate; I have used various translations of quoted passages (sometimes my own) in an effort to render as closely as possible the sense of the Latin. Hereafter, scriptural references follow quotation in the text.

3. C. H. Dodd, *The Parables of the Kingdom* (New York, 1961), p. 10.

parently harsh answer that Jesus gives his disciples concerning the parable of the sower: "To you it is given to know
the mystery of the kingdom of God: but to them that are
without, all things are done in parables: That seeing they
may see, and not perceive; and hearing they may hear, and
not understand: lest at any time they should be converted,
and their sins should be forgiven them" (Mark 4:11–12).
Apparently, Christ speaks in parables to prevent sinners from
repenting; yet elsewhere in the Gospels he is rebuked for
preaching repentance and forgiveness to innkeepers and
prostitutes, and the ministry on which he sends his disciples
is not just to the virtuous, but to the whole world. For the
Son of God, who came to bring forgiveness to fallen man,
this is a dark saying. But "there is nothing hid," he says
further, "except to be made manifest; nor is anything secret, except to come to light."

Bede suggests that we can understand this saying only as
itself a parable:

It is to be remarked in these words of the Lord that not only
those words which he spoke, truly, but also those things which
he did were parables, that is signs of mystical things, since
those to whom all things are done in parables are said to be
unable to understand either what they saw or what they heard.
For what would prevent observers from understanding those
things which they saw, his works or his wanderings, unless he
wished something greater to be understood spiriutally than in
these things was apparent to the eyes of the flesh? To those,
therefore, who are without and do not approach the feet of the
Lord to receive his teaching, all things are done in parables,
both the deeds, truly, and the words of the saviour, since
neither in those virtues which he manifested nor in those
secret things which he preached were they able to recognize
him as God, and therefore they do not merit to attain the remission of sins which is to be obtained by the grace of faith
alone.[4]

4. *In Marci Evangelium Expositio*, iv, 11–12, Bedae Venerabilis Opera,
Pars II Opera Exegetica 3, Corpus Christianorum, series Latina, vol. 120
(Tournhout, 1960): 482, my trans.

The nature of parables is *as though* an esoteric secret were hidden from those not intended to know it, lest knowing, they should profit by it. But that expression is a *likeness*, not a literal statement, since parables hide the truth only to reveal it. Christ's mission in the world was to forgive men their sins. Those who see and do not perceive are blind not because they cannot see but because they will not see, no matter how plainly truth is revealed to them. A lamp is brought out and put on a stand, but men turn away and look elsewhere. "For he that hath, to him shall be given: and he that hath not, from him shall be taken even that which he hath" (Mark 4:25). Here is still further parabolic elucidation of the nature of parables. Bede explains that Christ is admonishing us to "Pay attention . . . with the concentration of your whole mind to the word which you hear, and which is to be kept in memory and meditated, because whoever has love for the word, to him will be given also the sense to understand that which he loves, but whoever has no love for the hearing of the word, even if through natural ability or through the study of letters he seems to himself to understand, he will rejoice in no sweetness of true wisdom" (p. 485). Understanding, that is, springs from love; it involves the whole spirit. Thus, understanding and salvation are the same. The distinction between "those who are without" and "those who are within" is not really the physical distinction between those who happen to be in the house and those who happen to be outside. It is a likeness of the spiritual distinction between those who are saved and those who are not.

Marie de France, writing probably in the generation after Chrétien, also raises the question of obscurity, for the same reason—namely, to admonish her audience to apply more than casual attention to the fictions of the Bretons, and to labor diligently to understand their inner meaning. She begins the prologue to her lays with a theme that Curtius shows to be a standard rhetorical topos of the exordium:

"The possession of wisdom makes it a duty to impart it."[5] Her words seem meant to recall Christ's parable of the lamp:

> Whoever God has given wisdom
> And the eloquence of speaking well,
> Ought not keep it silent or hide it,
> Rather ought he willingly to show it forth.[6]

Good words bring forth flowers, she goes on, somewhat covertly employing the symbolism of the word as seed that Christ elaborates in the parable of the sower. Words are sown in the ears of those who hear them.

> When a great good is heard abroad,
> Then it has come into its first bloom,
> And when it is praised by still others,
> Then its flowers have spread.[7]

But the word must fall on good soil, as Christ explains; that is to say, in the ears of those "who hear the word and receive it, and yield fruit, the one thirtyfold, another sixty, and another a hundred" (Mark 4:20). It is diligence in laboring to discover the inner meaning within the outer "husk" of the letter that distinguishes good "soil" from bad. The ancients, Marie says, customarily wrote their books obscurely for the sake of those who should come after them, that they might diligently apply themselves to the interpretation of the letter, and supply the remainder, that is the inner meaning, from their own wisdom.[8] Such diligent study of the letter, as well as the author's own diligence in writing,

---

5. Ernst Robert Curtius, *European Literature and the Latin Middle Ages,* trans. Willard R. Trask (New York, 1963), p. 87.

6. Marie de France, *Lais,* ed. Karl Warnke (Halle, 1885), p. 3: "Qui deus a duné esciënce/e de parler bone eloquence,/ne s'en deit taisir ne celer,/ ainz se deit voluntiers mustrer" (ll. 1–4).

7. *Lais,* p. 3: "Quant uns granz biens est mult oïz,/dunc a primes est il fluriz,/e quant loëz est de plusurs,/dunc a espandues ses flurs" (ll. 5–8).

8. For a recent discussion of Marie's allusion to Priscian, see Mortimer J. Donovan, "Priscian and the Obscurity of the Ancients," *Speculum* 36 (1961): 75–80.

sharpens the intelligence and shows the way to eschew vice and sorrow, and therefore, for her own sake and the reader's, Marie has thought of drawing the lays of the Breton *conteurs* into French.

Marie's prologue is intended to reveal to the reader how the tales that follow are to be understood. The first tale is an adventure that she will show, she says, "according to the letter and the scripture."[9] These words underscore the need for the reader to supply the remainder from his own wisdom, as she has put it a few lines earlier, for in using the terms "letter," "scripture," "sense," and "gloss," to describe the method of reading she requires, she evokes, as Leo Spitzer has observed, a very particular model of interpretation, namely patristic exegesis. "Marie de France," he writes, "thinking 'medievally' . . . sees her own book as only another 'text,' which will be 'glossed,' after the model of the Old Testament commented on by Tertullian, Augustine, Jerome, etc.—after the model of Virgil and Ovid 'moralized.' "[10]

D. W. Robertson has argued that Marie's three terms *lettre, sens,* and *surplus* correspond precisely to the three parts of the standard exegetical reading of Scripture, *littera, sensus,* and *sententia,* that is, grammatical and syntactical analysis of the letter, determination of its literal signification, and determination of its spiritual, or allegorical meaning.[11] Spitzer takes the word *surplus* more literally to indicate simply an interpretation "super-added" to the literary work by the reader, but just the same, he concludes that Marie was thinking of "the gloss technique of biblical exegesis which, over the course of centuries, develops the whole meaning implied or latent in the text—the progress achieved by the latest readers being foreseen, as it were, by

---

9. *Lais,* p. 6: "sulunc la lettre e l'escriture" (l. 23).
10. Leo Spitzer, "The Prologue to the *Lais* of Marie de France and Medieval Poetics," *Modern Philology* 41 (1943–44) : 96–102.
11. D. W. Robertson, Jr., "Marie de France, *Lais,* Prologue, 13–16," *Modern Language Notes* 44 (1949) : 336–38.

divine inspiration: even such 'this-worldly' poets as Marie de France . . . could not help but see their secular works in the same light as that of the sacred book, the Bible" (p. 96) .

The exegetical expectations of these "secular" poets, moreover, were not limited to technique. Spitzer calls Marie *clerc*, and *poeta philosophus et theologus*, by which he means that she is a serious poet, and no mere versifier or entertainer. Marie's work ought to be approached, he argues, in light of the conventional Classical and medieval identification of poetry with philosophy, as well as with theology.[12] When in the prologues to both her lays and her fables Marie refers to ancient "philosophers" as her models, she is not distinguishing herself as poet from these "philosophers," but on the contrary identifying herself with them.

Marie's literary concerns are similar to those which Chrétien takes up in his prologue to *Erec*. He too makes the conventional assertion of the folly of hiding the light of one's wisdom. He does well who turns his efforts to wisdom, he says, for whoever foregoes such efforts often conceals something that gives great pleasure. Wisdom and pleasure, then, are the two aspects of the labor that Chrétien is about to undertake. We are perhaps more familiar with the same dichotomy under the terms *instruction* and *delight,* classically defined as the ends of poetry. Because it is right to turn one's endeavors to wisdom, as well as to give pleasure, "says Chrétien de Troyes" (1. 9), everyone ought to try to speak well and teach well, that is, give pleasure with the delightful configurations of words, and instruction with the wisdom of their meaning. Again, this dual function reflects the relation between inner meaning and outward form, and their paradoxical inseparability is expressed, as in the peasants' proverb, in the intentional ambiguity of the relative clause with which the sentence continues. Chrétien,

---

12. Spitzer bases his argument on Curtius; see his chapters 11 and 12, "Poetry and Philosophy," and "Poetry and Theology," *European Literature and the Latin Middle Ages,* pp. 203–27.

> . . . tret d'un conte d'avanture
> Une mout bele conjointure,
> Par qu'an puet prover et savoir
> Que cil ne fet mie savoir,
> Qui sa sciance n'abandone
> Tant con Deus la grace l'an done. (ll. 13–18)

The romance, that is, shows through the behavior of Erec, who ceases to function properly in the world of chivalry when he withdraws into the self-centered pursuit of pleasure with his new wife, that it is foolish not to use to the utmost the talents that God has given. But "one may know and show" this lesson as well by the example that Chrétien himself sets in writing the poem in the first place, spreading his own wisdom abroad under the guise of fiction. Similarly, Marie's labor in translating the Breton stories is exemplary of the very diligence she asks of her readers.

The seriousness of Chrétien's attitude toward his poetry, as well as the intimate relation of form and inner meaning, is attested by his passing remark that the story of Erec is often garbled by merely mercenary *conteurs*. The story of adventure is, after all, the apparently worthless thing that turns out to be of great value. In fact, he asserts, punning a little on his name, this story will be remembered so long as Christianity lasts—an expression by which he means "a very long time." But the relation also suggests that the story is imbued with a particularly Christian meaning.

There are really two prologues in *Yvain*, spoken by the two story tellers, Chrétien himself, and, within the fiction, Calogrenant; both take up the concerns that we have seen to be central in the prologues to *Erec* and to Marie's *Lays*. Chrétien explains in a digression that actually functions as a prologue (ll. 18–41), that what goes by the name of love today is a debasement of the true love that has flourished in the past. Calogrenant, the knight who tells a story "not to his honor, but to his shame," a story that incites Yvain to set out in quest of the same adventure himself, explains in his own prologue how to listen to what he is about to tell. But Calogrenant is obviously speaking for his author too, admonishing not only the knights who have gathered at Arthur's court, but Chrétien's audience as well, to listen not with the ears only, but with the heart.

Calogrenant's distinction between superficial and inner hearing parallels in a striking way Chrétien's earlier attack on contemporary love. "Çaus, qui an vie durent" (l. 30) have no understanding of true love because of a failure of the heart, which is to say, of true understanding. Love has been turned into a fable, he says, a hollow lie, like the story of Erec in the hands of inferior conteurs, a story torn apart and robbed of its inner truth. But Calogrenant intends to tell a true story, with meaning for those who have ears to hear. "Ears to hear," comments Bede on the passage from Mark cited above, "truly, are the ears of the heart, and ears to listen to and to do those things which have been commanded are the inner faculties of understanding" (p. 482). Calogrenant commands his audience:

> "Des qu'il vos plest, ore antandez!
> Cuer et oroilles me randez!
> Car parole oie est perdue
> S'ele n'est de cuer antandue." (ll. 149–52)

There are those, he goes on to explain, who praise even what they do not understand. Such people, whose hearts fail in understanding, have only the sounds of words, which pass like the wind.

> "As oroilles vient la parole
> Aussi come li vanz, qui vole;
> Mes n'i areste ne demore,
> Ainz s'an part an mout petit d'ore,
> Se li cuers n'est si esveilliez,
> Qu'au prandre soit apareilliez." (ll. 157–62)

Calogrenant's evocation in this context of the familiar scriptural admonition to be ever awake indicates the moral character of his tale. Moreover, his formulation even has the feel of a parable. Marie's assertion in her prologue that her work of rendering the lays into French has kept her awake many times is to be understood in the same figurative sense, as an indication of the moral value of her endeavor. The heart, Calogrenant continues, must receive and keep the word

> ". . . an son venir
> Prandre et anclorre et retenir." (ll. 163–64)

Calogrenant's directions to his audience echo Christ's figure when he tells his disciples, "Place these words in your hearts!" (Luke 9:44) ; or more closely, perhaps, God's commandment to Ezechiel, "Receive in thy heart, and hear with thy ears, all the words I speak to thee" (Ezechiel 3:10). The ears are only the pathway to the heart, which must enclose the word within the breast. Emphatically, he repeats his demand:

> " . . . Qui or me voldra antandre,
> Cuer et oroilles me doit randre." (ll. 169–70)

Calogrenant's theme of inner, that is to say, spiritual understanding contrasted with merely superficial, carnal understanding, and his imagery of the passage of words into the body, are variations on an idea that is basic to medieval biblical and literary interpretation, the distinction, epitomized by St. Paul, between the letter of a work and its spirit. Paul recalls the New Covenant, announced by the prophet Jeremiah as a covenant to be written, as Calogrenant wishes his words to be, on the hearts of the people. To the Corinthians he writes:

> You are our epistle, written in our hearts, which is known and read by all men: Being manifested, that you are the epistle of Christ, ministered by us, and written not with ink, but with the Spirit of the living God; not in tables of stone,

but in the fleshly tables of the heart. And such confidence we
have through Christ, towards God. Not that we are sufficient
to think any thing of ourselves, as of ourselves: but our suffi-
ciency is from God. Who also hath made us fit ministers of the
new testament, not in the letter, but in the spirit. For the letter
killeth, but the spirit quickeneth. (2 Cor. 3:2–6)

Paul's distinction between letter and spirit becomes, in
the patristic commentaries, the underlying principle of exegesis. The idea is expressed in innumerable analogies, from
the sublime analogy of the Incarnation—Christ's invisible divinity contained within yet shadowed forth by his visible
humanity—to the commonplace analogy of the kernel within
the shell, or as Chaucer's priest Sir John puts it, the "fruyt"
within the "chaf." Of course a scriptural text is true on the
literal level also, but the literal sense contains within it a
spiritual sense of higher, mystical truth, which it is the
function of exegesis to reveal.

Chrétien's contemporary, Alanus de Insulis, puts in the
mouth of his figure Natura a statement of poetics that
shows that this approach was not limited to the reading of
the Bible. "In the superficial shell of the letter," Natura
explains, "the poetic lyre sounds forth falsehood; but within, it speaks to those who hear, the secret of a higher understanding, so that the exterior shell of falseness having been
cast away, the reader may discover within secretely the sweet
kernel of truth."[13] Alanus here expresses the standard medieval approach to all serious literature.[14] W. A. Nitze has argued that Chrétien evokes this dichotomy explicitly in his
prologue to *Lancelot* when he speaks of "matiere et san," by
which he means the narrative material, and its signification.
Calogrenant implies the same distinction between the interior, spiritual meaning of his tale and the external letter of
it through the obvious parallel with the heart's interior un-

---

13. Quoted and translated in Bernard F. Huppé and D. W. Robertson,
Jr., *Fruyt and Chaf: Studies in Chaucer's Allegories* (Princeton, N. J.,
1963) , p. 5.
14. See chap. 1, "An Approach to Medieval Poetry," *ibid.,* pp. 1–31.

derstanding contrasted with the superficial hearing of the ear.

But the figure of the ear detached from the heart as a symbol of lack of understanding suggests affinity with another scriptural commonplace, found throughout the books of the prophets as well as the New Testament (including one of the passages from Mark cited above). Jeremiah, for example, exhorts his listeners:

> Hear, foolish people, who have no heart;
> Who, having eyes, see not,
> And ears, hear not. (5:21)

The adventure at the fountain is a tale calculated not only to entertain, then, but far more to enlighten Calogrenant's audience. After Kay's stupid affront to Calogrenant over his courtesy in rising at the Queen's entrance, he is reluctant to go on with his tale. It is not petulance, but the fear of casting his pearls before swine that moves him to beg the Queen's permission to remain silent. What he tells has to be taken to heart by those who hear; otherwise, his is like a voice crying in the wilderness. Calogrenant's prologue might not call to mind Christ's parable of the sower were it not for the remarkable thematic similarity among the prologues to *Erec* and *Yvain*, Marie's prologue, and Chrétien's prologue to *Perceval*, where the parable is more explicitly echoed.

Christ tells the parable to a large crowd that has gathered by the sea to hear him preach. To the crowd, as we have seen, he speaks only in parables, but to his disciples, privately, he reveals their meaning. "Listen!" he begins, "a sower went out to sow." A part of the sower's seed fell by the wayside and was eaten by birds; another part fell on rocky soil and was withered by the sun; another fell among thorns and was choked. But one part fell on good soil "and brought forth fruit that grew up, and increased and yielded, one thirty, another sixty, and another a hundred. And he said: He that hath ears to hear, let him hear" (Mark 4:3-9). The seed, Christ explains, is the word, which grows and bears fruit in those "who hear the word and receive it, and yield fruit" (4:20).

In his prologue to *Perceval*, Chrétien asserts that his "seed" will not fall on fallow ground. He has written the romance for Phillip, Count of Flanders, a man better even than Alexander the Great, possessing Alexander's famous virtues, but free of his notorious vices.

> Ki petit semme petit quelt,
> Et qui auques requeillir velt,
> En tel liu sa semence espande
> Que Diex a cent doubles li rande;
> Car an terre qui riens ne valt,
> Bone semence seche et faut.
> Crestiens semme et fait semence
> D'un romans que il encomence,
> Et si le seme en si bon leu
> Qu'il ne puet estre sanz grant preu,
> Qu'il le fait por le plus preudome
> Qui soit en l'empire de Rome.[15]

But Calogrenant is rightly skeptical about his audience and is reluctant to speak even in parables. He too is a sower of the word, and he wants his seed to fall on the heart, not on deaf ears. Possibly his very name hints at the figure of the sower. Loomis, in his etymological reading of the name *Calogrenant*, characteristically deals only with the meaning of putative sources at several removes from the text of *Yvain*, not with the meaning Chrétien himself may have intended. He judges that "Calogrenant, who plays the traditional role of Keu, is really Cai-lo-grenant, 'Kay the Grumbler.' Kay's churlish disposition is already familiar to us, and the very verb *grenir* is applied to him by Raoul de Houdenc. The fact that Calogrenant appears quarreling with Keu is merely an illustration of the doubling of characters

15. *Le Roman de Perceval ou Le Conte du Graal*, ed. William Roach, Textes Littéraires Français (Geneva, 1959), ll. 1–12.

not uncommon in Arthurian romance, so that more than once we find a figure fighting himself under a variant name."[16]

Clearly, Chrétien himself could not consciously have intended this identification of Calogrenant and Kay, characters who are diametrically opposed to one another in spirit as well as in deed. If Loomis's etymology is, from a genetic standpoint, correct, Chrétien must nevertheless have misinterpreted the name. I suggest as a possibility more consonant with the spirit of his role in the romance that Chrétien intended Calogrenant's name to appear a compound made from the Late Latin verb *calo* "I call," or "proclaim," and the present participle of the Old French verb *grener* "to germinate," or "sprout." Calogrenant is the sower of the seed that is the word. What he proclaims—his tale of adventure at the fountain—is meant to take root in the hearts of his audience, sprouting forth in faith and works. These are themselves, in turn, conventionally thought of as "seeds" that bring forth fruit. As St. Augustine comments on Psalm 125:5: "In that life, which is full of tears, let us sow. What shall we sow? Good works. Works of mercy are our seeds. . . . He who sows much, reaps much: 'He who soweth sparingly, shall also reap sparingly;' and he who sows nothing, reaps nothing. Why do you long for broad fields, where you may sow many seeds? There is no field broader for you to sow in than Christ, who wished you to sow in Him. Your ground is the Church; sow however much you can."[17]

Love and adventure are typically the subject of romance. If Chrétien wishes his audience to see not merely the shell of his fictions, but through them the kernel of meaning, is there some special sense in which we must understand these

16. Roger Sherman Loomis, *Chrétien de Troyes and Arthurian Tradition* (New York, 1949), p. 275; see also R. S. Loomis, "Calogrenanz and Chrétien's Originality," *Modern Language Notes* 43, (1928): 215–23.
17. St. Augustine, *Ennaratio in Psalmum CXXV, PL,* ed. J. P. Migne, vol. 37, col. 1664, my trans.

familiar terms? Chrétien himself, in the digressive prologue
to *Yvain*, expounds the distinction between, as it were, the
"shell" (which he actually calls the "fable") , which is taken
for love today, and the "kernel" of true love, which once
flourished. In keeping with the device of past-tense narrative
(only another element of fiction) , he translates what is really a qualitative distinction into a temporal one.

The knights and ladies of Arthur's court entertain themselves in speaking of love:

> Li autre parloient d'amors,
> Des angoisses et des dolors
> Et des granz biens, qu'an ont sovant
> Li deciple de son covant,
> Qui lors estoit riches et buens. (ll. 13–17)

The words of this passage have connotations that are apparently out of keeping with its sense. Chrétien seems to
be mildly satirizing the "anguish" and the "pain" of love by
associating with them figures of a religious nature, "disciples" and "covenant" (*covant* may also mean "religious order"). Thus, what is suffered in the name of love, and what
is gained, is seen in terms of what the disciples suffered and
gained in the name of—moreover, in imitation of—Christ.
The implication that success for the lover is "heaven" is a common metaphor. The real bite of Chrétien's little joke, however, is that he was perfectly serious in the first place. Love
is not after all being contrasted with spirituality, but rather
imbued with its meaning. "Diex est caritez (l. 47)," Chrétien tells us in the prologue to *Perceval*, quoting 1 John
4:16, "Deus charitas est."

The "shell" of the romance, then, presents a courtly conversation about lovers, metaphorically, disciples; the kernel,
Chrétien hopes we will see, is the truth that the great lovers
who lived in days gone by, *were* the disciples, who followed
the new commandment of Christ, "That you love one another; even as I have loved you, that you also love one an-

other (John 13:34)." In following Christ's commandment
to love, the disciples were rendered "the great blessings" of
his new covenant. The love exemplified by "Li deciple de
son covant" is spiritual love—in its earthly manifestation,
charity. But there is another kind of love, its opposite, the
only kind, complains Chrétien, to be found nowadays—
worldly love, or cupidity. Thus, he is not merely speaking
metaphorically, but distinguishing quite graphically, in terms
of the medieval cosmology, earthly from heavenly love when
he says that love is now abased. We must keep in mind,
however, the symbolic function of time in the romance. Ultimately, the two loves are distinguished not temporally, but
spiritually. Thus, we may all aspire to the love of Christ
by imitating the way of the disciples, as Paul instructs us,
"Be imitators of me, as I am of Christ" (1 Corinthians
4:16). Or directly: "Be imitators of God, as beloved children" (Ephesians 5:1).

Just as his use of double meanings reveals the true nature of the two loves, the poet's deliberate ambiguity in describing, presumably, Arthur is intended to reveal a double
meaning. The romance revolves around the courts of two
kings, on different planes, not just Arthur's.

> . . . Me plest a reconter
> Chose, qui face a escouter,
> Del roi, qui fu de tel tesmoing,
> Qu'an an parole pres et loing;
> Si m'acort de tant as Bretons,
> Qui toz jorz mes vivra ses nons;
> Et par lui sont ramanteü
> Li buen chevalier esleü,
> Qui an enor se traveillierent. (ll. 33–41)

About which king does it please Chrétien to tell a story?
He does not name him in this passage. The ambiguity indicates that although the narrative will start out from Arthur's court, its meaning will ultimately touch the court of
the King of Heaven; the earthly court partakes of the mean-

ing of the heavenly. Here too, the connotative words point to this double meaning, notably *tesmoing* and *esleü*. It is true that the Bretons in particular (the only explicit association with Arthur in the passage) spoke of Arthur, but obviously the Bretons also spoke in the same, or rather even greater terms, about the King of Heaven. Moreover, it was rather natural than otherwise in the twelfth century to associate the earthly king by analogy with his heavenly counterpart, whose representative he was, and whose spiritual nature his person adumbrated.[18]

Yvain begins at Pentecost; Arthurian romance conventionally uses the feasts of the church calendar as its setting. But conventions are not necessarily empty; they establish themselves, rather, because they are significant. Pentecost among Christians celebrates the descent on the disciples of the Holy Ghost—the completion of John's baptism with water—with fire and the spirit, that is, with love. The tongues of fire inspired the disciples to speak "in tongues," and sent them into the world to preach the "good news" of the Gospel. Chrétien may intend to suggest the scriptural figure of good news when he says of the conversation among the knights and their ladies about the "disciples" of love:

> Li un racontoient noveles,
> Li autre parloient d'amors. (ll. 12–13)

It comes to the same thing, really, for to tell the "good news" *is* to speak of love. What is more clearly significant is that Pentecost, the festival of divine love, provides the setting for Yvain's struggle to love, and imbues that earthly relationship with spiritual meaning.

Erec begins in the Easter season. If the Pentecostal season in *Yvain* is intended to supply a setting appropriate to the theme of love's advent, the Easter season in *Erec* suggests in a parallel way the theme of death and resurrection. The sequence of adventures begins, appropriately,

---

18. See below, chap. 3.

An la forest avantureuse. (l. 65)

The Forest of Adventure furnishes us with a useful figure in terms of which to see the relationship between what I have called the dual subjects of romance, love and adventure. Although Calogrenant sets out "seeking adventures," the ultimate quest in both romances is for love. Adventure is rather the form that this quest takes; love is its object. Adventure is, as it were, the medium, as the Forest of Adventure is the realm, in which the custom of the White Stag is pursued. We might liken the relationship further to that between the shell and the kernel of allegory. Adventure is the outer fiction, whose inner meaning is love.

Auerbach explains the function of adventure as the measure of personal worth in the new courtly scale of values. "The personal element in the courtly virtues," he writes, "is not simply a gift of nature; nor is it acquired by birth; to implant them now requires, besides birth, proper training too, as preserving them requires the unforced will to renew them by constant and tireless practice and proving. The means by which they are proved and preserved is adventure, *avanture*, a very characteristic form of activity developed by courtly culture."[19] In fact, Auerbach argues, adventure is the very essence of knighthood. He cautions against imposing on the medieval concept modern connotations of fortuity. "Although these perilous encounters called *avantures* now have no experiential basis whatever, although it is impossible to fit them into any actual or practically conceivable political system, although they commonly crop up without any rational connection, one after the other, in a long series, we must be careful not to be misled by the modern value of the term adventure, to think of them as purely 'accidental.' When we moderns speak of adventure, we mean something unstable, peripheral, disordered, or . . . a something that

---

19. Erich Auerbach, *Mimesis: The Representation of Reality in Western Literature,* trans. Willard Trask (Garden City, N. Y., 1957), p. 117.

stands outside the real meaning of existence. All this is precisely what the word does not mean in the courtly romance. On the contrary, trial through adventure is the real meaning of the knight's ideal existence" (pp. 117-18).

If adventure provides the real meaning of the knight's ideal existence, and if as I have suggested love is the object of adventure—love in the transcendental sense—then knighthood can be understood to be a type of the Christian soul, passing through the world, the "Forest of Adventure," in quest of salvation. The knight may indeed be misguided in his quest; as Boethius explains in the *Consolation*: although all men desire the true good, many are deceived concerning its nature. "All men," he says, "try by various means to attain this state of happiness; for there is naturally implanted in the minds of men the desire for the true good, even though foolish error draws them toward false goods."[20] In fact, the crises at the heart of both *Erec* and *Yvain* center around the knight's misguided pursuit of false love, Erec's selfish withdrawal into sensual delight, and Yvain's love of personal glory. Nevertheless, the ideal, if not always the realization of chivalry, is the Knighthood of Christ. How close Auerbach comes—although he does not see the final connection—to expressing the transcendental nature of knightly adventure and the election of those who achieve it! He cites the parallel but misses the real relationship between courtly and Christian election:

> The degrees of election, and specific election for a specific adventure, are . . . unmistakable wherever we have to do with courtly literature. The series of adventures is thus raised to the status of a fated and graduated test of election; it becomes the basis of a doctrine of personal perfection through a development dictated by fate, a doctrine which was later to break through the class barriers of courtly culture. We must not overlook the fact, it is true, that, contemporaneously

---

20. Boethius, *The Consolation of Philosophy*, trans. Richard Green (Indianapolis, Ind., 1963), p. 43.

with courtly culture, there was another movement which gave expression to this graduated proving of election, as well as to the theory of love, with much greater rigor and clarity— namely, Victorine and Cistercian mysticism. (pp. 118–19)

Auerbach stops short of connecting adventure and salvation. Nevertheless, the concept of adventure, which he describes so well, expresses perfectly the paradoxical, dual nature of salvation. The soul can achieve salvation only by actively seeking it. At the same time, it is possible only through grace, an unearned gift received passively from God. The knight, likewise, sets out *seeking* adventures, and yet these adventures, unforeseeable and even unexpected, *befall* him. The theological paradox thus adumbrated may be understood as a variation on the relation between faith and works, that perennial stumblingblock. "Faith . . . if it have not works, is dead in itself. . . . For even as the body without the spirit is dead; so also faith without works is dead" (James 2:17–26). James draws an apt analogy between faith and works on the one hand, and body and spirit on the other. Theologically, the same paradoxical unity informs them, as it informs the Creation itself—matter created from spirit, from the Word—or the mystery of the Incarnation. The fact that he reverses the terms of the analogy as we would expect them (that is, we would expect the analogy: faith is to works as *spirit* is to *body*) only underscores their essential unity.

As the body without the spirit is dead, so also is adventure that is divorced from love. Thus, Yvain goes mad and falls eventually into a state of unconsciousness that is taken for death itself as a result of his pursuit of empty adventures at the tournaments and his neglect of Laudine. In *Erec*, we have the converse: as faith without works is dead, so is the indulgence in love that withdraws a man from his mission in the world. Erec's mission, moreover, is the most crucial temporal mission, kingship. But love is not enough, as faith is not enough. "Thou believest that there is one

God. Thou dost well: the devils also believe and tremble" (James 2:19). Erec, like Yvain, falls into a state whose appearance is death, in the castle of *Limors*, whose name seems to mean "death," and is helplessly laid out on a bier, while the unscrupulous Count Oringle forces Enide to marry him. Erec's miraculous recovery in the nick of time can best be understood as a resurrection from the spiritual death into which he has let himself fall—an outward sign, that is, of the inner conversion that leads to his perfection as a knight and his coronation as king.

If adventure, in these romances, is the form of spiritual perfection, then it is a coincidence not without meaning that the gift of grace is conventionally thought of as a coming, an *advent*. "Adventure" and "advent" both derive from the Latin *advenire* "to come to," or "to happen." *Adventurus*, the Latin future participle, from which "adventure" most directly derives, characterizes that *which is to come*. The anticipation of advent, both the historical and the eschatalogical advents of Christ, as well as the advent of the Holy Spirit, of grace to the individual Christian as on the disciples at the first Christian Pentecost, is so central to the Christian faith and so pervasive a form of thought in its theology that it need not seem overly ingenious to suggest that the poet was conscious of this verbal connection. It is most explicit in *Erec*, where the sequence of adventures, the perfection of Erec as a knight, culminates in the season of Advent, so that the coronation of Erec on Christmas Day as earthly king is juxtaposed with the advent of Christ, the King of Heaven.[21] I have argued on other, more general and basic grounds that the meaning of adventure is equivalent to the meaning of advent. Word-play is in itself rarely crucial to a poet's meaning, but it may help to indicate a drift of meaning as it embellishes the texture of his verse.

---

21. The adventure of Sir Gawain and the Green Knight is similarly played out against the background of the Advent Season and its meaning. Arthur will not by custom begin to eat at this feast until he has heard "Of sum aventurus thyng," which turns out to be the advent of the Green Knight.

Chrétien employs the figure of advent in a passage cited above; the heart that is awake, Calogrenant directs his audience, receives the word "in its coming" ("an son venir"), and encloses and keeps it (ll. 157–66). This image of the word received and enclosed by the heart, we have seen, evokes Christ's figure of the word as seed. But further, the idea of the coming of the word suggests almost inevitably the meaning of "the Word" at the beginning of St. John's Gospel. The Word is the spirit of God enfleshed in the person of Christ. John's distinction between word and flesh is yet another variation on the distinction discussed above as that between spirit and letter of a text. Calogrenant, somewhat more covertly, is asserting no less than Dante when he writes of the *Commedia* that, "the aim of the whole and of the part is to remove those living in this life from a state of misery and to guide them to a state of happiness."[22] The *Commedia* is to be Virgil and Beatrice to each reader; the act of reading is to guide him to salvation. In exhorting his listeners to receive the word within themselves, Calogrenant suggests that true hearing is incarnation—the received word made flesh, become a living part of the man who hears it. He is affirming for Chrétien the seriousness, the spiritual efficacy of poetry. Poetry, properly taken to heart, leads to salvation.

Word and flesh are indeed a dichotomy parallel to the dichotomy between spirit and letter. But John's conception is the converse of Paul's. Paul wishes to distinguish the spirit from the letter, whereas John sees them as one. The distinction is where we must begin to understand, but the distinction is affirmed only in order to be transcended. Word is made flesh. Even Paul makes the distinction between spirit and letter only to transcend it after all. The thirteenth chapter of 1 Corinthians, well known excerpted from its context, is really the first half of an argument in which Paul asserts

22. Dante Alighieri, *A Translation of Dante's Eleven Letters,* trans. Charles Sterrett Latham, ed. George Rice Carpenter (Boston, 1891), p. 199.

the ultimate unity of spirit and letter. The letter empty of spirit is indeed dead. "Though I speak with the tongues of men and of angels, and have not charity, I am become as sounding brass, or a tinkling cymbal." But the spirit without the vehicle of the letter is equally sterile, because it remains fixed in itself, whereas the spirit is given in order to be spread abroad. "Follow after charity," Paul continues in the next chapter,

> but rather that ye may prophesy. For he that speaketh in an unknown tongue speaketh not unto men, but unto God: for no man understandeth him; howbeit in the spirit he speaketh mysteries. But he that prophesieth speaketh unto men to edification, and exhortation, and comfort. He that speaketh in an unknown tongue edifieth himself; but he that prophesieth edifieth the church. I would that ye all spake with tongues, but rather that ye prophesied: for greater is he that prophesieth than he that speaketh with tongues, except he interpret, that the church may receive edifying. (I Corinthians 14:1–5)

Paul's exhortation not merely to receive the spirit, but to make it wax and multiply in others is very likely one of the sources of the same theme in the prologues to *Erec* and Marie's *Lays*, for Paul too combines the theme of a man's duty to impart his wisdom with the image of fruitfulness. "If I pray in an unknown tongue, my spirit prayeth, but my understanding is without fruit" (1 Corinthians 14:14).

In the next chapter, Paul proceeds from the unity of spirit and letter to the unity of soul and body. Union of soul and body for Paul is conversion. "We shall not all sleep, but we shall all be changed (1 Corinthians 15:51)." He develops the idea, it is true, in affirming the resurrection of the dead, but we must remember that baptism (that is to say, spiritual conversion) is the death of an old life, the resurrection into a new, and that eschatalogical concepts are first of all figurative expressions of spiritual states in this life, here and now. The *Commedia* is only the most glorious and systematic example. Dodd calls the ministry of Christ, in which the Kingdom of God is proclaimed as already arrived, "realized eschatology." "This declaration that the Kingdom of God has already come," he writes, "necessarily dislocates the whole eschatalogical scheme in which its expected coming closes the long vista of the future. The *eschaton* has moved from the future to the present, from the sphere of expectation into that of realized experience" (*The Parables of the Kingdom*, p. 34).

The natural body Paul likens to a seed, whose tiny shape gives no hint of the unforeseeable fruit that it contains and brings forth when it is sown. "It is sown in corruption; it is raised in incorruption: it is sown in dishonor; it is raised in glory: it is sown in weakness; it is raised in power: it is sown a natural body; it is raised a spiritual body" (1 Corinthians 15:42–44). The paradox is wholly contained in that last, remarkable oxymoron, "a spiritual body." Spirit and body only appear to be separate entities, just as parables only appear to hide the meaning they actually contain and moreover reveal when they are "sown" in "good soil." In the same way, love and adventure appear to be different, even conflicting courtly ideals. But Erec and Yvain achieve the transcendence of this conflict in such a way that love and adventure become not only compatible but identical. Worldly adventure leads to strife. But spiritual adventure, by which is signified the advent of the Holy Spirit to earthly affairs, *is* love, and in true love there is no strife. If adventure is the fictional shell of which the sweet kernel of truth is love, or, to give one turn more to the metaphor, if adventure is the body whose spirit is love, the body and the spirit nonetheless are one.

2

The Hart Hunt

The romance of Erec begins at Easter, in "the new time" (l. 27), that is, in spring. Anyone familiar with medieval romance recognizes the opening as conventional: a sequence of knightly adventures is initiated at Arthur's court during the celebration of a major Christian feast, Christmas or Easter or Pentecost. But patterns become conventional only when their meanings are widely understood, and can be taken for granted. Their very self-evidence makes understanding at our remove from Chrétien's audience difficult, but by the same token necessary. Certainly, that the royal court should celebrate sacred holidays lavishly does not in itself ask much explanation; Chrétien's descriptions of Arthur's festivals reflect perhaps quite accurately the celebrations to which he was accustomed at the court of Champagne. But the care that he and other writers of romance take to specify the relation of their narratives to the liturgical calendar suggests more particular connections between the meaning of a romance and the sacred events with which it is identified. The real convention is this: the medieval writer of romance conventionally sets his narrative in some particular relation to the liturgical calendar in order to indicate major themes around which his work is built.[1]

Easter is the central feast of the Christian year, and the theme that its meaning suggests is clear—death and resurrection. In this context is set the opening episode of the romance, the hunt of the white stag. This episode undoubtedly has its roots in Celtic mythology or folklore, in which the figure of the stag plays a prominent role. Two studies of narrative materials related to the hunt of the white stag indicate that the hunted animal is typically magical or divine, and that it leads its pursuer to an encounter with inhabitants of the Other World. Harris argues more particularly that the source of "the custom" of the stag in *Erec*, associated as it is with Easter, was an annual spring ritual connected with the worship of a Celtic deity identifiable with the Roman Diana.[2]

The spiritual character of the White Stag, by virtue of both its mythological origin and its association in Chrétien's poem with Easter, is consistent with the physical setting of the hunt. The temporal setting is the yearly celebration of the death and resurrection of Christ; the spatial setting is "la forest avantureuse" (l. 65). The White Stag is hunted in no ordinary forest, but in the Forest of Adventure, a realm in which the marvelous is ordinary, although none the less marvelous for that. The Forest of Adventure, the setting in which the "matter of Britain" typically is acted out, is the literary descendant of the Other World of Celtic mythology, and just as Easter is a time of heightened spiritual meaning, so this realm of marvels is a place of heightened

---

1. Schneider, *Sir Gawain and the Green Knight,* shows that this fourteenth-century romance, for instance, is built around the meaning of Christmas and New Years (feast of the Circumcision) .

2. Carl Pschmadt, *Die Sage von der verfolgten Hinde* (Greifswald, 1911) ; S. Cigada, "La Legende medievale del Cervo Bianco e le origini della 'matiere de Bretagne,'" *Atti della Accademia Nazionale die Lincei,* Memorie, classe di scienze morali, storiche e filologiche, series 8, vol. 12 (1965) : 363; R. Harris, "The White Stag in Chrétien's *Erec et Enide,*" *French Studies* 10 (1956) : 55–61.

spiritual meaning. The meaning, precisely because of the marvelous nature of events, is obscure, but we sense its presence as we sense the presence of obscure meaning in the fragments that remain to adumbrate the mythology from which these fictional marvels themselves derive. As noted in the previous chapter, this obscurity, which paradoxically hides meaning in order to reveal it, and which, by posing the conundrum of its meaning makes us more than usually aware of the presence of an inner reality that permeates also the everyday world, is the characteristic obscurity of allegory. Mythology is not obscure in this sense, for it is the direct, idiomatic expression in figurative language of experience. Only at the touch of archaeology does mythology turn obscure; to those who do not share the experience of which it is the natural expression, mythology appears to function allegorically.[3]

It is often said that Chrétien, through ignorance or indifference, put his poems together without regard to the meaning and coherence of the Celtic materials that he received from the *conteurs*. Thus he produced elegant but essentially garbled pastiches, notwithstanding his own unequivocal denunciation of those who garble the story of Erec, for instance. While it is true that Chrétien's interests in his materials did not reflect the ideology of the Celts, it does not follow that he could not use them in a new way, coherent in terms of an ideology of his own time.

The figure of the hunted stag, for example, plays a prominent role in the mythology in which this episode in *Erec* apparently has its source. But the figure was likely to have conveyed a different meaning to the twelfth-century court poet at Troyes. For the stag plays an equally prominent role in the long figurative tradition of patristic commentary and the representation of its imagery in medieval art. Chrétien, educated as a clerk, possibly ordained as a priest, can

---

3. See Owen Barfield, *Poetic Diction: A Study in Meaning* (New York, 1964), esp. chaps. 3 and 4.

be assumed to have been perfectly familiar with these figurative traditions, from theological studies as well as from
the art of the Church and manuscript illuminations.

The adaptation to Christian purposes of motifs from Celtic mythology was not unique with Chrétien. We have an
example in the representations of stag hunts carved on pre-
Norman Irish high crosses. Françoise Henry believes that
these representations derive from mythological motifs associated with the stag-horned god, Cernunnos, but were used
on the crosses as figures of Christ pursuing the soul.[4] This
interpretation rests on the figure of Psalm 41: "As the hart
longs for the fountains of water, so my soul longs for thee,
O Lord" (Psalm 41:2).

The Bestiary applies a similar symbolism to the stag,
which it likens to the faithful Christian. Stags in herds
cross large bodies of water, each supporting its head on the
rump of the animal in front; in the same way, the Bestiary
tells us, Christians who abandon the comforts of this world
for the spiritual pastures of the Church help and support each
other in their passage by example and good works. As stags
pass over these waters in a hurry so as not to become befouled, faithful Christians hurry over occasions to sin. Finally, as the stag was thought to shed sickness and old age by
devouring snakes, so faithful Christians "after snuffing up the
devil-snake, i. e., after the perpetration of sin . . . run with
Confession to Our Lord Jesus Christ, who is the true fountain, and, drinking the precepts laid down by him, our
Christians are renovated—the Old Age of Sin having been
shed."[5]

The stag at the fountain is the central image in the complex of the animal's religious symbolism. From the commentaries of Augustine and Jerome, exegesis of the second
verse of Psalm 41 remains consistent throughout the Middle
Ages. The thirsting hart is a type of the catechumen, who

4. Françoise Henry, *Irish High Crosses* (Dublin, 1964), esp. pp. 50–52.
5. *The Bestiary*, trans. T. H. White (New York, 1954), pp. 38–39.

longs for the renewing water of baptism. We may take as representative Peter Lombard's commentary, based on the earlier commentaries of Augustine, Jerome, Cassiodorus, and Alcuin:

> This likeness of the hart is fitted to the catechumen in this manner: just as the hart, burning from the snake it has ingested, seeks the fountain in order to put out the fire, so the catechumen, knowing himself to be burning with the poison of the collective sins of the earth, longs for and seeks the fountain of baptism, where he sheds the hair of sins and the horns of pride, and is thus rejuvenated, made a new man. It applies to the perfect, however, in this manner: just as the hart draws in the snake, and destroys that which he has ingested, whereby because of that which it has destroyed it seeks the fountain to drink—so the man of faith, because of the faults and sins destroyed within him, longs for the fountain of contemplation, at which he is restored. Both the perfect and the catechumen, however, strive to reach the same fountain, namely Christ, who is the fountain of living waters.[6]

Through this traditional symbolism, and the use of the Psalm itself in the liturgy of baptism, the figure of the hart became closely associated with the administration of the sacrament.[7] Baptism was normally administered on Holy Saturday, the Easter vigil, in a smaller annex to the church proper, the baptistery. Its shape conventionally was round, sometimes eight-sided to signify the resurrection (Sunday reckoned as the day after the Sabbath, or the eighth day). The baptistery was frequently fed by its own natural spring, and the interior walls surrounding the central font were commonly decorated to represent a forest filled with animals, principally harts—figuratively, the paradise of the Church to

---

6. *PL,* ed. J. P. Migne, vol. 191, cols. 415–16, my trans.

7. See articles on *baptistère* in *Dictionnaire D'Archéologie Chrétienne et de Liturgie,* ed. dom Fernand Cabrol (Paris, 1910); *baptismal font* and *baptistery* in *The Catholic Encyclopedia.* See also J. G. Davies, *The Architectural Setting of Baptism* (London, 1962); and Paul A. Underwood, "The Fountain of Life in Manuscripts of the Gospels," *Dumbarton Oaks Papers,* no. 5 (Harvard University, 1950), pp. 43–138.

which the sacrament of baptism gives entrance. Sometimes the harts were free-standing sculptures placed around the font, or in the font itself to serve as water spouts.[8]

The stag hunt is also closely associated with baptism. The illumination of Psalm 41 in the ninth-century Utrecht Psalter, for instance, shows a stag pursued by two hounds.[9] In the twelfth-century reception hall of Roger in the Palazzo Reale in Palermo, a lunette mosaic depicts a paradise at the center of which is a *fons vitae* (of which the baptismal font is a type); facing peacocks drink from the fountain, and above them, archers aim their bows at two stags. Baptism, figuratively the "door" to the Church, is an appropriate theme for the decoration of a reception hall. A baptismal font from the middle of the twelfth century at Dalby in Sweden shows a stag pursued by a hunter with a horn and a leashed hound in relief on its circumference.[10] The pre-Norman font at St. Mary Church, Torquay, on the Dorsetshire coast also depicts a stag hunt. This baptismal motif presumably expresses the same allegory as that on the Irish high crosses: the stag is the soul, pursued by the hunter Christ to the waters of the font.

But patristic tradition applies another symbolism to the stag; we find it in commentaries on Psalm 21, specifically on the title given the psalm in Hebrew, rendered in Latin, *pro cerva matutina*, "for the hind of the morning." This is the psalm that begins with the words repeated in Matthew's Gospel as the seven last words of Christ. Its association with the crucifixion makes it logical that the hind of the Hebrew title be taken by the patristic exegetes to signify Christ. In his commentary on this psalm, Peter Lombard quotes Alcuin: "The hind, namely, is the human nature of

---

8. Underwood, pp. 50–51.

9. E. T. DeWald, *The Illustrations of the Utrecht Psalter* (Princeton, London & Leipzig), fol. 24. v.

10. Illustrated in Lars Tynell, *Skanes Medeltida Dopfuntar* (Stockholm, 1913), PL. XLIII, and see pp. 95, 168; also Monica Rydbeck, *Skanes Stenmästare före 1200* (Lund, 1936), pp. 88–96.

Christ, which leapt over the mire and thorn bushes of the sins, and in the morning, in the glory of the resurrection, was as it were taken into heaven."[11] This iconography, incidentally, is not affected by the difference of sex; any member of the deer family may assume such meaning. For example, in his commentary on Psalm 41, Bede calls Christ, whom we have seen likened to the hind, *cervus cervorum*, "hart of harts."[12] Masculine and feminine forms are used as equivalent by Alanus de Insulis in the entry for *cervus* in his theological dictionary. The stag, he explains, signifies the human nature of Christ; his allegory is based on the standard interpretation of the hind of Psalm 21.[13]

The symbolism of the stag as Christ is carried over into hagiographic tradition in the popular legend of St. Eustace, the wealthy and powerful Roman commander who was converted when, as he was hunting, the stag that he pursued turned to face him, revealing between its antlers the sign of the cross. Here the stag hunt is a type of the conversion experience.[14] Howard Helsinger shows that the Saint's legend is an important source of the typical romance motif (of which the "custom of the White Stag" in *Erec* is a clear example) of the stag hunt that is the initiatory experience of the hero, and leads to a surprising and crucial turn of events (Helsinger, p. 194).

In romance tradition, too, we find the religious symbolism of the stag used in explicit allegory. In the early thirteenth-century *Queste del Saint Graal*,[15] Galahad, Bors, and Perceval and his sister pursue a white stag and four lions to a hermitage. There they enter a chapel, and watch the stag miraculously become a man and take a seat on the altar, as the lions become man, lion, eagle, and ox, the sym-

---

11. *PL*, ed. J. P. Migne, vol. 210, col. 737, my trans.
12. *PL*, vol. 93, col. 702.
13. *Distinctiones Dictionum Theologicum, PL*, vol. 210, col. 737.
14. Howard Helsinger, *"The Book of the Duchess* and the Hunt of the *Hart,"* Ph.D. diss. (Princeton, 1970).
15. Ed. Albert Pauphilet (Paris, 1923), pp. 234–36.

bols of the evangelists, and take their places (as we see them typically in visual art) around the seated figure. The hermit explains the vision to the knights, in Malory's rendering of the French: "A, lordys . . . well oughte oure Lorde be signifyed to an harte. For the harte, whan he ys olde, he waxith yonge agayne in his whyght skynne. Ryght so commyth agayne our Lorde frome deth to lyff, for He lost erthely fleysshe, that was the dedly fleyssh whych He had takyn in the wombe of the Blyssed Virgyne Mary. And for that cause appered oure Lorde as a whyghte harte withoute spot."[16] The hermit indicates the commonplace nature of this symbolism when he adds that, "oftyntymes or thys hath oure Lorde shewed Hym unto good men and to good knyghtes in lyknesse of an herte."

The stag, then, is identified on the one hand with the catechumen approaching baptism, and on the other with Christ, particularly in connection with the central events of his humanity, the crucifixion and the resurrection. This apparently ambivalent iconographic tradition, however, actually reflects in a precise way the meaning of Christian initiation. For the catechumen, baptized ideally on Holy Saturday,[17] the commemoration of Christ's descent into Hell, himself assumes the nature of the crucified Christ, and participates in his resurrection. "For we are buried together with him by baptism into death; that as Christ is risen from the dead by the glory of the Father, so we also may walk in newness of life. For if we have been planted together in the likeness of his death, we shall be also in the likeness of his resurrection" (Romans 6:4–5).

The Fathers elaborate St. Paul's identification of baptism with death and resurrection. Not only does the catechumen "die" to sin in baptism in imitation of Christ's death; "un-

---

16. *Works,* ed. E. Vinaver (London, 1964), p. 718.
17. At least the holy water used in the administration of the sacrament must have been consecrated on Holy Saturday or Pentecost. The important relation between Pentecost and baptism will be further discussed in connection with *Yvain.*

der the waters" he struggles with the devil and overcomes him, in imitation of the harrowing of Hell.[18] Thus, baptism must be seen not only as the passive reception of grace by the catechumen, but as a militant and painful struggle with the forces of sin and death within himself.[19] Thus, the stag hunts on the crosses and the stag hunts on the baptismal fonts represent not separate iconographic traditions, but on the contrary share the complex meaning of Christ's sacrifice and the sacrament by which it is made effectual in the soul.

The episode of the hunt of the White Stag in *Erec* encompasses also Erec's pursuit of Yder and his victory over him in the tournament for the sparrow-hawk, as well as his winning of Enide and return with her to Arthur's court. For not until Arthur bestows the prize kiss on the fairest maiden of the court is the "custom" of the White Stag fulfilled. Indeed, the entire episode functions as the initiation to what we will see is a coherent sequence of events culminating in Erec's coronation at the end of the romance. The iconography of this adventure reveals, moreover, that Erec's initiation, the beginning of a long and arduous process of preparation for the sacred crown, is not primarily a secular initiation, but a spiritual one, and pertains typologically to the initiatory rites of the Church.

The season is Easter, ". . . au tans novel" (l. 27), the time of newness, the time, as St. Paul puts it, "to put off . . . the old man, who is corrupted according to the desire of error . . . [to] be renewed in the spirit of your mind, and put on the new man, who according to God is created in justice and holiness of truth" (Ephesians 4:22–24). By the same token, the hunt for the White Stag begins early in the morning (see ll. 67–74). The same commentaries on Psalm 21 that help to establish the iconography of the stag also

---

18. See Jean Daniélou, "La symbolisme des rites baptismaux," *Dieu Vivant* 1 (1945) : 10.

19. The catechumen's identification with Christ is also reflected in the liturgy for the consecration of baptismal water on Holy Saturday, in which the font is likened to the immaculate womb of the Virgin.

elucidate the spiritual meaning of this otherwise realistic detail. In commenting on the title in the Vulgate, *pro susceptione matutina*, Bede writes: "An early morning undertaking, moreover, indicates the time of the resurrection, when he himself, glorified, assumed for the sake of greater glory, a mortal body, the refuse of the old man."[20]

Gawain's objection to the hunt, that it will cause strife among the maidens of the court, who will each claim the right as the most beautiful to the kiss that is to be bestowed by the slayer of the stag, reveals how the court stands in need of spiritual renewal. The strife that Gawain foresees has its source in pride, chief of the sins, and is typical of the unregenerate old man under the Old Law. It is the same strife that we find frequently pictured in marginalia—hirsute or semi-bestial men, sometimes apes, attacking each other with clubs or other weapons, often pointedly below the principal illumination and, in contrast with it, a Nativity, for example, to indicate the victory of grace over strife. Gawain's admonition is worldly wisdom, to be sure, and Arthur's bullish insistence seems to arise from the very pride that Gawain warns will throw the court into dissension. Arthur knows all that, he says, but a king's word once spoken ought not to be contradicted. In spite of Arthur's folly, Gawain's worldly wisdom is superseded by events, because the events themselves take on a sacred and providential character.

Arthur appears even more foolish when, having had his way against the counsel of Gawain—having slain the stag and brought on rumblings of the trouble he has been warned of —he begs his nephew now to get him out of the jam:

> "Biaus niés Gauvains! conselliez m'an
> Sauve m'enor et ma droiture!" (ll. 308–9)

His "honor" is saved, not by Gawain after all, but by the

---

20. *PL*, vol. 93, col. 590, my trans.

queen's suggestion that they wait the three days in which Erec has vowed to carry out his vengeance and return to court. Arthur's behavior may surprise us, but we are meant to view it ironically. He had been depicted in a contemptible light before Chrétien's time. In fact, we find two parallel traditions concerning Arthur: in one, he is the great *dux bellorum*, the once and future king who is Britain's savior; in the other, he is a fool. In a mosaic dated 1165 in the Cathedral of Otranto, for instance, he is shown riding a goat, the animal of Venus, symbol of lechery, and hardly a dignified mount for a king.[21]

We think of Chrétien's romances as "Arthurian," yet ironically the British king plays no significant role in the action, and cuts at his best an unimposing figure. In *Erec* Arthur is meant to serve as contrast to the ideal of holy kingship to which the young knight, in the course of his adventures, attains. Arthur is the model of what a king should not be. Thus, the king appears to carry out the "custom" of the White Stag by himself slaying the stag and bestowing the kiss. But it is Erec, not Arthur, who is profoundly affected by it, and who partakes of the sacramental substance of the adventure. It is fitting that the king and his court merely wait around while Erec thrusts himself into the real, the decisive action.

The "custom" is fulfilled, as it happens, in three days. Erec seems to know how long it will take, for he tells the queen that he will return within that time, "joyous or sad," and the queen calms the court by telling them that they need wait only the three days for her avenger to return. On the first of the three days the stag is slain. This hunt is typologically imbued with the meaning of the crucifixion, on Good Friday. On the second of the days, Erec vanquishes his

21. Reproduced in Roger Sherman Loomis, *Arthurian Legend in Medieval Art* (New York, 1938), PLs. 9, 9 (a) ; on the dual tradition of King Arthur, see E. Faral, *Légende Arturienne* (Paris, 1929), 1: 236–42; C. Grant Loomis, "King Arthur and the Saints," *Speculum* 8 (1933) : 478–80.

enemy, Yder, son of Nutt, and in his victory we may see by analogy the meaning of Christ's descent into Hell on Saturday, and his victory there over death and sin. On the third day, Erec returns to the court in triumph as Christ in triumph rose on the third day, Easter Sunday. This pattern of death and resurrection in the "custom" of the stag pertains in turn, we have seen, to the initiatory rites of baptism, the sacramental participation of each Christian in the crucifixion, the harrowing, and the resurrection of Christ.

If we consider the episode of the White Stag as a whole, we see that Erec's accomplishment of the adventure functions not only as his personal initiation, but also as the restoration of harmony to the court. Erec's inner state is reflected in the world about him, and this relationship between inner and outer is closer than mere analogy; it is the basis of the ideal of kingship to which Erec aspires: the state of the kingdom reflects exactly the spiritual state of its king. Thus, Arthur's court is unstable because its king is foolish. But Erec's kingdom will prosper harmoniously because he learns, in the course of his adventures, to bring order to his own life.

The pride that threatens to disrupt Arthur's court is typified by Yder, son of Nutt, in his discourtesy to the Queen's messengers, as well as his arrogant defense of the sparrowhawk on the silver perch:

> Mout chevauche orguelleusemant
> Vers l'esprevier isnelemant. (ll. 795–96)

But the crowd is so thick around the perch that the count of the castle has to clear the place with his whip. The dwarf has voiced the same arrogant pride earlier when he warned the Queen's maiden,

> "Alez arriere! n'est pas droiz
> Qu'a si buen chevalier parloiz." (ll. 173–74)

Erec then perceives Yder as, "Mout felon et desmesuré" (l. 228); if he strikes back at the dwarf, Erec thinks to himself, unarmed as he is, "Tost m'oceïst par son orguel" (l. 243). Pride is typified still more graphically by the dwarf, hunchbacked and cruel, who rudely strikes Erec and the Queen's maiden with his whip as they approach the stranger knight and his lady. Although the catechumen's struggle "under the waters" in baptism is figuratively with an objective adversary, it must be understood spiritually as an inner struggle against the "devil" within the catechumen himself. Erec's first adventure centers around his struggle with Yder in the "custom" of the sparrow-hawk. But when the dwarf strikes Erec with his whip, he strikes him on the neck, the proverbial seat of pride, indicating the inner nature of the struggle which lies ahead.

Yder's arrogance, and the prideful dissension of Arthur's court are pointedly contrasted with the modest demeanor of Enide, the wise and beautiful daughter of the impoverished vavasor who shelters Erec and lends him arms for the tournament of the sparrow-hawk. When she sees Erec for the first time, she blushes:

> Quant ele le chevalier voit,
> Que onques mes veü n'avoit,
> Un petit arriere s'estut
> Por ce qu'ele ne le conut.
> Vergoigne an ot et si rogi. (ll. 443–47)

Chrétien gives Enide an unusually extensive and full description. The contrast he notes between the outer covering of her clothes and the beautiful body that it conceals is reminiscent of the opening words of the romance, which caution the audience not to be deceived by outward appearances:

> Povre estoit la robe defors,
> Mes dessoz estoit biaus li cors. (ll. 409–10)

Just as the peasants' proverb covertly expresses the nature of allegory, this parallel instance of the same principle suggests that the description of Enide will reveal more than may at first appear, if we take care to look beyond the surface.

Enide is a child of nature—nature's most perfect creature, in fact:

> Mout estoit la pucele jante,
> Car tote i ot mise s'antante
> Nature qui fait l'avoit. (ll. 411–13)

Nature herself was astonished at the unparalleled beauty of her work:

> Ele meïsme s'an estoit
> Plus de cinc canz foiz mervelliee,
> Comant une sole foiiee
> Tant bele chose feire sot,
> Ne puis tant pener ne se pot
> Qu'ele poïst son essanpleire
> An nule guise contre feire. (ll. 414–20)

Chrétien contrasts Enide with the most famous, certainly the most notorious heroine of medieval romance in order to set off her innocence against Iseult's deceit and lust:

> De cesti tesmoigne Nature,
> Qu'onques si bele creature
> Ne fue veüe an tot le monde.
> Por voir vos di qu'Iseuz, la blonde,
> N'ot tant les crins sors ne luisanz,
> Que a cesti ne fu neanz. (ll. 421–26)

The same contrast is drawn later in the romance, when Enide is described as

> . . . une dame si bele,
> Qu'Iseuz sanblast estre s'ancele. (ll. 4945–46)

To underscore the contrast, Chrétien compares the whiteness of Enide's forehead with the white of the lily, symbol of purity:

> Plus ot, que n'est la flors de lis,
> Cler et blanc le front et le vis. (ll. 427–28)

The same comparison appears in the description of Nature herself in the contemporaneous *De planctu Naturae* of Alanus de Insulis: "But in truth her forehead, wide and full and even, was of the milk-white lily in color, and seemed to vie with the lily."[22]

Chrétien's description of Enide parallels other aspects of Alanus's Nature. The white of her face is flushed with rose:

> Sor la blanchor par grant mervoille
> D'une color fresche et vermoille,
> Que Nature li ot donee,
> Estoit sa face anluminee. (ll. 429–32)

Alanus is more expansive: "The glowing fire of her cheeks, kindled with the light of roses, with soft flame cheered her face; and this in turn chastened the pleasing warmth with cool whiteness—like rose-color on fine linen" (p. 6).

Enide's eyes are like stars:

> Li oel si grant clarté randoient
> Que deus estoiles ressanbloient. (ll. 433–34)

Alanus says of Nature: "The clear calm of the eyes, which

---

22. No more precise dating is possible than that each of these poems must have been composed within the same twenty-year period, 1150–1170. Raynaud De Lage, *Alain De Lille: Poète du XIIᵉ Siècle* (Montreal & Paris, 1951), conjectures roughly that the *De planctu* precedes the *Anticlaudianus* (1183–84) by a dozen to twenty years, but that guess is based on his sense of the relative literary sophistication of the two works. Foerster (introduction to cited text) admits the possibility of a date for *Erec* as early as 1150, but Mario Roques (introduction to his edition *Erec et Enide*, Les Classiques Français du Moyen Age (Paris, 1963) sets the *terminus a quo* at 1155, the date of Wace's *Brut*. Roques admits the possibility of a date as late as 1170. Translation is from *The Complaint of Nature*, trans. Douglas M. Moffat, Yale Studies in English (New York, 1908), p. 5. Alanus's text may be found in *PL*, vol. 210, cols. 429–82.

attracted with friendly light, offered the freshness of twin stars" (p. 6).

Finally, Chrétien despairs of his ability to convey in words what was really made to be seen:

> Que diroie de sa biaute?
> Ce fu cele par verite,
> Qui fu feite por esgarder;　(ll. 437–39)

for she was like a mirror in which one might see himself:

> Qu'an li se poïst an mirer
> Aussi come an un mireor.　(ll. 440–41)

On the face of it, this likeness seems a curious way to compliment a lady on her singular loveliness. The figure suggests that Enide shows every man his own image, that she is thus not unique, but representative—the image of man. But Chrétien says one *might* see himself in her—one might, that is, if one looks with the proper intention and in the proper way. Enide is not simply the passive receptacle of whatever chance qualities the viewer—king, or tradesman, or riffraff—happens to possess and set before her. She is, rather, a paragon, and shows any man his own image by implication only if he will consider her perfect beauty, and his own deformity in relation to it.

The simile of the mirror is a philosophical and literary commonplace,[23] and a quick survey of this convention, despite its ambivalence and complexity, will illuminate Enide's role in the romance. Among the great variety of things lik-

---

23. A useful brief survey of the philosophical background of the mirror figure is Sister Ritamary Bradley, C. H. M., "Backgrounds of the Title *Speculum* in Medieval Literature," *Speculum* 29 (1954): 100–115. On the mirror in visual art, see G. F. Hartlaub, *Zauber des Spiegels: Geschichte und Bedeutung des Spiegels in der Kunst* (Munich, 1951). A comprehensive work on the philosophical sources and uses of the figure in the twelfth century is Robert Javelet, *Image et Ressemblance au douzième siècle de Saint Anselm à Alain de Lille* (Strasbourg, 1967). See also Hans Leisegang, "La connaissance de Dieu au miroir de l'âme et de la nature," *Revue d'Histoire et de Philosophie réligieuses* 17 (1937): 145–71.

ened by medieval writers to a mirror, conspicuous in the present context is the idealized lady of the courtly love lyric. The simile arises naturally and universally in love poetry from the actual physical reflection of the lover in the eyes into which he gazes. In this sense, the lady is literally a mirror, or more precisely, two mirrors. But in the poetry of the Provençal troubadours, argues Frederick Goldin, she is made a mirror metaphorically in that she is the sum, the paragon of the virtues to which the poet and his audience aspire, the objectification, or rather the embodiment of otherwise invisible spiritual qualities. These spiritual qualities, however, are no less ideal for being embodied in her. Thus, she is a "mirror" by virtue of the perfection or clarity of that which is revealed in her, as well as by the revelation itself. "We look to her to know what we ought to be, and therefore what we are. It is for *us* that she exists. She is there to be consulted, like a mirror, by every courtly person. She reflects our future condition, the goal of our striving. She makes visible for us what would otherwise be mere concepts dissociated from experience: *ricor, pretz, valor, cortesia, digz belhs, grans onors*; we know what these things are because we know *her*."[24]

Although the simile was conventional among the troubadours, it certainly did not originate with them. The tradition with which we are here concerned may be traced back through the philosophical currents of Platonism to Plato himself, not only in his use of the figure of the mirror, but more fundamentally in the concepts about the relation of spirit to matter that underlie the figure. In Platonic philosophy, the mirror expresses the relationship of correspondence that pertains between the spiritual realm of immutable forms and the material realm of visible creation. The mirror expresses moreover the correspondences that pertain among all the levels of the hierarchy of creation, all the links in the "great

24. Frederick Goldin, *The Mirror of Narcissus in the Courtly Love Lyric* (Ithaca, N. Y., 1967), p. 78.

chain of being." Macrobius, who transmitted much of the Plotinian neoplatonic doctrine to the Latin Middle Ages, epitomizes this figurative convention in likening the multiple correspondences among hierarchical levels of being to the multiple reflections of a single face in a series of mirrors. "Since, from the Supreme God Mind arises, and from Mind, Soul, and since this in turn creates all subsequent things and fills them all with life, and since this single radiance illumines all and is reflected in each, as a single face might be reflected in many mirrors placed in a series; and since all things follow in continuous succession, degenerating in sequence to the very bottom of the series, the attentive observer will discover a connection of parts, from the Supreme God down to the last dregs of things, mutually linked together and without a break."[25]

But the Platonic mirror is an ambivalent figure. Goldin distinguishes among the three conventional types of mirror similes, "the mirror of the ideal," "the mirror of matter," and "the ambivalent mirror" (see pp. 4–15). The radically different uses to which the figure was put stem from the paradoxical nature of the mirror, itself material, but able to show immaterial images. If the ideality of the image is stressed, the mirror's virtue is its revelation of the immutable forms of the realm of spirit. The figure may be used in the opposite sense, however, if the materiality and passivity of the mirror are stressed. "Then we condemn it as a snare of vain images that seduce us with a false vision of beauty and leave us with nothing, further away than ever from the ideal to which we aspired" (Goldin, p. 4). In the third instance, we apprehend both the seductively material nature of the mirror and its ability to reveal the otherwise invisible forms. The "ambivalent mirror" reflects most precisely the proper relationship between matter and spirit. We must use the world of matter, avoiding the temptation to

---

25 *Commentarium in Somnium Scipionis*, I, xiv, 15, trans. in Arthur O. Lovejoy, *The Great Chain of Being* (New York, 1960), p. 63.

pursue it for its own sake, in order to attain the world of spirit. As the twelfth-century Richard of St. Victor puts it, "When we wish to ascend, we naturally use a ladder, we who are men and unable to fly. Then let [us] use as a ladder the similitude of visible things, so that the things we cannot see by direct vision we may become able to see from this watchtower and as though in a mirror" (trans. in Goldin, p. 8, from *De Trinitate*, V, vi) .

The most famous example of the mirror simile from this cautionary, if not pessimistic point of view is St. Paul's glass through which we see but darkly, or as the Vulgate reads, *in aenigmate*, "in mysteries," or, we might say, in allegories. The sensible world is an allegory which, properly perceived, reveals the intelligible. There is a delicate balance in this "ambivalent mirror" between contempt for the inferiority of matter, and praise of its capacity to reveal the eternal; the use of the figure leans now this way, now that. Plato concludes the *Timaeus* by declaring the universe to be no less than a "perceptible god." "For having received in full its complement of living creatures, mortal and immortal, this world has thus become a visible living creature embracing all that are visible and an image of the intelligible, a perceptible god, supreme in greatness and excellence, in beauty and perfection, this Heaven single in its kind and one."[26]

The balance depends on the maintenance of just order in the universal hierarchy—most fundamentally in the relationship of matter to spirit. Matter, in Christian neo-Platonism, is not inherently evil, but can only be put to evil uses by the corrupted will of fallen man. When matter is used for the purpose of elevating mind and spirit to the contemplation of and participation in eternal forms, its use conforms with the Good. The subject of Chrétien's romance is Erec's initiation and education to kingship; the true relationship of matter to spirit is his fundamental lesson. How must a king

---

26. *Plato's Timaeus*, ed. & trans. Francis M. Cornford (Indianapolis, Ind., 1959) , p. 117.

govern his realm so as to maintain his people in their proper relation to both earthly and divine authority? But a parallel, not to say prior question is how must a man govern himself so as to maintain his own body—on which he depends to promote even the most spiritual ends, even to pursue a life of contemplation—in its proper relation to his soul?

Platonic idealism can easily lead the philosopher to contempt for the merely sensible world, an imperfect and corrupt copy of the eternal, but not so easily the king. For him, the fruit of contemplation must be active leadership of his people. Moreover, the neo-Platonism closest to hand for Chrétien, the naturalism of the school of Chartres and its followers, notably Bernard Silvestris and Alanus de Insulis, was not even philosophically ascetic. Quite the reverse. It celebrated the place of the Creation in the hierarchical scheme of providence. This world cannot be contemptible if it indeed gives man the image of a perfect world, and is informed and infused by the essence of its perfection.

One of the most influential works associated with Chartrian neo-Platonism is the *De mundi universitate* of Bernard Silvestris. In this *prosimetrum* (modeled formally on Boethius and Martianus Capella) Bernard sets forth a cosmogony under the veil of an allegory based on classical figures, but revealing a Christian philosophy. Incidentally, here is another parallel to the Christian use that the writers of romance make of an alien mythology. Gilson argues that the work is in effect a philosophical commentary on the six days of creation, and that it must be seen in the tradition of patristic commentary on Genesis. We must not be deceived by appearances, he warns; "le paganisme de la forme risque de dissimuler le christianisme du fond."[27]

In the first of the two books into which Bernard's work is divided, entitled "megacosmus," Noys, a spiritual emana-

---

27. E. Gilson, "La cosmogonie de Bernardus Silvestris," *Archives d'histoire doctrinale et littéraire du Moyen Age* 3 (Paris, 1928) : 9.

tion of God identifiable with the Word, imposes order and
form on the chaotic matter of the universe at the behest of
Nature, whose figure expresses "the female longing of matter to receive . . . form."[28] In the second book, entitled "mi-
crocosmus," Nature fulfills the design of Noys by fashioning
man. The realm of Noys is the realm of forms, but within
her is the potentiality of the realm of Nature, the realm
of physical bodies. "Noys, therefore, is the intellect of the
supreme, most excellent God, and from his divinity was born
her nature, in which images of life in actuality, ideas of the
eternal, the intelligible world, and knowledge of things were
all pre-fixed. Thus in her might be seen as in a more pol-
ished mirror whatever concerning generation, whatever concerning His Creation the more secret disposition of God had
ordained."[29]

"L'âme du monde produit les âmes des choses," writes
Gilson; "Nature produit leurs corps" (p. 18). Nature *pro-*
creates in time and space what God has created in eternal
spirit. "Nature . . . est donc le principe fécondant de la matière" (p. 18). Thus, Noys addresses her: "Nature, blessed
fruitfulness of my womb" (Book I, ii, 3–4). Man the mi-
crocosm corresponds to the macrocosm, and the same relation holds within him as between the intelligible and the
sensible in the universe at large. Man's soul is of a higher,
more perfect essence than his mortal body. But the soul
depends on a body properly subordinated to it. Thus, although the body dies, the principle of procreation that resides in it, and that transcends its death, partakes of the
supreme Good. The *De mundi universitate* concludes with
sober praise of the genitals, instruments of that procreation:

---

28. C. S. Lewis, *The Allegory of Love* (New York, 1958), p. 90. For a
fuller description of the *De mundi universitate* and its tradition, see Lewis,
chap. 2, "Allegory," pp. 44–111; and E. R. Curtius, chap. 6, "The Goddess
Natura," *European Literature and the Latin Middle Ages*, pp. 106–27.

29. *De mundi universitate*, Book I, ii, 152–57, ed. Carl Sigmund Barach
and Johann Wrobel (Innsbruck, 1876), p. 13: my trans.

Pleasant and fitting both their use will be
When time and mode and measure do agree,
Else withering from the root all lives would fail
And that old Chaos o'er the wreck prevail.
Conquerors of Death! they fill each empty place
In Nature and immortalize the race.[30]

"Here at last," exclaims C. S. Lewis of Bernard's measured optimism, "we find a whole man" (p. 98).

Wholeness depends on the familiar medieval virtue *mesure*, descendant of the classical golden mean. Moderation is the course advised the dreamer in the *De planctu Naturae*. " 'I do not deny the essential nature of love honorableness if it is checked by the bridle of moderation, if it is restrained by the reins of sobriety' " (Prose V, p. 49), Alanus's Nature declares. This work (an allegorical *prosimetrum* like the *De mundi universitate*) is an attack on the perversion of sexual love from its proper function in marriage of contravening fated death. Alanus attacks particularly the perversion of homosexuality, the ultimate dead-end of sterility in the pursuit of pleasure for its own sake. Indeed, procreation is for Alanus a "tithe" and a duty within "the rule of marital coition, with its lawful embraces" (Prose V, p. 50). If the *De planctu* is a condemnation of perversion, it is by the same token a celebration of marriage, whose joys are not to be shunned, but embraced under the guidance of reason. Like Plato in *The Republic*, Alanus expresses the just relation of faculties in man by a political allegory. "The loins, like outlying districts, give over the extreme parts of the body to passionate pleasures. These, not daring to oppose the direction of magnanimity, serve her will. In this realm, then, wisdom assumes the place of commander, magnanimity the likeness of the administrator, passion acquires the appearance of the servant" (Prose III, p. 28). In the whole man, the body is the soul's servant. But Nature advises against ascetic rejection of the body's needs:

---

30. Book II, xiv, 155 ff., trans. in Lewis, p. 97.

"To the end . . . that Scylla of the greedy whirlpool do not whelm thee in the deep night of self-indulgence, apply the curbs of moderation to thy palate, pay thy belly its due most temperately. . . .That the despot who always exults in the flesh may drive thee the less, let quiet Cupid take his rest. Let the bridles of love be checked in thee, and the sting of the flesh faint and be numb, and let the flesh thus become the handmaid of the spirit" (Metre VIII, pp. 75–76).

This same relationship between body and soul is expressed in terms of marriage. The marriage simile, moreover, is familiar from the Pauline epistle, inserted in the nuptial mass, which likens the man's love for his wife on the one hand to Christ's love for his Church, and on the other, to the man's natural love for his own body:

> Let women be subject to their husbands, as to the Lord: Because the husband is the head of the wife, as Christ is the head of the church. He is the saviour of his body. . . . Husbands, love your wives, as Christ also loved the church, and delivered himself up for it. . . . So also ought men to love their wives as their own bodies. He that loveth his wife, loveth himself. For no man ever hated his own flesh; but nourisheth and cherisheth it, as also Christ doth the church: Because we are members of his body, of his flesh, and of his bones. (Ephesians 5:22–30)

Nature tells the dreamer, ". . . Arranging the different offices of the members for the protection of the body, I ordered the senses, as guards of the corporeal realm, to keep watch, that like spies on foreign enemies they might defend the body from external assault. So would the material part of the whole body, being adorned with the higher glories of nature, be united more agreeably when it came to marriage with its spouse the spirit; and so would not the spouse, in disgust at the baseness of its mate, oppose the marriage."[31] (Prose III, pp. 24–25)

---

31. On nature and the body in prescholastic philosophy, see Javelet, chap. 6, "L'homme à l'image et à la ressemblance," esp. secs. 6, "Nature et corps, vestige de Dieu," and 7, "Homme et femme à l'image de Dieu?" pp. 224–45.

The correspondence between marriage and the relation of body to soul was turned into an allegory by medieval philosophers.[32] Javelet cites various sources, from John the Scot[33] to Peter Lombard and William of Conches, as well as the more popular *Glossa Ordinaria*, to illustrate the conventional character of the analogy between man and woman, and spirit (or reason) and flesh. Peter Lombard puts it succinctly: "Mulier typus carnis, Adam rationis" (*PL*, vol. 192, col. 342). Medieval writers on the subject often worked variations on a common formula: as man is the image of God, so woman is the image of man, the image of an image. Thus, she represents in her greater remove from divinity, exteriority—the body. Nevertheless, even as the sign of the body's exteriority she is the image of man. Godfrey of Admont declares that man may see his condition reflected in woman as in a mirror (*PL*, vol. 174, col. 360).

In turn, as man is the microcosmic mirror of the universe, so the body itself mirrors everything. Nature tells the dreamer, "I am she who have fashioned the form and eminence of man into the likeness of the original mundane mechanism, that in him, as in a mirror of the world itself, combined nature may appear" (*The Complaint of Nature*, Prose II, p. 25). To say that Enide is an allegorical figure of the flesh in its relation to spirit is to oversimplify a complex of meaning in Chrétien's romance. But that she reflects this relation in an exemplary way is certainly the key to her role. She is both the most perfect work of nature and the image (Chrétien actually says the pattern, *essanpleire*, l. 419) of man. Like Nature herself, Enide is a worker; she and her mother,

> . . . an un ovreor ovroient;
> Mes ne sai, quel oevre feisoient. (ll. 399–400)

---

32. See Javelet, p. 241 and n. 559.
33. On John the Scot's use of the marriage of Adam and Eve and the Fall of Man as an allegory of human nature, see D. W. Robertson, Jr., *A Preface to Chaucer* (Princeton, N. J., 1962), pp. 69–72.

Gilson sees as a crucial characteristic of Bernard's *Natura* her role as artificer, *ouvrière* (p. 22n.) ; Enide is the image not only of man, but of nature itself.

Like the body that is properly the servant of the spirit, Enide serves humbly and faithfully. She is particularly skillful with horses. Chrétien devotes nine lines to a description of the way she cares for Erec's horse (not an occupation, incidentally, for a courtly lady!), how she unharnesses and unsaddles it, combs it, and feeds it. The horse itself is a commonplace figure for the flesh. Representative is this passage from Gregory: "Indeed the horse is the body of any holy soul, which it knows how to restrain from illicit action with the bridle of continence and to release in the exercise of good works with the spur of charity."[34] Alanus uses the same figure implicitly in several of the passages quoted above in phrases like, "the bridle of moderation," and "the reins of sobriety." This explains the otherwise curious emphasis on Enide's horses throughout the romance. When Erec is about to return with Enide to be married at Arthur's court, her uncle, the count of the castle where Erec has overcome Yder, wishes to give his niece fine clothes to replace the humble clothes she is wearing. Erec refuses to have Enide accept the clothes, but allows her to accept the substitute gift of a horse—a horse as perfect and unique as only Enide herself. The Count's description of the horse exemplifies the submission of passion to the governance of reason. It runs swift as the birds fly, but so gently a child can ride it:

> "Li oisel qui volent par l'er
> Ne vont plus tost del palefroi;
> Et si n'est pas de grant esfroi,
> Teus est come a pucele estuet:
> Uns anfes chevauchier le puet;
> Qu'il n'est onbrages ne restis,
> Ne mort ne fiert ne n'est ragis.

34. *PL,* vol. 76, col. 588, trans. in Robertson, *Preface,* p. 254.

> Qui mellor quiert, ne set qu'il viaut.
> Qui le chevauche, ne se diaut,
> Ainz va plus eise et plus soef
> Que s'il estoit an une nef." (ll. 1392–1402)

This last likeness of the horse to a ship is apt. The ship is a type of the Church, which is in turn (as we saw in the passage from St. Paul) the body of Christ.

As Erec vanquishes each of his adversaries in the sequence of adventures that he undertakes to restore his tarnished honor, he gives their horses to Enide to lead and care for. Near the end of the romance, Enide is given a horse by Guivret to replace the one she has lost at the castle of Limors, a horse as fine as the one her uncle had· given her, to which Chrétien devotes an even longer description, forty-three lines in all. The most notable feature of this horse is the decoration carved on the ivory saddle-bow with which it is furnished. The carving depicts, presumably in a series of pictures, the story of Aeneas, particularly his coming to Carthage, his love affair with Dido, his deception, and Dido's suicide:

> Li arçon estoient d'ivoire,
> S'i fu antailliee l'estoire,
> Comant Eneas vint de Troie,
> Comant a Cartage a grant joie
> Dido an son lit le reçut,
> Comant Eneas la deçut,
> Comant ele por lui s'ocist,
> Comant Eneas puis conquist
> Laurente et tote Lonbardie,
> Dont il fu rois tote sa vie. (ll. 5337–46)

Notice that each element in the series is connected to the next only by its quite neutral parallel structure until in line 5344 *puis* underscores the critical juncture at which Aeneas frees himself from the bonds of passion that keep him from fulfilling his divinely appointed mission. Implicitly, it is *be-*

cause he leaves Dido that he conquers Laurentum and all of Lombardy, and rules them the rest of his life.

Medieval readers, guided by the commentaries of Fulgentius and Bernard Silvestris (Bernard's written only a matter of decades before Chrétien's romance), saw in the *Aeneid* an allegory of the soul's passage through life. The meaning of the decoration on Enide's saddle-bow, then, is exemplary. It shows us the weakness to which the flesh (signified by the horse itself, as well as by the representation of Dido) is subject, and it teaches us by example how the soul must flee entrapment in inordinate passions if it is to achieve its true end, and escape despair and death. Aeneas's liberation from passion to the duties of kingship is a particularly relevant exemplum for Erec, whose career it parallels. The cautionary tale is appropriately engraved on the device whereby the human rider subdues and governs the unreasonable animal. The story of Aeneas is thus a variation (or amplification) of what the bridled horse already signifies, and what in turn the submission of Enide to her husband signifies.

There are other indications that Enide is meant to represent the natural body. Just as she knows how to care for horses, she cares for the sparrow-hawk that Erec wins for her; Chrétien shows her holding it on her hand after Erec's victory and feeding it. It is Enide who arms Erec for the battle—that is, who attends to his bodily needs. Chrétien devotes seventeen lines to telling how Enide laces his armor, puts on his helmet, girds him with his sword, and gives him shield and lance. Enide is thus consistently associated with animals, and with the body's exteriority (in this case suggested also by the knight's armor, which encloses him).

Her association with the flesh is not to her discredit, however. On the contrary, although her father declares in praise of her physical beauty, " 'Je n'aim tant rien come son cors' " (l. 546), he has already affirmed that her wisdom surpasses her beauty:

"Mout est bele, mes miauz assez
Vaut ses savoirs que sa biautez.
Onques Deus ne fist rien tant sage." (ll. 537–39)

Her uncle, the count, says of her likewise, " 'La pucele est
et bele et sage' " (l. 1277), and Chrétien tells us that the
people of Erec's land rejoiced,

Por la grant biauté qu'an li virent,
Et plus ancor por sa franchise.
. . . .
Aussi iere Enide plus bele
Que nule dame ne pucele
Qui fust trovee an tot le monde,
Que le cherchast a la reonde;
Tant fu jantis et enorable,
De sages diz et acointable,
De buen estre et de buen atret.
Onques nus ne sot tant d'aguet,
Qu'an li poïst veoir folie
Ne mauvestié ne vilenie. (ll. 2404–22)

Chrétien's emphasis on her surpassing wisdom does not con-
tradict the interpretation of Enide's role suggested here, although it may seem mysterious, in the usual manner of
paradox. Javelet cites Richard of St. Victor to epitomize the
attitude of the prescholastic philosophers toward physical
beauty: "Quant a la beauté des créatures, elle vient du
Verbe, image du Père; elle en manifeste la Sagesse" (p. 229).
Beauty is thus a mirror in which he who has eyes to see may
behold the image of divine wisdom. It cannot be stressed
too much that the division between body and soul is only
a manner of speaking; the philosophy underlying the romance is not dualistic. Rather, matter is informed by spirit,
and is its image. We need only recall the supreme manifestation of this mystery in the Incarnation whenever the
naturalism of Chartres begins to seem heretical, or "pagan."
Thus, King Arthur's praise of Enide to his assembled knights
has a double meaning. She is the most beautiful maiden

from here, he says, to that place where heaven meets the earth.

> "Cest est et de cors et de vis
> Et de quanque estuet a pucele
> La plus jantis et la plus bele,
> Qui soit jusque la, ce me sanble,
> Ou li ciaus et la terre assanble." (ll. 1782–86)

The truth is that in Enide, as in the body of man, heaven and earth (that is, spirit and matter) *are* joined.

Erec has set out to avenge an insult. As we have seen, however, the adventure takes on a far deeper spiritual meaning in the context of the iconographic stag hunt, particularly in light of the adventure's initiatory function in Erec's passage toward kingship. His victory over Yder, moreover, accomplishes more than redress for the dwarf's discourtesy. It liberates Enide and her parents from the bonds of poverty and dishonor, and restores them to their rightful place in the world. As baptism is participation in the death and resurrection of Christ, the three days of Erec's adventure correspond to Good Friday, Holy Saturday, and Easter. The battle for the sparrow-hawk occurs on the day that corresponds, then, to Christ's descent into hell to liberate the descendants of Adam. Adam is man, as Enide is the image of man. This explains why Erec so perversely refuses the count's gift of new clothes for his fiancée.

> "Sire! n'an parlez mie!
> Une chose sachiez vos bien:
> Ne voudroie por nule rien
> Qu'ele eüst d'autre robe point,
> Jusque la reïne li doint." (ll. 1372–78)

Clothes are, on the one hand, the sign of the fall. Thus, the finest gown the count might give Enide would represent only more pointedly the corruption that Erec has sacramentally overcome. On the other hand, clothes are often used iconographically to represent the virtues whereby we repair the effects of the fall; such is the robe that Erec wears at his coronation, which will be discussed in chapter 6. More obviously relevant here is the white linen robe given the catechumen to wear at baptism, symbolizing the purity of the soul that has been cleansed of original sin. For a white linen gown and a white tunic over it are the only clothes Enide has on.

> Povre estoit la robe defors,
> Mes dessoz estoit biaus li cors, (ll. 409–10)

says Chrétien, working yet another variation on the parallel themes of concealed virtue and allegorical truth.

Enide's father tells Erec that had he only consented, Enide might have married any one of the wealthy barons of his land. But he has awaited instead the advent of a king:

> " . . . J'atant ancor mellor point,
> Que Deus greignor enor li doint,
> Que avanture ça amaint
> Ou roi ou conte qui l'an maint.
> A dons soz ciel ne roi ne conte,
> Qui eüst de ma fille honte,
> Qui tant par est bele a mervoille
> Qu'an ne puet trover sa paroille?" (ll. 529–36)

We should note the coincidence here of the word *avanture* and the idea of advent. *Adventure* will lead a king to Enide. Furthermore, it is God who brings about the *adventure* of a king's *advent* (ll. 530–32). Adam and his descendants also awaited a king's advent; the king would free them from hell, and lead them to a better country. This liberation from hell is repeated within the soul of each catechumen, although it is not the historical Adam who is liberated, but rather the spiritual "Adam" within, of whom the historical Adam is the type. To speak of the liberation of Adam from hell is simply a figurative way of expressing the func-

tion of baptism—the cleansing of the spirit of original sin.
Enide is the spouse whom the savior weds. Her father is
also liberated and led into a far country, the kingdom of
Erec's father. There, Erec promises, he will be given two
castles,

> "Mout buens, mout riches et mout biaus.
> Sire seroiz de Roadan,
> Qui fu fez des le tans Adan,
> Et d'un autre chastel selonc,
> Qui ne vaut mie mains un jonc.
> Les janz l'apelent Montrevel;
> Mes pere n'a mellor chastel." (ll. 1334–40)

The rhyme word *Adan* not only reminds us of Adam, but
underscores that name as an element in the name of the
castle. Could the name be meant to suggest *rue Adan*, "the
way of Adam?" The second castle is called *Mont/revel*,
"Mount Joy." The "way of Adam" leads to hell, but beyond hell, it leads to the joy of salvation.

On the morning of the third day, when Erec is to return
with Enide to Arthur's court, the tears shed by Enide and
her parents over their parting (which Chrétien attributes to
nature and love) appear in marked contrast with Erec's joy
over his adventure:

> Li pere et la mere autressi
> Les beisent sovant et menu.
> De plorer ne se sont tenu:
> Au departir plore la mere,
> Plore la pucele et li pere.
> Teus est amors, teus est nature,
> Teus est pitiez de norreture.
> Plorer les feisoit la pitiez
> Et la douçors et l'amistiez,
> Qu'il avoient de lor anfant;
> Mes bien savoient neporquant
> Que lor fille an tel leu aloit,
> Don granz enors lor avandroit.
> D'amor et de pitié ploroient,

> Quant de lor fille departoient;
> Ne ploroient por autre chose.
> Bien savoient qu'a la parclose
> An seroient il enoré.
> Mout ont au departir ploré:
> Plorant a Deu s'antrecomandent;
> Or s'an vont, que plus n'i atandent, (ll. 1458–78)

This lachrymal deluge is abruptly juxtaposed to Erec's impatience and joy:

> Erec de son oste depart;
> Que mervoilles li estoit tart
> Que a la cort le roi venist.
> De s'avanture s'esjoïst:
> Mout estoit liez de s'avanture. (ll. 1479–83)

Chrétien obviously has his tongue in his cheek here. This is not a touchingly realistic vignette of the exigencies of courtly life, but rather a burlesque of exaggerated sentiment. The contrast between Enide's tears and Erec's joy, moreover, underscores the correspondence of their relationship with the relation of passion to reason, or body to soul. Inordinate, unreasonable grief is one manifestation of the weakness of flesh, the weakness that its marriage with reason is meant to overcome. But Chrétien does not use his irony to condemn Enide and her parents; he is only having a bit of fun at their expense. And the humor arises precisely because of— not in spite of—its connection with the most serious themes of the romance.

If Enide reveals in an amusing way her association with Nature by her tears and her "pitiez de norreture," she reveals it more deeply by restoring order to Arthur's court. Three days earlier, the court was in dissension over the kiss of the White Stag, each knight prepared to maintain his own lady's right to the honor. But just as Nature fashions order from chaotic matter, as the whole natural creation in Alanus's *De planctu* resolves itself into order at Nature's ap-

proach so that even "Juno, who but a little while before
had scorned the embraces of Jove, was so carried away with
joy that, with many a laughing glance of her eyes, she al-
lured her husband to the delights of love" (Prose II, p.
20), so, in the same way, Arthur's court is restored to unity by the appearance of Enide. It is Guenivere herself,
otherwise notoriously subversive of marriage and order, who
first affirms Enide's right to the kiss. Enide sits in the place
of honor on the king's right hand;

> De la senestre part s'assist
> La reïne, qui au roi dist:
> "Sire, si con je cuit et croi,
> . . . .
> Or poez vos le beisier prandre
> De la plus bele de la cort.
> Je ne cuit que nus vos an tort:
> Ja nus ne dira, qui ne mante,
> Que ceste ne soit la plus jante
> Des puceles qui ceanz sont
> Et de celes de tot le mont." (ll. 1763–76)

Similarly, Enide's right to the sparrow-hawk was recognized
spontaneously by the people who lined the way to the tournament:

> Li uns dit a l'autre et consoille:
> "Qui est, qui est cil chevaliers?
> Mout doit estre hardiz et fiers,
> Qui la bele pucele an mainne.
> Cist anploiera bien sa painne,
> Cist puet bien desresnier par droit
> Que ceste la plus bele soit."
> Li uns dit a l'autre: "Por voir
> Ceste doit l'esprevier avoir." (ll. 752–60)

With order, even unity restored to the court, it is with
considerable irony that Chrétien has Arthur recite the duties of kingship in a long speech (ll. 1783–1814) whose
pomposity is set in relief by the spontaneity of the court's

response to Enide's appearance. He continues to show himself a buffoon. The first duty of a king, to which all other duties pertain, is to guide his people on a course of order and unity. But Arthur has shown himself to be on the contrary reckless, and dependent on others to extricate him from the difficulties his policies lead him into. A fitting commentary on the example Arthur offers might be that passage in St. James where he admonishes, "Be doers of the word, and not hearers only, deceiving yourselves. For if someone is a hearer of the word, and not a doer, he may be likened to a man regarding his natural face in a mirror: for he looked at himself, and went away, and immediately forgot what manner of man he was" (James 1:22–24).

But the irony of Arthur's pompous speech would have little real bite if it did not revolve around the central themes of the romance. Erec undergoes initiation to kingship, and its duties are the lesson he must learn. Arthur is, willingly or not, his master in this lesson, not only by his easy pieties, but more graphically by his own negative example—by the discrepancy between his words and his deeds. What is even more important is the relation of Enide to the institution of kingship. Just as she restores unity to Arthur's court, and just as her presence inspires Arthur's speech on a king's duties, so her marriage with Erec is crucial in his development as a king. The model of government to which he must aspire is suggested in the unanimous response of the court to Arthur's choice of the fairest maiden:

> Tuit s'escrïent a une voiz:
> "Sire, par Deu et par sa croiz!
> Bien la poez beisier par droit;
> Que c'est la plus bele que soit.
> An cesti a plus de biauté
> Qu'il n'a el soloil de clarté.
> Beisier la poez quitemant:
> Tuit l'otroions comunemant." (ll. 1881–28)

The court is governed by its own, unifying consent.

3
The Thigh Wound

If the interpretation of *Erec and Enide* thus far proposed has seemed to deromanticize the romance, it is not meant to ignore the "real," flesh-and-blood love of Erec, the man, for Enide, the woman. Chrétien does not delineate for his audience the emotional microchanges of psyches in love. Nevertheless, the very fact that the allegory I have indicated adumbrates the relation of flesh and blood to spirit requires an understanding of the place of sexual love in the scheme of meaning that the poem expresses.

The relationship between Erec and Enide is not simple, however. Its ambivalence is nowhere more pointed than in the allegory of the stag hunt with which the romance begins, which we have just examined in the light of Christian iconography. Although it is convenient (if not inescapable) to consider different aspects of this allegory separately, it is essential that other meanings be understood to function simultaneously, if paradoxically so. For the iconographic tradition which attaches to the hunt of the deer is a complex of sacred and profane meanings. The hunt is conventionally associated with Venus, for instance, and the dual sense of

"venery" has long provided a pun that rests on this tradition. D. C. Allen, surveying the history of the figure of the
deer hunt, shows that already in classical tradition the deer
("venison" when slain) was associated variously with lovers
and with divinities, and that it could thus express both sensuality and holiness. Moreover, this basic ambivalence remains characteristic of the figure of the hunt throughout
medieval and renaissance tradition.[1] Thus, while in certain
contexts the hunt of the deer or the stag symbolizes the
soul's pursuit of Christ, or Christ's pursuit of the soul, or
baptism, in other contexts it symbolizes the pursuit of the
earthly lover, or in a moralistic sense, the pursuit of lust.[2]

The ambivalent iconography of the hunt seems at first
inconsistent, but it is rather a case of double meaning. The
figure pertains to heavenly love in one case, as it pertains
to earthly love in the other, and its ambivalence has a counterpart in the dual Venuses and Cupids of Christian myth-
ographic tradition.[3] St. Augustine, whose outline in the *De
doctrina Christiana* of the techniques of exegesis was a basic
text, notes the common use in Scripture of one sign to mean
contrasting, even opposite things. In one place, a figure may
be used *in bono*; in another, the same figure may be used
in malo (Bk. III, xxv, 36).

Moreover, it is quite a universal phenomenon that things
—often the most important things—are pervaded by opposite meanings. We must not confuse this inherent ambivalence with a tendency toward religious dualism, Manichean
or otherwise. It is rather the result of the gap between language and experience—language, which is broken up into
separate words and phrases and meanings, and experience,
which is felt as whole. Opposing meanings reside together
in the same thing; they do not face each other across a gulf,

---

1. D. C. Allen, *Image and Meaning* (Baltimore, Md., 1960), pp. 91–104.
2. See Howard Helsinger, "*The Book of the Duchess* and the Hunt of the
Hart," Ph.D. diss. (Princeton, N. J., 1970), pp. 91–104.
3. See D. W. Robertson, Jr., *Preface to Chaucer* (Princeton, N. J., 1962),
pp. 125–27; Erwin Panofsky, chap. 4, "Blind Cupid," *Studies in Iconology*
(New York, 1962), pp. 95–128.

and if they are in constant struggle with one another, it is the struggle itself that is the essence of the thing's meaning. A notable example of the attempt to express this paradoxical relation is the mystical figure of the Cross in the Old English "Dream of the Rood," which the dreamer visualizes as shifting continuously back and forth from the ugly and terrifying instrument of Christ's death to the radiant symbol of his victory over death. Any cross, however simple, however ornate, is redolent with the same contradictory meanings, although the Anglo-Saxon poet expresses them more graphically than usual. In the same way, we have to do with opposing meanings in the figure of the stag hunt, but both meanings may be subsumed under a single word. Both as expressive of sensuality and as expressive of spirituality, the hunt means love.

The spirit in which both the "custom" of the White Stag and the "custom" of the sparrow-hawk are undertaken is at least on the surface the spirit of what is commonly understood by the term "courtly love," that thoroughly worldly and idle, if not decadent, ethos in which the relation between men and women became an elaborate, all-consuming game. The sparrow-hawk—more generally, the falcon—is, like the deer, a common symbol of the lover, on whose wrist it is frequently seen in medieval art.[4] Chrétien gives us such a picture of the couple departing for Arthur's court:

> Erec chevauche lez le conte,
> Et delez lui sa douce amie,
> Qui l'esprevier n'oblia mie:
> A son esprevier se deporte,
> Nule autre richesce n'an porte. (ll. 1440–44)

The figure of the hawk shares with the figure of the stag the motif of the hunt, symbolically the "hunt of Venus." Chrétien leaves no doubt that he intends this figurative meaning, for in a striking figure he describes the embraces

---

4. See Robertson, *Preface*, pp. 190–95.

of the lovers on their wedding night in terms of the very stag and sparrow-hawk that provide the symbolic setting of the romance:

> Cers chaciez, qui de soif alainne,
> Ne desirre tant la fontainne,
> N'espreviers ne vient a reclaim
> Si volantiers, quant il a faim,
> Que plus volantiers ne venissent
> A ce que nu s'antretenissent. (ll. 2081–86)

This repetition of the hunt motif, as well as the actual outcome of the adventure, which is Erec's marriage, establishes a symbolic context in which Erec's pursuit of Yder takes on a meaning beyond mere vengeance for his and the Queen's honor. The key words giving us the figure of the stag thirsting for the fountain are almost certainly intended as an echo of Psalm 41: "Quemadmodum desiderat cervus ad fontes aquarum,/Ita desiderat anima mea ad te, Deus." In the psalm, the soul's love for its god is likened to the thirsting stag; in *Erec*, it is a man's love for a woman. The scriptural echo, and the exegetical tradition it carries with it, imbue Erec's marriage with the spiritual meaning of baptism. Moreover, we can say that the pursuit of Yder is itself a "hunt," and that it embodies the whole man's pursuit of fulfillment, on all levels of his being—spiritual, social, and sexual.

But although sexual love has its proper place in the order of things, the children of Adam are always liable to the weakness whereby reason is corrupted and made subject to passion. On the one hand, Erec's adventure leads to marriage and kingship. On the other, it leads to luxury and dishonor. If the demons with whom the catechumen struggles under the waters were not real and powerful, the sacrament would be trivial. We noted earlier that the adversary of the soul is only figuratively external to it; the real adversary is within the soul, and the manifestations of its power are in the flesh.

Erec does not leave the combat with Yder unscathed, although he wins the victory. Yder wounds him in the thigh:

> Jusqu'a la char li est colez
> Sor la hanche li aciers froiz.
> Deus le gari a cele foiz!
> Se li cos ne tornast defors,
> Tranchié l'eüst parmi le cors. (ll. 946–50)

The thigh wound is a familiar motif in romance literature. Lancelot's thigh wound, received in a "perilous" bed from a flaming lance, more clearly reveals the sexual meaning of this figure.[5] A more notorious thigh wound of the same iconographic type is suffered by Tristan, and the analogy with Erec's is not arbitrary, since Chrétien himself discreetly draws attention to it three hundred lines later. At this point, Erec has vanquished Yder, and sent him to Arthur's court. Yder's arrival there, and his news of Erec's victory and plans to return, take up most of the intervening lines. Erec, meanwhile, is still at the tournament ground, and with characteristic irony Chrétien implicitly draws the parallel with Tristan by declaring with a straight face:

> Onques, ce cuit, tel joie n'ot
> La ou Tristanz le fier Morhot
> An l'Isle saint Sanson veinqui,
> Con l'an feisoit d'Erec iqui. (ll. 1247–50)

Tristan comes away from his battle with Morholt victorious, indeed, but with a wound in the thigh that soon festers and stinks so that he can no longer be in company. He sets off in a boat adrift (here, a figure like the unbridled horse for the loss of reason's guidance of the passions). His only hope is to find the one person in the world who, as Morholt has declared, can cure his stinking wound—a person with the name Iseult. The romance from that point on tells how Tristan continues to "cure" his "wound" with Iseult in the manner of one who would quench a fire with gasoline.

---

5. On the thigh wound, see Robertson, *Preface,* pp. 450–52.

The unquenchable passion of Lancelot and Tristan for an ultimately unattainable woman, pursued at the cost of honor, duty, and loyal love, is not put forth by medieval poets as a romantic ideal (as it has been taken by later readers), but rather as exemplary of the folly of idolatry. Gower reminds his readers of this:

> Comunes sont la cronique et l'istoire
> De Lancelot et Tristrans ensement;
> Enquore maint leur sotie en memoire,
> Pour ensampler les autres de present:
> Cil q'est guarni et nulle garde prent,
> Droit est qu'il porte mesmes sa folie.[6]

As Lancelot and Tristan betray their kings in pursuit of their idolatrous passion, Erec, the wound in his thigh emblematic of the same idolatrous passion, betrays as it were the king he is to become (to say nothing of Arthur, the king he is bound as a knight to serve) when he neglects his duties as a knight in order to indulge in the carnal pleasures his marriage makes available to him. But unlike them, Erec is shocked by his realization of the truth about himself into a course of action that leads to the restoration of reason, to his regeneration as a knight, and ultimately to his ascension of the throne as true king of his people. Thus, his fall is properly the hell through which the soul must pass as the only way—as Virgil shows Dante—to salvation. This is the deeper meaning of what Enide exclaims somewhat desperately when Erec, whose true condition she has revealed to him, determines to set off in quest of penance:

"Ne set qu'est biens, qui mal n'essaie." (l. 2610)

The figure of the thigh wound itself expresses this paradox. For there are two kinds of thigh wounds. If Lancelot's and Tristan's are signs of their shame, Jacob's is the sign of his blessedness. Jacob is tested by the angel with whom he

---

6. *Traitié*, 15, I, 1–7, quoted in Robertson, *Preface*, p. 452.

wrestles (Genesis 32:24–32), and although the sign in his
flesh maims him, it is a sign of the honor he finds in the
angel's—and God's—sight. Erec and Enide are married on
Pentecost, the festival of Christian love, commemorating the
advent of grace to the apostles. Erec and Enide on their
way to Arthur's court exemplify the ideal of marriage—itself a sacrament—according to which Adam says: "This is now
bone of my bones, and flesh of my flesh. . . . Therefore shall
a man . . . cleave unto his wife: and they shall be one flesh"
(Genesis 2:23–24). Erec and Enide, Chrétien tells us, are of
one substance:

> Mout estoient igal et per
> De corteisie et de biauté
> Et de grant deboneireté:
> Si estoient d'une matiere,
> D'unes mors et d'une meniere,
> Que nus qui le voir vossist dire,
> N'an poïst le mellor eslire
> Ne le plus bel ne le plus sage.
> Mout estoient d'igal corage
> Et mout avenoient ansanble. (ll. 1504–13)

Their wedding night is explicitly *un*like Iseult's, for their
marriage is founded on love, not deception:

> La ne fu pas Yseuz anblee,
> Ne Brangiens an leu de li mise. (ll. 2076–77)

The joy of their physical union is innocent; the lovers are
naked (l. 2086) like Adam and Eve in the verse following
those quoted above: ". . . naked, the man and his wife, and
were not ashamed" (Genesis 2:25). Their love *restores*
them to what they long have waited for:

> Cele nuit ont bien restoré
> Ce que il ont tant demoré. (ll. 2087–88)

True marriage is thought of as return to paradise, the restoration, that is, of lost innocence.

To underscore the paradoxical nature of love, Chrétien echoes, as we have seen, the opening lines of Psalm 41 in describing the joys of the naked lovers. If the joys of marriage entail a danger to the soul (a danger to which Erec succumbs), so does baptism, the "struggle under the waters." Like baptism, marriage is a sacrament, not an indulgence. As the catechumen emerges from the waters a "new man," Enide, in losing the name of maiden, awakens a "new woman."

> Eincois qu'ele se relevast,
> Ot perdu le non de pucele;
> Au matin fu dame novele. (ll. 2106–8)

Both of the figures in this passage, "awakening" and "newness"—figures that commonly express spiritual regeneration —serve to emphasize the sacramental character of Enide's marriage. This is holy wedlock, not "courtly love."[7]

Chrétien has no difficulty shuttling from one side of the moral ambivalence of Erec's position to the other because he writes from the perspective of hindsight—he knows that it comes out alright in the end. At one point he ironically compares Erec to Absalom, Solomon, and Alexander the Great (ll. 2266–70), three notoriously flawed exemplars of history.[8] While appearing to praise Erec's beauty, his speech, his boldness, and his magnanimity, Chrétien is actually rather drily suggesting his vulnerability to the same weaknesses that brought low those great men before him. On the other hand, he anticipates the triumphant conclusion of the romance in his description of Erec's arrival in his father's land. The Middle Ages adopted from the Romans the elaborate ceremonies that attended the return of a ruler to his city. But for Christians, the advent of the temporal lord had

---

7. On courtly love, see Robertson, chap. 5, "Some Medieval Doctrines of Love," i, ii; *Preface,* pp. 391–463.
8. Hartmann von Aue, in his Middle High German version of *Erec,* adds Samson, whose fatal weakness is consistent with the others, and Foerster, following Hartmann, emends *lion* of l. 2268 to read *Sanson.*

a further significance by analogy with the advent of Christ, first with his historical advent on Palm Sunday into Jerusalem, and second with the expected eschatalogical advent in the last days, the Second Coming. The arrival of a lord to his castle was the earthly type of the coming of the King of Heaven.

Numerous examples survive, particularly from the Carolingian period, of poems of the type *In Adventu Regis*, written to celebrate the politically important and spiritually meaningful reception of the earthly lord by his city.[9] E. Baldwin Smith stresses how natural and important it was for the people of the Middle Ages to experience the earthly event in relation to its spiritual counterpart, and how difficult it is for modern students to enter into that experience:

> It is easily understood why an age of pageantry and hieratic formalities would have continued the Roman ceremonies intended to dramatize a ruler's godlike nature and heavenly authority. It is more difficult for the modern reader to comprehend why the medieval man continued to see a messianic promise of peace, prosperity, and happiness in the triumphal Coming of his earthly Lord, and why as a Christian he believed that his city would enjoy a heavenly distinction from the presence in it of a ruler whom he was accustomed to equate with the Son of God. . . . In the medieval world every terrestrial city had come to be thought of as another Jerusalem at the Advent of the Anointed, who on the occasion of his royal visitation was ritualistically, at least, identified with Christ.[10]

Throughout the long description of Erec's reception, Chrétien emphasizes the joy of the people at his coming:

> Onques nus rois an son reaume
> Ne fus plus lieemant veüs
> N'a greignor joie receüz. (ll. 2398–2400)

---

9. Ernest H. Kantorowicz, "The King's Advent," *Art Bulletin* 26 (1944): 207–31.
10. E. Baldwin Smith, *Architectural Symbolism of Imperial Rome and the Middle Ages* (Princeton, N. J., 1956), p. 152.

He is not yet actually king, but he is king to be, and his presence brings his people together:

> Tote la janz est aünee
> Por veoir lor novel seignor. (ll. 2370–71)

Novel here carries with it (as in the phrase *dame novele*, noted above) the spiritual meaning of newness appropriate to the Christian initiate. Erec's approach is called "son avenemant" (l. 2362), and as Christ's way into Jerusalem was strewn with clothing and with branches cut from trees (Matthew 21:8),

> De jons, de mantastre et de glais
> Sont totes jonchiees les rues. (ll. 2364–65)

Finally, the advent of the king's son to his father's realm is given an explicitly spiritual turn:

> Premiers sont au mostier venu,
> La furent par devocion
> Receü a procession.
> Devant l'autel del crocefix
> S'est Erec a genoillons mis.
> Devant l'image Nostre Dame
> Menerent dui baron sa fame. (ll. 2374–80)

In the history told in the Old Testament, the multitude of names and places and epic events may obscure the recurrence of a very simple pattern. Israel is chosen by God, and blessed by him; but Israel sins, and the Lord punishes her with exile and bondage. After a time, he relents, and blesses a redeemer through whom Israel is brought out of bondage and into his favor once again. The history is cyclical, but time is really a fiction. For behind the motion of the pattern is a conception of human experience that encompasses the whole cycle at once. Man is not blessed at one moment, and damned the next. The paradox of his nature (or rather the poverty of language to express it) is that he is blessed and damned simultaneously and always. Narrative form separates out the elements of this complexity, and arranges them along a fictional axis of time, but time betrays its fictional nature by repeating itself. Salvation is not a goal, but a continuing process, a way of life.

Thus, Chrétien's view of Erec, constantly shifting back and forth between admiration and irony, is not inconsistent, although it is complex. Erec is no sooner seen in the light of an analogy with Christ than he falls into the temptations of luxury. He has lost hold of the bridle whereby passion is properly checked. His companion knights sadly shake their heads and talk behind his back. He has lost his reputation as a knight, and has thus lost the ability to function in the world, a situation we see the consequences of in the example of the foolish King Arthur. Often, it is past noon before Erec rises now (ll. 2446–47). It is left to Enide, in whom "one might see himself as in a mirror," to show him the image of himself as he has become:

> "Sire! . . .
> La verité vos an dirai,
> Ja plus ne le vos celerai;
> Mes je criem bien, ne vos enuit.
> Par ceste terre dïent tuit,
> Li noir et li blont et li ros,
> Que granz damages est de vos,
> Que voz armes antreleissiez;
> Vostre pris an est abeissiez.
> Tuit soloient dire l'autre an
> Qu'an tot le mont ne savoit l'an
> Mellor chevalier ne plus preu;
> Vostre parauz n'estoit nul leu.
> Or se vont tuit de vos gabant,
> Vieil et juene, petit et grant;
> Recreant vos apelent tuit.
>
> . . . .
>
> Autre consoil vos covient prandre,
> Que vos puissiez cest blasme estaindre
> Et vostre premier los ataindre.
>
> . . . .

> Sovantes foiz, quant m'an sovient,
> D'angoisse plorer me covient.
> Tel pesance or androit an oi,
> Que garde prandre ne m'an soi,
> Tant que je dis que mar i fustes." (ll. 2540–75)

When the woman for whom a man—by loving her too much
(l. 2445)—has lost his reputation mourns his behavior and
shows him the image of his folly in order to induce him to
abandon it, we are not dealing with romantic sentiment.
Erec is not a great lover, but a foolish one, and he recognizes his folly at once.

> "Dame!", fet il, "droit an eüstes,
> Et cil qui m'an blasment ont droit." (ll. 2576–77)

At once he sets out on a quest to regain the honor without which he is not truly a man, or able to assume the duties of the throne. It is his "first honor" that Enide admonishes him to regain, and man's "first honor" is his innocence
before the Fall. Adventure, and the glory that accrues to it,
is the visible type of spiritual conversion, which must happen not once, but continually.

4

Rising from Death

Erec is shocked into action by the image he sees of himself. But what he does at first is just to turn the same coin to its other side. If he has fallen from knightly honor by giving himself wholly to the pleasures of the body, he sets out to regain his honor by subjecting the body to the absolute tyranny of will. His excessive (and misdirected) love is turned to equally excessive hate. Balance, proportion, *mesure* are the ideal of the knightly ethos. The word that haunts this section of the romance, however, is *trop*. Erec has loved Enide *too much*; but Enide blames herself for her change in fortune; she was *too happy*; pride lifted her *too high* (ll. 2589–2610). Erec impatiently sends a valet to hurry Enide who, he says, has made him wait *too long*; she is spending *too much* time preparing herself (ll. 2665–71), and so on.

Erec's dilemma, his excessive behavior in both luxury and asceticism, may be understood in terms of St. Augustine's distinction between things that are to be enjoyed and things that are to be used, and the further distinction that follows from it between use and abuse: "To enjoy something is to cling to it with love for its own sake. To use something, however, is to employ it in obtaining that which you love, provided that it is worthy of love. For an illicit use should be called rather a waste or an abuse."[1] That which is to be "enjoyed" or loved for its own sake is God. God's creation, on the other hand, should be *used* toward the attainment of that which we love. When we love for its own sake that which should instead be used to attain the love of God, we abuse it. Evil does not inhere in things; "evil" describes rather the perverse delight that arises from an improper relation of the soul to things. How then according to St. Augustine should other human beings be loved?

> This is the divinely instituted rule of love: "Thou shalt love thy neighbor as thyself," He said, and "Thou shalt love God with thy whole heart, and with thy whole soul, and with thy whole mind." Thus all your thoughts and all your life and all your understanding should be turned toward Him from whom you receive these powers. For when he said "With thy whole heart, and with thy whole soul, and with thy whole mind," He did not leave any part of life which should be free and find itself room to desire the enjoyment of something else. But whatever else appeals to the mind as being lovable should be directed into that channel into which the whole current of love flows. . . . Thus, loving his neighbor as himself, he refers the love of both to that love of God which suffers no stream to be led away from it by which it might be diminished. (Bk. I, xxii, p. 19)

The inordinate nature of Erec's passion comes from his failure to understand how to love Enide—how to love her in such a way that love of her becomes a part of "the whole current of love" of God, and leads beyond her own mortality to participation in immortality. Erec dwells in excessive love of her for her own sake—of the pleasures that their bodies momentarily afford them. The sudden reversal of his

---

1. St. Augustine, *On Christian Doctrine*, Bk. I, iv, trans. D. W. Robertson, Jr. (New York, 1958), p. 9.

feelings is not a true conversion, but rather a shifting of affect from the person of Enide to the knightly honor he has lost because of his relation with her. At the point of reversal, as Erec sets out to regain his honor, he pursues it *for its own sake* in the same misdirected way he has pursued his love for Enide. Thus, as he was before excessively sensual, he is now excessively severe with Enide, whom he chastises for his own spiritual blindness.

Erec forbids Enide to speak to him unless he first addresses her, no matter what she may see. Enide correctly feels this to be a sign of his hatred, the inversion—not the conversion—of his inordinate love.

> " . . . Mes sire m'a anhaïe.
> Anhaïe m'a, bien le voi,
> Quant il ne viaut parler a moi." (ll. 2789–92)

Although her breaches of his prohibition are obviously expressions of natural, spontaneous affection and concern, Erec threatens her with vague but increasingly dire consequences. He confirms her feelings that his former love has turned to hatred. When for the second time Enide is unable to suppress her fear for her husband's life, and warns him of the attack of five robber knights, he rebukes her rudely,

> "C'est servises mal anploiiez;
> Que je ne vos an sai nul gre,
> Ainz sachiez que plus vos an he.
> Dit le vos ai, et di ancore.
> . . . .
> Je n'aim mie vostre parole." (ll. 3002–10)

In terms of the Pauline analogy, a man who hates his wife is like the thoroughly unnatural phenomenon of a man who hates his own body. If "he that loveth his wife loveth himself," then it is likely also that he whose love for his wife turns to hate comes to hate himself. And this is precisely the image we have of Erec—a man driven by self-hatred. Yet the apostle declares, "no man ever yet hated his own flesh; but nourisheth and cherisheth it, even as the Lord the church." St. Augustine explains this paradox; the love of one's body *is* natural and imperative,

> And that which some say, that they would rather be without a body, arises from a complete delusion: they hate not their bodies but the corruption and solidity of their bodies. . . . Those who seem to persecute their bodies with continence and labors, if they do so correctly, do not act so that they may not have bodies but so that their bodies may be subjugated and prepared for necessary work. . . . Those who seek to do this perversely war on their bodies as though they were natural enemies. In this way they have been deceived by the words, "The flesh lusteth against the spirit: and the spirit against the flesh; for these are contrary to one another." For this was said on account of the unconquered habit of the flesh against which the spirit has a concupiscence of its own, not that the body should be destroyed, but that its concupiscence, which is its evil habit, should be completely conquered so that it is rendered subject to the spirit as the natural order demands. (Bk. I, xxiv, pp. 20–21)

"The natural order" is the key phrase here, and it is the lesson that Erec still must learn. When he prohibits Enide to speak to him, even to warn him of danger to his life, he is like a man who wishes to pass through the dangers of this world without the benefit of his senses, like a man who, in St. Augustine's words, "would rather be without a body." But this wish is a delusion, not to say a presumption against providence. It is as subversive of the natural order as the inordinate pursuit of pleasure. We see here an ironic equivalence between lust and misguided asceticism—each the pursuit of self-love at the expense of charity.

It seems ironic, too, that Enide, who corresponds in the analogy to the body, is in harmony with the natural order. She is dutiful and obedient in everything but that which is so unnatural as to threaten the natural order. She shows miraculous restraint and humility. Moreover, although she blames herself for talking too much, we know perfectly well that this is not a defect but a virtue in her. In a charming passage, Chrétien describes Enide's experience of her dilemma—how she is torn by conflicting feelings:

> De deus parz est mout a mal eise,
> Qu'ele ne set le quel seisir,
> Ou le parler ou le teisir.
> A li meïsme se consoille:
> Sovant del dire s'aparoille
> Si que la langue se remuet,
> Mes la voiz pas issir n'an puet;
> Car de peor estraint les danz,
> S'anclot la parole dedanz.
> Einsi se justise et destraint:
> La boche clot, les danz estraint,
> Que la parole fors n'an saille. (ll. 3726–37)

She struggles against her nature, but she loses the struggle and speaks. Later, when Erec lies on the ground, apparently dead, she blames herself for her speech. She is Erec's murderer through her words, she tells herself.

> "Ha!" fet ele, "dolante Enide,
> De mon seignor sui omecide,
> Par ma parole l'ai ocis.
> Ancor fust or mes sire vis,
> Se je come outrageuse et fole
> N'eüsse dite la parole,
> Por quoi mes sire ça s'esmut.
> Ainz teisirs a home ne nut,
> Mes parlers nuist mainte foiiee.
> . . . .
> . . . Trop ai mespris,
> Qui la parole ai maintenue,
> Don mes sire a mort receüe,
> La mortel parole antoschiee.
> . . . .
> . . . Nus n'i a coupes fors moi;
> Je sole an doi estre blasmee." (ll. 4623–51)

If our own good sense does not tell us that she is wrong to

blame herself, we should recall that Chrétien himself in his prologue has already condemned those who keep silent when they might speak to the advantage of others.

It may be ironic that it is Enide who reflects natural order while Erec is spiritually disordered, but it is consistent with Christian doctrine. For it was reason and will that were corrupted by the Fall, not the body. It is only as the corrupted reason allows the body to go ungoverned, or to be misgoverned, that it falls into sin. Obviously it is not government of the body, but abuse of it to deny it its just place, and the abuse consists in undeserved punishment as well as simple neglect. Thus, the despised body becomes the prey of vice, as Enide becomes the prey of the lecherous count who plans Erec's murder to obtain her. Enide does not herself incline to the count's advances, but Erec's neglect leaves her vulnerable to him. The count sees his opening:

> "Bien sai et voi que vostre sire
> Ne vos aimme ne ne vos prise.
> A buen seignor vos seroiz prise,
> Se vos avuec moi remenez." (ll. 3330–33)

This time, through Enide's perfect loyalty, Erec escapes with her. In fact, her loyalty is so striking that it effects the conversion of the count himself, though not yet of Erec. Later, in the castle of Limors, where Erec lies unconscious, apparently dead from the wounds he has sustained in his quest of self-chastisement, Enide is left helplessly in the hands of the unscrupulous Count Oringle, who marries her by force. Enide unwittingly sums up Erec's excessive behavior (showing herself again a mirror in which one may see his condition reflected) when she remarks sympathetically,

> "Je voi bien que mes sire panse
> Tant que lui meïsmes oblie." (ll. 3762–63)

We may be touched by Enide's sympathy for her husband,

but we must also recognize how disastrous such a mental fog would be in a king.

The beginning of Erec's real conversion coincides with his battle with the stout-hearted little Guivret le Petit. Several things about this encounter indicate some change in the course of his adventures. First, Guivret challenges Erec not out of malice, but out of an exuberant love of chivalrous adventure and knightly prowess. Second, the battle is evenly matched, unlike Erec's previous encounters, in which he has taken on three and five armed knights in a row (and beaten them handily). The encounter's position near the center of the romance and the evenly matched nature of the battle suggest the equilibrium of a turning-point. More important, Erec's harshness toward Enide finally begins to relent. When she warns him this time of the knight's approach, his menacing gesture is only a pretense:

> . . . Cil la menace,
> Mes n'a talant que mal li face;
> Qu'il aparçoit et conoist bien
> Qu'ele l'aimme sor tote rien,
> Et il li tant que plus ne puet.   ll. 3765–69)

The knights are evenly matched, but their swords are not. Guivret's breaks, and leaves him at Erec's mercy. We have here an exemplum of the reality of a man's dependence on material things. Chrétien's description of Guivret stresses rather the transcendence of spirit over material limitations:

> De lui vos sai verité dire,
> Qu'il estoit mout de cors petiz,
> Mes de grant cuer estoit hardiz. (ll. 3678–80)

Nevertheless, there are material limits that even a great spirit—at least in the life of a knight—cannot transcend. When his sword breaks, Guivret throws away the useless hilt that remains:

> Peor ot; arriers l'estuet treire;
> Que ne puet pas grant esforz feire
> An bataille ne an assaut
> Chevaliers, qui s'espee faut. (ll. 3837–40)

We are surprised to hear Erec, after he has defeated him, ask Guivret for help, but actually his request marks the beginning of the restoration of order within his soul.

> " . . . Itant solemant vos pri,
> Que se nus besoinz m'avenoit
> Et la novele a vos venoit,
> Que j'eüsse mestier d'aïe,
> Adonc ne m'obliessïez mie." (ll. 3908–112)

It is a vital lesson for a king to learn just how he must depend on those over whom he rules, as it is a vital lesson for any man to learn how he must depend on his own body. Erec has begun to learn, and perhaps Guivret's name, which means "little serpent" (*guivre* < L. *vipera*), indicates the wisdom that the initiate takes away from this encounter. The serpent is one of the figures that St. Augustine points out as typical of the ambivalence of scriptural allegory. In Genesis, the serpent is the familiar figure *in malo* of the devil. But in Matthew, Christ uses the same figure *in bono* when he admonishes the faithful to be "wise as serpents, and harmless as doves" (Matthew 10:16).[2] The episode closes with a touching picture of the two reconciled knights, embracing and kissing one another ("harmless as doves"?), and cutting strips of cloth from their tunics to bandage each other's wounds:

> Li uns l'autre beise et acole.
> Onques de si dure bataille
> Ne fu si douce dessevraille;
> Que par amor et par franchise
> Chascuns des panz de sa chemise

---

2. I heard Professor Robertson suggest the connection between Guivret's name and the serpent from Matthew in a graduate seminar in 1964.

Trancha bandes longues et lees,
S'ont lor plaies antrebandées.
Quant li uns ot l'autre bandé,
O Deu sont antrecomandé.   (ll. 3922-30)

Just how far Erec has progressed appears in considerable
relief against the background of Arthur's court in the next
episode. In striking juxtaposition with the picture of charity with which we are left in the preceding section, we see
Arthur and his queen idly amusing themselves in the forest
—the same forest that for Erec is the Forest of Adventure—
hunting deer. The context tells us clearly that Arthur's deer
hunt is not the sacramental experience that has initiated the
change in Erec's life, but rather the other side of the iconographic tradition, the hunt of Venus, pursuit of worldly delight. In keeping with the earlier behavior of the foolish
king, his seneschal Kay now plays the buffoon in a scene
that borders on slapstick. With the shield and lance of the
truly doughty knight Gawain, and mounted on Gawain's famous horse, Guingalet, Kay rudely accosts Erec, who easily
unhorses him with the butt end of his lance. Kay has to
beg Erec desperately for the return of the horse that does
not belong to him.

Even if Erec has been initially misguided, his quest in this
forest is profoundly serious. Against his real spiritual struggle Chrétien plays off the tomfoolery by which Gawain and
Arthur trick Erec into joining them, for one night at least.
Gawain detains him in conversation while Arthur has his
entire encampment, tents and all, picked up and moved several leagues and set up again squarely across the road that
Erec must travel. Surely it is with irony that Chrétien has
Erec declare his admiration for Gawain's remarkable wisdom
in engineering this prank:

"Haï! Gauvains!" fet il, "haï!
Vostre granz sans m'a esbaï.
Par grant san m'avez retenu."   (ll. 4149-51)

We see how far Erec has come through this reminder of where he started from. The Forest of Adventure is not a geographical location, but a spiritual direction; his struggles with visible adversaries there adumbrate inner struggles. There is no adventure, only idleness and foolery in the forest in which Arthur and his court amuse themselves. And Erec is not returning to the court in this episode—just passing through.

But Arthur urges him to stay on with them. He fears lest Erec should die of his wounds.

> "Mout iert granz diaus et granz damages,
> Se vos an cez forez morez." (ll. 4252–53)

When he departs early the next morning, the king and his knights mourn as though he had in fact already died:

> Lors les veïssiez toz plorer
> Et demener un duel si fort,
> Con s'il le veïssent ja mort. (ll. 4290–92)

This fear echoes the same court's reaction to his earlier departure from them, when he first set out on this penitential adventure. The poet remarks:

> Ne cuit que plus grant duel feïssent,
> Se mort ou navré le veïssent. (ll. 2751–52)

The setting of Easter has furnished the romance with the theme of death and resurrection. Now that spiritual theme is visibly manifested in Erec's collapse and apparent death, and his astonishing recovery at the castle of Limors. From the vantage of this episode we see that what seemed essentially a figurative idiom to express the apprehension the court feels for Erec in fact foreshadows the actual events, and pertains to the major theme of the romance.

Erec's encounter with Arthur's court is on Saturday; Chrétien specifies the day (as he does nowhere else in the romance) in order really to identify the following day, on which Erec collapses, overcome with weakness from the wounds he has sustained. On Sunday at dawn he sets out. Presently he comes upon a damsel who begs him to save her hapless lover. He has been taken captive by two giants, who have stripped him naked and are leading him away between them, flogging him mercilessly as they go. For the first time Erec fights to save not himself but another—he becomes a savior. Several details in this episode underscore the Christlike role that he has assumed. The giants scornfully liken him to a lamb:

> "Se vos estiiez or tel quatre,
> N'avriiez vos force vers nos
> Ne qu'uns aigniaus contre deus los." (ll. 4432–34)

Of course, if Erec's act of charity is an imitation of the sacrifice of Christ, it is precisely the power of the lamb that assures his victory. When Erec has killed the giants, the captive knight, Cadoc de Tabriol, declares that he has been sent from heaven.

> Li chevaliers de joie plore
> Et reclaimme Deu et aore,
> Qui secors anvoiié li a. (ll. 4475–77)

Cadoc declares Erec his lord because he has saved his life, which otherwise he would have lost in suffering and martyrdom:

> "Mon seignor vuel feire de toi
> Et par reison feire le doi;
> Que tu m'as sauvee la vie,
> Qui ja fust del cors partie
> A grant tormant et a martire." (ll. 4485–89)

Erec's coming is a great adventure, he says:

> "Queus avanture, biaus douz sire!

> Por Deu, t'a ça a moi tramis,
> Qui des mains a mes anemis
> M'as gité par ton vasselage?" (ll. 4490–93)

"Delivered from the hands of my enemies" is a phrase that echoes innumerable scriptural passages—particularly in Psalms—praising God as the savior of his people. Literally, one might read Cadoc's exclamation, "What *chance* . . . has brought you here to me?" But we know that there is no chance, that chance is a figment of the imagination that serves only to bridge our inability to discern providence pervading all things. Especially in the Forest of Adventure adventure is not mere chance. On the contrary, an "adventure" is an event whose meaning is extraordinary.

Chrétien's word play here with *adventure,* and its figurative sense of *advent,* lend contextual significance to Erec's earlier retort to the giants' blustering threats.

> "Ne sai que iert," Erec respont;
> "Se li ciaus chiet et terre font,
> Donc sera prise mainte aloe.
> Teus vaut petit, qui mout se loe." (ll. 4435–38)

Erec's quip is a variation of the Old French proverb, "Se les nubz cheent, les aloes sont toutes prises."[3] Chrétien has added the dissolution of the earth to the original, more lucid proverb in which only the falling of the sky catches the larks. The addition obscures the proverb's original meaning, but it does make unmistakable the apocalyptic nature of the image. We might read Erec's response in the following way: he is not so presumptuous as to think he can know the outcome of their battle; but in the end, when "the sky falls and the earth dissolves," all shall stand before God, and justice shall then be served on such as the giants. But the apocalypse is the time not only of judgment, but of the Second Coming, that is, the Second Advent. And the advent of

3. *Proverbes Français Antérieurs au XVe Siècle,* ed. Joseph Morawski, *Les Classiques Français du Moyen Age* (Paris, 1925), #2243.

Christ is reenacted in every work of charity, like Erec's self-less rescue of Cadoc. Time is once more seen to be fictional —that is, transcended by the spiritual reality it serves. The eschatalogical Advent and Judgment first of all signify something spiritual, which occurs continually in the lives of the faithful.

It should not be thought to detract from his act, incidentally, that Erec makes Cadoc pledge to report what he has done at Arthur's court. Erec has lost the honor without which he cannot function as a knight, certainly never as king. His passage toward the throne demands that he restore his reputation. An act of charity ought not to be hidden under a bushel any more than a wise saying or an edifying tale, but ought to be placed like a lamp on a stand. Don't *hide* it, Erec says:

> " . . . Gardez, ne li celez ja,
> De quel peril je ai mis fors
> Et vostre vie et vostre cors." (ll. 4538–40)

Sunday is the day of the Resurrection. On Sunday, Erec collapses in the likeness of death. But Erec's "death" to his former life *is* his resurrection to the new life he must assume as king. It is characteristic of Chrétien's deep sense of humor that he laces such a crucial scene, the completion of Erec's conversion in his quest to restore his reputation, with slapstick. Appropriately, it is "un jor de mai" (l. 4779), the time when the whole earth is resurrected. The setting is the castle of Limors, whose name ominously means "the dead."[4] Oringle, its wicked count (ruler of the dead?), becomes impatient with Enide's refusal to leave off mourning her apparently dead husband and become his wife in more than name (although the forced marriage of a woman still actually married to another is obviously invalid).

---

4. For Celtic and romance analogues and sources, see R. S. Loomis, *Arthurian Tradition and Chrétien de Troyes* (New York, 1949) pp. 162–68.

> "Dame!" fet il, "il vos estuet
> Cest Duel leissier et oblïer." (ll. 4792–93)

The dead cannot be raised, he says:

> "Certainnemant poez savoir,
> Que morz hon por duel ne revit;
> Qu'onques nus avenir nel vit." (ll. 4796–98)

It can't happen (*avenir*), he asserts. But of course it can
happen that the dead are raised. All the dead shall be
raised at the Second Advent. Christ was raised on Easter.
The fact is that resurrection from a kind of death is precisely what the romance is about, and it is what happens to
Erec in that room.

Enide refuses to eat, although the Count orders her to.
Nevermore in her life will she eat or drink, she declares,
before she first sees her lord ("mon seignor" l. 4818) eat.
Oringle again uses the word *avenir* in his assertion of the
impossibility of resurrection:

> "Dame! ce ne puet avenir.
> Por fole vos feites tenir,
> Quant vos si grant folie dites." (ll. 4819–21

Enide refuses even to answer him. In his rage, he slaps her
face, and then slaps her again in defiance of his own barons,
who are shocked by his discourteous behavior, and condemn
him for it.

In the midst of this confusion, Erec, who has been laid
out on a bier in the same hall, suddenly regains consciousness, and, hearing the distress of his wife, jumps to the
floor, draws his sword, and kills Oringle. The barons and
squires and servants in the hall, seeing a dead man rise from
his bier, believe him to be a devil, and panic-stricken, fall
over each other in their desperate attempts to escape:

> Li uns devant l'autre s'an fuit,
> Quanqu'il pueent, a grant eslés.

Tost orent vuidié le palés,
Et crïent tuit, et foible et fort:
"Fuiiez, fuiiez! vez ci le mort."
Mout est granz la presse a l'issue:
Chascuns de tost foïr s'argue,
Et li uns l'autre anpaint et bote. (ll. 4874–81)

Chrétien whimsically echoes the scriptural admonition that
"if any man desire to be first, the same shall be last of all"
(Mark 9:35), when he further describes the barons' rush for
the exit:

Cil qui deriers est an la rote,
Vossist bien estre el premier front. (ll. 4882–83)

Erec and Enide escape on a horse that has been abandoned
by a terrified groom. Erec's conversion is now complete. He
declares his renewed love for his wife, greater even than before.

. . . Erec, qui sa fame an porte,
L'acole et beise et reconforte;
Antre ses braz contre son cuer
L'estraint et dit: "Ma douce suer!
Bien vos ai del tot essaiiee!
Ne soiiez de rien esmaiiee,
Qu'or vos aim plus, qu'ains mes ne fis,
Et je resui certains et fis,
Que vos m'amez parfitemant." (ll. 4917–25)

The poet is being ironical at Erec's expense in this declaration that he has tested Enide, and has finally discovered
her love to be perfect. Her love was obvious from the beginning. It is rather Erec's love that has needed to pass a
test. From now on, he continues, he is wholly at her commandment, just as in the past:

"Tot a vostre comandemant
Vuel estre des or an avant,
Aussi con j'estoie devant." (ll. 4926–28)

Erec sounds a bit like the typically unmanned lover, willingly dominated by his lady, whose interests are the pursuits of Venus. But Erec has it backwards. It was not Enide who "commanded" Erec to abandon chivalry for the delights of love. On the contrary, she loyally mourned his loss of manly reputation, while he chose to sleep till noon. Chrétien's irony turns to farce when Erec goes on to forgive his wife for anything she may have said against him during their trials:

> "Et se vos rien m'avez mesdite,
> Jel vos pardoing tot et claim quite
> Del forfet et de la parole." (ll. 4929–31)

It is of course Erec himself who stands in need of forgiveness for the repeated bullying threats and insults he has spoken to Enide.

The seriousness of meaning is not contradicted or undercut by Chrétien's continual ambivalence toward even his most heroic characters. It is rather the mark of insight into the inescapable weaknesses of the human condition. But it is the mark also of sympathy, for his irony arises from a profoundly comic view of original sin. We laugh even at his heroes, not only at the obvious buffoons like Sir Kay. But the very fact that we can laugh at their foibles—not only cry over them—reflects the poet's faith in man's salvation, the comic ending that transcends even the laughter in beatitude. As we laugh at Erec's ludicrous condescension toward the admirable Enide, we recognize the deeper meaning of the episode at Limors. Erec has undergone death, and has been reborn; the meaning of baptism, with which his victory over Yder is infused, has been completed by his symbolic resurrection. The fiction has made visible for us an image of spiritual initiation. And Chrétien has taken his tongue from his cheek when he once more affirms the renewal of Erec's love after Guivret's sisters have healed his wounds:

Or fu Erec et forz et sains,
Or fu gariz et respassez.
Or fu Enide liee assez,
Or ot totes ses volantez,
Or li revient sa granz biautez;
Car mout estoit et pale et tainte,
Si l'avoit ses granz diaus atainte.
Or fu acolee et beisiee,
Or fu de toz biens aeisiee,
Or ot sa joie et son delit;
Que nu a nu sont an un lit
Et li uns l'autre acole et beise;
N'est riens nule, qui tant lor pleise.
. . . .
Or ont lor amor rafermee
Et lor grant dolor obliëe. (ll. 5238–58)

When they depart Guivret's castle for Arthur's court, Enide rides the palfrey with the ivory saddle bow depicting the story of Aeneas. Like Aeneas, Erec has successfully turned away from spiritual enslavement to passion, and, guided by reason, pursues his way to the throne for which he is destined.

5
Joie de la Cort

The adventure called *La Joie de la Cort* is the culmination of Erec's quest, and it is the greatest of his trials. It is an adventure veiled in mystery, whose true nature is revealed to Erec only by actually undergoing it, although the innuendoes of Guivret and Evrain whet his desire for it irrevocably. The more perilous it comes to seem, the more fixed becomes Erec's determination to achieve it. Greatness, he has learned, is purchased at a great price—a price that must be paid continually.

> . . . Con plus granz est la mervoille
> Et l'avanture plus grevainne,
> Plus la covoite et plus se painne. (ll. 5644–46)

Evrain tries to dissuade Erec from undertaking what he fears will end in his destruction, but he acknowledges that if he is successful, he will have achieved what no man can surpass:

> "Se vos a joie an esploitiez,
> Conquise avroiz si grant enor,
> Qu'onques hon ne conquist greignor." (ll. 5664–66)

118

Erec too, although he is ignorant of the nature of his peril, senses that this is to be a supreme test, to which he must dedicate supreme effort:

> ". . . Ja de rien que j'aie anprise,
> Ne ferai tel recreantise,
> Que je tot mon pooir n'an face
> Einçois que j'isse de la place." (ll. 5653–56)

If we read this episode strictly on the literal level, we are surprised—after the innuendo and mystery and awe—to find that the perilous adventure turns out to be just another joust with just another knight, albeit a formidable one. We have seen Erec prevail too often against greater odds for his victory over Mabonagrain in itself to impress us much. It is not in the one more proof of his knightly prowess that the meaning of this episode lies, however. For the *Joie de la Cort* is figuratively the image, as it were in a mirror, of the spiritual condition that it has been Erec's quest first to flee, but then to confront and overcome. It is the image of the willing enslavement of reason to the whims of passion.

After he has been vanquished, Mabonagrain reveals to Erec the nature of his imprisonment in the garden of delights of the *Joie*. He has blindly promised to grant his lover a secret wish; no matter what the wish may be, he reasons, a man can deny his lover nothing, if he loves her truly:

> "Qui veeroit rien a s'amie?
> N'est pas amis, qui antreset
> Tot le buen s'amie ne fet
> Sanz rien leissier et sanz faintise,
> S'il onques puet an nule guise." (ll. 6058–62)

But the man, we know from St. Paul, is properly the head over the woman, and ought to guide her passionate nature by his own superior reason; when the man gives over the sovereignty of reason to the dictates of passion, natural or-

der between the sexes is subverted. Once Mabonagrain has
committed himself to act on any whim of his lover, he has
relinquished the reins of reason. To be ruled by a woman,
or more generally to be ruled by passion, was thought of in
the Middle Ages as "effeminate" behavior, since, quite simply, if the woman had assumed the man's legitimate role,
the man must needs have assumed the woman's. Thus, Mabonagrain is appropriately hamstrung in his knightly function at the very moment of his assumption of manhood as
a knight. King Evrain has chosen the magic garden for the
ceremony of Mabonagrain's dubbing to knighthood. Immediately, his lover reminds him of his pledge, and now reveals to him what he has unwittingly vowed.

> "Ma damoisele qui siet la,
> Tantost de ma foi m'apela
> Et dist que plevi li avoie,
> Que ja mes de ceanz n'istroie
> Tant que chevaliers i venist,
> Qui par armes me conquëist." (ll. 6073–78)

Now we understand the meaning of the marvelous wall of
air that encloses the garden:

> El vergier n'avoit anviron
> Mur ne paliz se de l'er non;
> Mes de l'er est de totes parz
> Par nigromance clos li jarz
> Si que riens antrer n'i pooit,
> Se par dessore n'i voloit,
> Ne que s'il fust toz clos de fer. (ll. 5739–45)

A "wall" of air, as any fool could see, is no wall at all. Like
the Emperor's new clothes, it is a desperate fantasy that can
imprison only those whose own wills give it the appearance
of reality. Mabonagrain has surrendered his will to the
whims of his lover, but that surrender was itself an act of
perverted will. Wryly, Chrétien says that one can escape this
"magic" wall only by flying over it; but while the will has

the power to imprison the body in thin air (or to dissolve the "wall" again) , it cannot make the body fly.

Once the soul has surrendered the function of reason to the dictates of passion, passionate behavior comes to appear reasonable. Chrétien plays with this inversion at Mabonagrain's expense when he has him argue that his obviously foolish submission to his lady's outrageous demand is the "reasonable" thing for an honorable knight to do:

> "Reisons fu, que je remassisse,
> Ainz que ma fiance mantisse,
> Ja ne l'eüsse je plevi." (ll. 6079–81)

On the contrary, it is only to compound folly to carry out a foolish (not to say wicked) promise merely in order not to break faith. Mabonagrain's conception of knightly honor is pitiably shallow. The irony is repeated, more grimly, in his defensive apology for the deaths of those knights who have come against him to try the adventure, and whose heads are chivalrously impaled on stakes about the garden:

> " . . . Miens n'an est mie li torz,
> Qui *reison* i viaut esgarder:
> De ce ne me poi je garder,
> Se je ne vossisse estre faus
> Et foi mantie et desleaus." (ll. 6110–14; emphasis mine)

Mabonagrain's disavowal of responsibility implicitly raises a thorny moral dilemma for him, although he does not even recognize, much less confront it. If he is not to blame for the gruesome consequences of his misguided "faith," who is? From the viewpoint of his own perverted sense of honor, he could no more place the blame with his lady than as a Christian he could place it with God. Yet he himself admits that a wrong has been done. Clearly, he is blinding his conscience to his own responsibility as before he blinded his reason to the folly of passion. He *is* to blame.

Furthermore, Mabonagrain's lame rationalization is only

a very transparent cover for his real motive, his fear that his lady might withdraw her favors if he displeases her. He suppresses even the semblance of protest at her extravagant whim:

> "Des que je soi le bien an li,
> A la rien que je plus ai chiere,
> N'an dui feire sanblant ne chiere,
> Que nule rien me despleüst;
> Que, s'ele s'an aparceüst,
> Tost retreissist a li son cuer;
> Et je nel vossisse a nul fuer
> Por rien qui deüst avenir." (ll. 6082–89)

Mabonagrain's desperate clinging, at the expense of reason and justice, arises from the same all-pervading fearfulness that is the first characteristic of the lover described by Andreas Capellanus. Fear is only a part of the complex of folly that he describes and analyzes in order to reveal to the "Walter" for whom the book is written the precise nature of the behavior he must shun. "Any man who devotes his efforts to love loses all his usefulness," Andreas declares, putting his finger directly on the predicament of Erec when he neglects his knightly duties, and of Mabonagrain when he willingly imprisons himself in a wall of air.[1] On the other hand, St. John affirms that true love is without fear: "There is no fear in love; but perfect love casteth out fear: because fear hath torment. He that feareth is not made perfect in love" (1 John 4: 18).

Mabonagrain's moral blindness is the crucial point of difference between his lapse in the garden of delights, and Erec's lapse into sensuality in the garden of delights of marriage. Erec is made conscious of his error, and liberates himself; Mabonagrain remains blind, and must be liberated by another. Mabonagrain's predicament reflects Erec's as the inversion of it. Erec overcomes the "enchantment" of the gar-

---

1. Andreas Capellanus, *The Art of Courtly Love*, trans. John Jay Parry (New York, 1957), p. 44.

den of the *Joie* as he has already overcome passion's enchantment of reason and manhood within himself. The
adventure of the *Joie* is the emblem of this final, inner victory.

It is no mere off-hand likeness to call this adventure an
emblem. Like a true emblem, the elements of which it is
composed are signs whose meanings, taken together, form a
larger pattern of meaning of an essentially moral nature. The
hedging of Guivret and Evrain, the sense of mystery arising
from the incongruity of their innuendoes on the one hand,
and the pleasant name of the adventure on the other, serves
to prepare our expectation of some deep significance.

Guivret indicates the treacherous nature of the adventure's
name; like the little book of prophecy given John to eat in
Revelation 10:9–10, it is sweet in the mouth, but in the
fulfillment it is bitter:

> "Li nons est mout biaus a nomer,
> Mes mout est griés a assomer." (ll. 5461–62)

The "joy" is a deception, Erec is warned by the people of
the castle:

> . . . Les granz janz et les menues
> Disoient tuit: "Haï! haï!
> Chevaliers! Joie t'a traï,
> Cele que tu cuides conquerre;
> Mes ton duel et ta mort vas querre." (ll. 5704–8)

Chrétien is playing on the double meaning of joy. For the
adventure of the *Joie* does not after all betray Erec for the
very reason that the joy he sought with Enide, the joy of
sensuality has already betrayed him, and he has learned from
that betrayal the nature of true joy. Mabonagrain, on the
other hand, has indeed been betrayed by what he thought
was joy, and he may properly be said to have sought his
sorrow and his spiritual death in pursuing foolishly the love
of his mistress.

As sensuality seems first a joy, but reveals itself to be a spiritual death, the garden of the *Joie* appears a paradise, but is really the anti-type of the true paradise, as the people of the castle indicate when they call the adventure a *misadventure* (l. 5519). It is a garden enclosed, in which flowers bloom and ripe fruits grow year round. All manner of birds sing for the pleasure of those in the garden. Whatever herbs and roots are good for healing grow there in abundance. The gate, like the way to salvation, is strait. The birds' song, Chrétien says, is in itself a sign of the joy that Erec desires:

> Erec . . .
> . . . .
> . . . mout se delitoit el chant
> Des oisiaus qui leanz chantoient;
> Sa Joie li represantoient,
> La chose a quoi il plus beoit. (ll. 5768–73)

But immediately, he sees the severed heads of Mabonagrain's adversaries impaled on sharpened stakes. And then he sees another sign, a stake on which there hangs a horn, although,

> Il ne set que ce senefie. (l. 5787)

Evrain explains the meaning of the sign:

> "Amis!", fet il, "savez que monte
> Ceste chose que ci veez?
> Mout an devez estre esfreez,
> Se vos amez rien vostre cors[2]
> Car cil seus peus qui est defors,
> Ou vos veez cest cor pandu,
> A mout longuemant atandu,
> Mes nos ne savons mie, cui,
> Se il atant vos ou autrui.
> Garde, ta teste n'i soit mise;
> Car li peus siet an tel devise." (ll. 5792–5802)

---

2. This pun on *cor* "horn" and *cors* "body," etc., is discussed below.

Evrain has touched on the ambivalent meaning of the sign. On the one hand, the horn signifies liberation from the enchantment of the garden; it awaits the coming of one who will redeem those imprisoned there. Probably the horn is meant to be identified with the trumpets of Revelation, which announce the Second Advent, and Judgment. On the other hand, the stake on which it hangs is a grim reminder of the risks the redeemer must be prepared to accept. This ambivalence reflects the dual nature of love, too: holy love is salvation, sensuality is death.

The opposing knights represent the same ambivalence. As Mabonagrain's imprisonment itself is his love for the lady on the silver bed—emblem of luxury—So Erec attributes his strength to the faithful love of Enide:

> "S'an moi n'avoit de hardemant
> Fors tant con vostre amors me baille,
> Ne doteroie je sanz faille
> Cors a cors nul home vivant." (ll. 5856–59)

Erec's victory thus expresses figuratively the victory of heavenly over sensual love, of reason over passion, of natural order over the folly that returns the world to primeval chaos. It is no accident that Chrétien ironically has Mabonagrain, when he accosts Erec, swear by his own salvation, "se je soie saus" (l. 5908) and "se Deus me saut!" (l. 5935). Salvation is unlikely so long as he persists in the pernicious folly of his submission to his lady. Submission to Erec, however, *can* mean his salvation.

We are all the more justified in seeing parallels between Mabonagrain and Erec in light of the revelation of their close connection (Mabonagrain was a young squire at the court of Erec's father), and of the blood relationship between Mabonagrain's mistress and Enide. These relationships are not the arbitrary whim of a poet who wishes to knit up loose ends, but the outward sign of spiritual kinship, whether by way of likeness or contrast. In Mabonagrain, Erec may

see the image of his former self. He may see it in Mabonagrain's luxurious mistress too. Her reason for contriving the
imprisonment of her knight was to monopolize him for her
own amorous desires. Mabonagrain tells Erec,

> "Einsi me cuida retenir
> Ma dameisele a lonc sejor;
> Ne cuidoit pas, que a nul jor
> Deüst an cest vergier antrer
> Vassaus qui me poïst outrer.
> Por ce me cuida a delivre
> Toz les jorz que j'eüsse a vivre,
> Avuec li tenir an prison."   (ll. 6090–97)

We have here the image of Erec's own abandonment of duty
for the joys of love-making.

   When everyone else is celebrating the joy of Mabonagrain's liberation, only his mistress is inconsolable. She is sad
and angry, and tears stream down her face,

> Cui la joie enuie mout fort,
> Por ce qu'il li estoit avis,
> Qu'or ne seroit mes ses amis
> Avuec li tant come il soloit,
> Quant del vergier issir voloit.   (ll. 6214–18)

Her present grief is as excessive and foolish as her past luxury; it is simply the other side of the same passionate coin.
Only the natural love that arises when Enide reveals their
kinship subdues her immoderate feelings, and leads to her
reconciliation with the fulfillment of the *Joie*.

   Our first view of her is intended to reveal her passionate nature. In sharp contrast to the humble condition in
which we first saw Enide, Mabonagrain's mistress sits on a
silver bed, spread with gold brocade, in the shade of a sycamore tree. Robertson has shown that the person who rests
under a shade tree in the garden of earthly delights is to be
identified with Adam and Eve who, after they had eaten

the forbidden fruit, "hid themselves from the face of the Lord God amidst the trees of paradise" (Genesis 3:8). His discussion of a sermon by Hugh of St. Victor in which the same figure is used is strikingly applicable to Mabonagrain's mistress: "Here the leaves of the tree are the objects of worldly vanity . . . and the shade is the deceitful comfort which things of this kind afford. . . . But the leaves ultimately fall, leaving the person seeking shelter fully exposed to the heat and light from which he sought to escape. . . . This light is the sunshine of God's justice."[3]

In addition, medieval commentary on the nature of the sycamore tree made it a figure that expresses here the spiritual condition of the lady in its shade. As Curtius observes in his discussion of the *locus amoenus*, the flora of landscape description in medieval poetry derives not from the actual flora of northern Europe, but from the models of classical rhetoric.[4] The sycamore that appears in medieval literature is not the tree with which we are familiar in Europe and America, but the Asiatic sycamore, *ficus sycamorus*, also mentioned in Scripture. The leaves of this tree resemble those of the fig, and its fruits are even somewhat of the sweetness of the wild fig, but they are held not to be good for the stomach. Its nature thus corresponds precisely with the foolishness of sensuality, which is superficially sweet, but whose sweetness is overcome by bitterness in the soul. Evrain has warned that the *Joie*'s "name is very sweet to say,/But most grievous to fulfill."

Alanus, in the *Distinctiones*, associates the sycamore with folly and transitoriness: "The sycamore is a tree similar to the fig, whence the sycamore is like a foolish fig [*ficus fatua*], since it is like the fig not in its fruits but in its leaves. . . . Also that which is transitory is signified, whence Isaiah: 'They

---

3. D. W. Robertson, Jr., "The Doctrine of Charity in Medieval Literary Gardens: A Topical Approach Through Symbolism and Allegory," *Speculum* 26 (1951) : 26.
4. Chapter 10, "The Ideal Landscape," *European Literature and the Latin Middle Ages* (New York, 1963), pp. 183–202.

have cut down the sycamores, but we will change them for cedars' " (*PL,* Vol. 210, col. 891) .[5] The sycamore expresses figuratively the foolish and transitory pleasures in whose "shade" Mabonagrain and his mistress wish to hide from the moral and civic obligations of life—that is to say, from the sun of justice.

Mabonagrain's mistress, Chrétien tells us wryly—if obliquely—is more than four times as beautiful as Lavinia (l. 5891). This is a curious compliment. It evokes again the thematically important story of Dido's fatal passion, and of Aeneas's fulfillment of his heavenly destiny in abandoning her and marrying Lavinia. Aeneas's marriage with Lavinia is not a passionate affair at all, but what we would call a "political" marriage, designed precisely to quell the passions of war, and to restore the order of peace. Moreover, Lavinia is not in Vergil a paragon of beauty, against whom it makes much sense to compare a lady you wish to pay a compliment. It is on the contrary Dido whose beauty is matchless —whose beauty is also her undoing. Thus, Chrétien suggests by this garbled compliment that the real likeness is to Dido, not Lavinia. We may also recall the now significant word with which Chrétien described the pleasures of Dido's love, depicted on the saddle-bow:

> . . . A Cartage a grant *joie*
> Dido an son lit le reçut. (ll. 5340–41; emphasis mine)

In light of the *Joie de la Cort,* the word is not simply a manner of speaking, or even a euphemism, but is imbued with the ironic ambivalence of love.

In tracing mythological sources of the *Joie de la Cort* episode, Loomis accounts in an ingenious way for the confusion in the tradition that leads up to Chrétien's poem among the homonyms *cors* "court," *cors* "horn," and *cors* "body."

---

5. See also Robertson, "The Doctrine of Charity in Medieval Literary Gardens," p. 29.

The *joie* stemmed from the Celtic mythological vessel of plenty conceived as a horn, *cors*, Loomis argues. This horn became confused with the Eucharistic *cors*, the body of Christ, with which the communicant is fed spiritually; and it became confused also with the *cors*, "court," of King Bran and of the Rich Fisher.[6] The precise nature of the *joie* in *Erec* is purposely left obscure. The adventure's name rings with grim irony after Guivret's hints about its dangers. But Erec sanguinely jumps to the conclusion that "Deus! an joie n'a se bien non!" (l. 5466). We fear that Erec's enthusiasm is hasty, however, when the people of the castle warn him, "Joie t'a traï" (l. 5706).

Loomis assumes that Chrétien was unaware of the thematic connections among these homonyms. While it may be true that the poet had no knowledge (or even interest) in the intricacies of transmission of the themes that he employed, it is improbable that he was not consciously punning with the multiple meanings of *cors* and their thematic implications for his poem. Thus, the *joie dou cors* "joy of the body" is the joy that Dido offers Aeneas in her bed, and the joy that Mabonagrain has sought with the lady on the silver bed. The *joie de la cort* "joy of the court"—Mabonagrain finally explains to Erec—is the joy at his liberation from imprisonment in the garden. The *joie dou cor* "joy of the horn" is the signal of that liberation in the joyous sound of the trumpet, related typologically with the trumpets of Revelation. Finally, *joie dou cuer* "joy of the heart" is the true, inner joy whose source is holy love. Christ brings such love and joy to the world, and Erec's redemption of Mabonagrain, his bringing of joy to the court, repeats Christ's advent. As the world awaited the coming of the Messiah, the court of Evrain has long awaited the joy of Mabonagrain's redemption, and Erec's coming fulfills that expectation as though fulfilling a prophecy. Mabonagrain tells him:

6. Roger Sherman Loomis, *Arthurian Tradition and Chrétien de Troyes* (New York, 1949), pp. 168–75.

> "Mout avez an grant joie mise
> La cort mon oncle et mes amis,
> Qu'or serai fors de ceanz mis;
> Et por ce que joie an avront
> Tuit cil qui a la cort seront,
> Joie de la Cort l'apeloient
> Cil qui la joie an atandoient.
> Tant longuemant l'ont atandue,
> Que ore lor sera randue
> Par vos, qui l'avez desresniee." (ll. 6118–27)

There is an important parallel between the *Joie de la Cort* and the adventure that opens the romance, the pursuit and conquest of Yder. In both, Erec liberates by his victory—Enide and her parents from poverty and obscurity, Mabonagrain from passionate enslavement to his mistress. Both adventures last exactly three days, symbolic of the days of Christ's death and resurrection, through which he liberated man from death. As Erec restored order to Arthur's court when he returned with Enide, he has restored joy to Evrain's court. In superlatives, Evrain's people bless their redeemer:

> "Deus saut celui, par cui ressort
> Joie et leesce a nostre cort!
> Deus saut le plus buen eüré
> Que Deus a feire et anduré!" (ll. 6375–78)

Erec has healed the court of Evrain, but the court of King Arthur to which he at last returns is sick once more. Erec's victory over Yder and marriage with Enide restored order there momentarily, but the foolish Arthur is still head of the body politic, and if the head is diseased, the body must suffer with it. The day before Erec's return, Arthur has been bled "privately" in his chambers, Chrétien quips, with only five hundred barons in attendance (ll. 6416–19). There is a truly pathetic quality to Arthur's vanity:

> Onques mes an nule seison

Ne fu trovez li rois si seus,
Si an estoit mout angoisseus,
Que plus n'avoit jant a sa cort. (ll. 6420–23)

But Erec's advent heals the court once more. When Arthur hears of his approach with Guivret, he cheers up at once: "D'aus iert mout ma corz amandee" (l. 6437). Chrétien puns here quite unmistakably on *cors*. The feminine possessive, it is true, fixes the literal meaning: "My *court* will be greatly healed by them." But the king is sick, and it is his own body that actually needs to be healed. Moreover, the court *is* the body of which he is head, as Christ's "body" is his Church. Chrétien works a variation on the same pun when, before Erec's coronation, Arthur gives new clothes to his knights, "Por ce que sa corz miaudre apeire" (l. 6666). Arthur's *court* will look better if the *bodies* of his knights are more stylishly adorned; and the bodies of his knights, collectively, are his *body*.

John of Salisbury develops the figure of the "body" politic, which he ascribes to an otherwise unknown work of Plutarch (*Policratus*, Bk. V, 2). In the same work he explains the relationship between the health of the Prince and health of the state: ". . . The happiness of no body politic will be lasting unless the head is preserved in safety and vigor and looks out for the whole body."[7]

This figure illuminates the meaning of the allegory whereby Enide is understood as signifying the body. The natural body, which she represents on one level of the allegory, is in turn to be understood as corresponding to the king's "body," his people, whom he must learn to govern as reason governs the flesh. He must also learn to care for it. Erec's slow, agonizing struggle to come into and maintain the proper relationship of a man to his wife is the figurative expression of the education of a king to rule his people.

---

7. *Policratus*, Bk. VI, 22, trans. in D. W. Robertson, Jr., ed., *The Literature of Medieval England* (New York, 1970), p. 218.

Incidentally, the passage quoted above from *Policratus* gives us a further insight into the meaning of the exemplum from Vergil. The story of Dido and Aeneas offers not only the positive example of Aeneas for Erec to follow; Queen Dido's is as crucial an example of behavior for him to eschew. The passage continues:

> Learn from the example of Dido. For with what careless and irresponsible levity did she admit Aeneas, what favor did she too quickly bestow on an unknown stranger, an exile, a fugitive, of whose plight and motives she was ignorant, and whose person was suspicious. . . . These things brought forth fruit in fornication, in the burning down of the city and the desolation of its citizens, and bequeathed to future generations the seeds of undying enmity. This was the end of the effeminate rule of a woman, which, though it had a beginning and basis in virtue, could not find an issue into subsequent prosperity. (pp. 218–19)

6

The King's Advent

Erec's adventures have brought him to the Christmas day on which he is crowned king. At the beginning of Advent, twenty days before Nativity, messengers reach Arthur's court with the news that Erec's father, king of his land, has died. Erec is the king to be, "li novel roi" (ll. 6859, 6867), and his journey back to his father's land to assume the throne is filled with the meaning of Christ's advent.

With characteristic irony, Chrétien has Arthur crown Erec, who has now acquired the wisdom that Arthur himself still lacks. But the foolishness of King Arthur does not detract from Erec's dignity; rather, it underscores it. When Erec learns of his father's death he is grief-stricken, but he bridles his natural emotions (which is not to repress them), as it becomes a king to do.

> Erec an pesa plus assez,
> Qu'il ne mostra sanblant as janz;
> Mes diaus de roi n'est mie janz,
> N'a roi n'avient qu'il face duel. (ll. 6524–27)

As the king can expect no more submission from his own

subjects than he himself shows whatever authority is over him, Erec does wisely to accept his land in fief from Arthur. Although Arthur is foolish, God has established the throne he occupies and determined its place in the social hierarchy, which is in its turn a part of the universal hierarchy of creation. Erec's deference to the order of which Arthur is only a small part, then, is not submission to folly, but to reason:

> Aprés fist un mout grant savoir,
> Que del roi sa terre reprist;
> Aprés si li pria et dist
> Qu'il le coronast a sa cort. (ll. 6544–47)

On Christmas Eve, Erec and Enide arrive at court; on Christmas day, they are crowned king and queen. "Nor tongue nor mouth of any man could tell," says Chrétien, "a third or a fourth or a fifth part of the preparations which were made for his coronation" (ll. 6702–6) . It is foolish for him to try, but since he must, he says, punning on the theme of advent, "Or avaingne qu'avenir puet" (l. 6710).

Arthur himself has brought the thrones, two finely carved ivory folding chairs, marvelously identical. Each is carved with the representation of a leopard and a crocodile. Erec appears earlier in the romance seated on the image of a leopard. Before he sets out on his penitential adventures, he has a Limoges carpet spread on the ground with his arms arrayed on it.

> Erec s'assist de l'autre part
> Dessus l'image d'un liépart,
> Qui el tapit estoit portreite.
> Por armer s'atorne et afeite. (ll. 2633–36)

Rabanus Maurus, in the *De Universo,* explains that the leopard signifies the Devil, who is "full of diverse vices, or any sinner covered with the spots of crimes and of diverse errors" (Bk. VII, *PL,* Vol. 111, col. 220). Alanus, in the *Distinctiones,* adds to these meanings the heretic, "who beguiles by diverse frauds, as the pard is adorned with diverse colors" (*PL*, Vol. 210, col. 891) .

We have noted in another context the significance in medieval art of relative position. When a saint, for instance, appears standing on the small figure of a dragon or a lion or a grotesque of some sort, his victory over some evil is signified. The picture of Erec seated on the image of a leopard is an emblematic representation of this kind, which shows outwardly his inner struggle to subdue vice. Of course, the context affects the meaning of the emblem. At the beginning of his quest, the emblem can properly indicate only intention; at his coronation, the same emblem indicates achievement. Perhaps it is to show the genuineness of his conversion, to indicate that his quest has not been merely an outward show and that the reputation he has regained is not the vanity of worldly glory but the virtuous reputation that a king requires to fulfill his mission, that Chrétien adds the figure of the crocodile to the coronation scene. For the Bestiary tells us that "hypocritical, dissolute and avaricious people have the same nature as this brute—also any people who are puffed up with the vice of pride, dirtied with the corruption of luxury, or haunted with the disease of avarice—even if they do make a show of falling in with the justifications of the Law, pretending in the sight of men to be upright and indeed very saintly. Crocodiles lie by night in the water, by day on land, because hypocrites, however luxuriously they live by night, delight to be said to live holily and justly by day."[1]

Perhaps the most curious, if not downright startling detail for the casual reader of the romance is the decoration of Erec's coronation robe, which Chrétien goes to some lengths to describe. On the robe are pictured the arts of the quadrivium: geometry, arithmetic, music, and astronomy. We are only *told* they are "pictured," however; there is nothing

---

1. *The Bestiary*, trans T. H. White (New York, 1954) , pp. 50–51.

visual about Chrétien's description of them. Instead of a visual, emblematic representation of the four arts, like Lady Philosophy's gown in Boethius, for instance, Chrétien gives us quite abstract explanations of the realm and function of each art. He shows no interest in evoking a sensuous mental picture of the robe, even though he praises the workmanship of the four fairies who have made it. His interest is entirely in the thematic import of the quadrivium and the source of his description of it, which he identifies as Macrobius's *Commentary on the Dream of Scipio.*

Macrobius's work bears an obvious relevance to the romance whose theme is the initiation of a king. For Cicero's "Dream of Scipio," actually only a fragment of his otherwise lost *Republic,* is explicitly an exhortation to statesmen to govern according to the precepts of justice. Scipio Africanus the Elder appears in the dream to his grandson (by adoption) and charges him to conquer Carthage and restore and maintain order in the city. Carthage, we recall, is the city of Dido, and thus particularly susceptible to the disorder of the passions. He assures Scipio the Younger that there is a special place reserved in heaven for those statesmen who govern their people well—who, in governing, serve them. "Nothing that occurs on earth," he says, "indeed, is more gratifying to that supreme God who rules the whole universe than the establishment of associations and federations of men bound together by principles of justice, which are called commonwealths."[2] Thus Chrétien's identification of the *Commentary* as his source for the description of the four arts veils *in order to reveal* the political relevance of Cicero's work and Macrobius's commentary to his romance.

But how is a statesman to serve the commonwealth? His grandfather charges Scipio to support the commonwealth with deeds of virtue and valor, but virtue and valor in turn proceed only from a life molded according to the precepts of

---

2. *Commentary on the Dream of Scipio,* trans. W. H. Stahl (New York, 1952) , p. 71.

philosophy. Macrobius anticipates the objections of those who will fail to see the relationship of philosophy to politics; Cicero's discussion of the spheres, of heavenly bodies, of the immortality of the soul, and so on, as well as his own discussion of physics, mathematics, music, astronomy, and metaphysics, is not, he stoutly maintains, the padding of a prolix philosopher to fill out an essentially brief ethical and political tract. It is rather of necessity that the "Dream of Scipio," "embraces the entire body of philosophy," and "that there is nothing more complete than this work" (*Commentary*, Stahl, p. 246).

Justice in the commonwealth is the image of divine order in the universe as a whole. Moreover, the earthly king stands at the apex of the hierarchy that includes the whole visible creation. The king who rules justly acts in harmony with the entire creation. This is the meaning of Erec's sceptre, which is decorated with all manner of fish and beasts and men and birds; the true king rules over the whole realm of nature:

> . . . An tot le mont nen a meniere
> De peisson ne de beste fiere
> Ne d'ome ne d'oisel volage,
> Que chascuns lonc sa propre image
> N'i fust ovrez et antailliez. (ll. 6877–81)

Enide, over whom Erec rules as husband, is in this light, too, appropriately associated with nature. As she symbolizes his body and his people, she symbolizes also his realm. Erec's sceptre is made of a single emerald, which medieval lapidaries agree symbolizes faith.[3] As a Christian king, anointed "according to the Christian Law" (l. 6860), it is through faith that his legitimate authority derives.

Only that king can rule wisely who knows his realm. If the earthly king rules God's visible creation, moreover if that

---

3. Leon Baisier, *The Lapidaire Chrétien, Its Composition, Its Influence, Its Sources* (Washington, D. C., 1936), pp. 79–82.

creation in all its variety is nonetheless ultimately a unity, then the wisdom that the king requires must proceed from "physical" and "rational" as well as "moral philosophy."

> Moral philosophy is a guide to the highest perfection in moral conduct, physical philosophy is concerned with the physical part of the divine order, and rational philosophy discusses incorporealities, matters apprehended only by the mind. Accordingly, Cicero included all three in *Scipio's Dream*. (*Commentary*, p. 246)

For Macrobius, "instruction in moral philosophy" (Africanus's "exhortation to do virtuous deeds, to love one's country, and to despise glory") is not in itself the sum of philosophy necessary to govern wisely. Justice in the commonwealth is the reflection of divine order in the universe; the wisdom of the statesman must proceed from insight into the principles of that universal order, and insight is achieved when the mind is led from contemplation of the visible things to a spiritual understanding of the invisible forms with which they are infused.

Number is the principle that informs the creation of order from chaos; a passage from Wisdom provided medieval philosophers the text for this conception: "Thou hast ordered all things in measure, and number, and weight" (Wisdom 11:21).[4] And if number is the fundamental principle of divine order—the order of which justice is the image—then the key to wisdom is mathematics. In fact, the four arts of the quadrivium were thought of as four branches of mathematics. This is how Cassiodorus defines the quadrivium:

> Mathematical science . . . is that science which considers abstract quantity. . . . It has these divisions: arithmetic, music, geometry, astronomy. Arithmetic is the discipline of abso-

---

4. For a brief survey of this idea and its ramifications, with extensive bibliographical notes, see Otto von Simson, "Measure and Light," *The Gothic Cathedral* (New York, 1962), pp. 21–58.

lute numerable quantity. Music is the discipline which treats of numbers in their relation to those things which are found in sounds. Geometry is the discipline of immobile magnitude and of forms. Astronomy is the discipline of the course of heavenly bodies; it contemplates all figures and with searching reason considers the orbits of the stars about themselves and about the earth.[5]

We are not surprised, then, to find that Chrétien stresses the principle of number, certainly in his descriptions of the first two arts. Geometry measures the extent of heaven and earth, the depth and the breadth of the sea; she measures the whole world. Arithmetic in her turn numbers the days and the hours, the sea, drop by drop; she numbers the grains of sand, the stars, rank on rank, the leaves of the trees. Music, the third art, is also governed by the principle of number, of which harmonious sounds are only the sensible image; the sounds, moreover, ought not to be dwelt on for their own sake, but should lead the hearer to mystical contemplation of the inner mathematical harmonies they adumbrate. Finally, astronomy, who consults the heavens for whatever she desires to know, represents the mind's aspiration to heavenly wisdom, to the opening of divine mysteries.

Order through number is the theme suggested by the quadrivium depicted on Erec's robe; justice through order may be said to be the major theme of the romance as a whole. The female personifications of the four arts are allegorical figures of a familiar kind. But beyond the explicit allegory *on* the robe, there is an allegory of the robe, which may be understood as the figurative representation of the wisdom and justice that Erec has struggled to attain. It is useless to try to figure out in a literal-minded way when Erec, with all his knightly adventures to attend to, has had time for the library or for lectures in philosophy, or even, if the adventures are themselves in some sense "educational"

---

5. *Institutiones* II, 3, para. 21, trans. in Oliver Strunk, ed., *Source Readings in Music History: Antiquity and the Middle Ages* (New York, 1965), p. 88, n.6.

allegories, which battle goes with which art of the quadrivium, and so on. The practical ramifications of Chrétien's vision of just government—its implications for the education of princes, for instance—are considerably less important in the context of romance than the vision itself: the identification of wisdom and justice. Whatever the particular place of scholarship ("philosophy" in the medieval sense) in society may be, it is not separable from politics, or is only as separable as the head is separable from the body—at the cost of life.

Everything is connected to everything else in the unity of creation. Only man has fallen into disarray—the spiritual disarray that it is his peculiar struggle to transcend or succumb to. Erec has won the struggle, for himself and for his people. He has put together the "whole man" within him, soul and body; he is truly wed to Enide, as man to woman, and figuratively as man to nature; and he is the true king as surely as he is the husband—head of his body, the people. Because he is a king, Erec's struggle to attain wisdom and justice is peculiarly crucial. Yet it pertains not only to princes, for it is exemplary to each man of his own struggle to be saved.

7

The Fountain of Storms

Yvain begins on Pentecost, commemoration of the descent of the Holy Spirit; in the digression that functions as a prologue, Chrétien takes up the theme of love, which the festival lends the romance. The opening words of this Arthurian romance appear to honor the famous king when Chrétien introduces him as

> Artus, li buens rois de Bretaingne,
> La cui proesce nos ansaingne,
> Que nos soiiens preu et cortois. (*Yvain*, ll. 1–3)

To be "preu et cortois," though, is really to love well, as we discover from the digression on the decadence of modern love:

> Car cil, qui soloient amer,
> Se feisoient cortois clamer
> Et preu et large et enorable. (ll. 21–23)

Thus, if we pay attention, the example of Arthur's *proesce* can teach us to love.

Arthur's *proesce,* however, is immediately manifested in his behavior. To the amazement of his knights, the king chooses to accompany the Queen to bed. In the middle of the court celebration of Pentecost, Arthur "forgets himself" with the Queen and falls asleep:

> . . . Cel jor mout s'esmerveillierent
> Del roi, qui d'antre aus se leva,
> S'i ot de tes, cui mout greva
> Et qui mout grant parole an firent
> Por ce, que onques mes nel virent
> A si grant feste an chanbre antrer
> Por dormir ne por reposer;
> Mes cel jor einsi li avint,
> Que la reïne le detint,
> Si demora tant delez li,
> Qu'il s'oblia et andormi. (ll. 42–52)

Arthur is the same foolish king we have seen in *Erec,* and he "teaches" in the same way, by his own negative example.

Pentecost gives us the pattern of true love; Arthur demonstrates the pattern of foolish love. Arthur is, then, very much the earthly king in contradistinction to the heavenly king, and he stands in the same relation to Christ (with whom Chrétien through verbal ambiguity allows us to confuse him) as modern to old-fashioned love. This intentional contrast explains why Guiot's manuscript can read *eincois* instead of *d'antre aus* in line 43, intensifying the logical opposition to the preceding passage (ll. 33–41, discussed above in chapter 1 as applicable to Christ) suggested by the introductory *mes* (l. 42). Arthur is thus *distinguished from* the king "qui fu de tel tesmoing . . . Que toz jorz mes vivra ses nons" by his incongruous behavior.

If Arthur is the worldly king, his court is the worldly court, or, figuratively, worldliness, or perhaps the world itself. A. C. L. Brown concludes in his source study of the poem that *Yvain's* source is a Celtic Other-World tale that

Chrétien "rationalized," and "dressed . . . up in the costume
of the twelfth century."[1] Brown assumes that Chrétien did
not care about the meaning of his sources, and that he picked
up this Other-World tale rather casually, because it was a
"good story." But Brown's viewpoint serves us as objective
corroboration of the interpretation that we are here pursuing. The place from which both Calogrenant and Yvain set
out on their journey to the Other World is Arthur's court,
which must therefore represent *this* world even in Brown's
conception of the Celtic source. I would argue, however, that
Chrétien was aware of the transcendental motif of the story,
and that he did not so much "rationalize" it as see in it a
specifically Christian meaning.

Actually, we know that it was not Chrétien who Christianized the Other-World landscape of the fountain of
storms. The paradisiacal islands of the Irish *imrama* show
us the pattern of Chrétien's landscape, and Brown himself
notes that the landscapes of the later *imrama* were conventionally identified with the Christian paradise (*Iwain*, p.
57). Specifically, verbal correspondence makes it clear, as
Kölbing showed, that Chrétien's description of the fountain
of storms derives from the description of the Paradise of
Birds in the Latin *Navigatio Sancti Brendani*, or the Anglo-
Norman version of Benedeit.[2]

The extraordinary, spiritual character of Calogrenant's
journey is indicated from the beginning of his tale:

"Il avint, pres a de set anz,
Que je seus come païsanz
Aloie querant avantures,
. . . .
Et trovai un chemin a destre
Parmi une forest espesse." (ll. 175–81)

Medieval numbers are characteristically less precisely quan-

1. *Iwain*, p. 146.
2. Kölbing, "Christian von Troyes *Yvain* und die *Brandanuslegende*,"
Zeitschrift für vergleichende Literaturgeschichte 11 (1897) : 442–48.

titative than qualitative; the spiritual number seven lends its connotations to Calogrenant's story. In the same way, Calogrenant's discovery of the road that leads off to the right indicates the moral, rather than the geographical direction his journey takes. Auerbach notes that the direction "to the right" makes no sense when it is used absolutely, and must therefore have an ethical significance. "Apparently it is the 'right way' which Calogrenant discovered. And that is confirmed immediately, for the road is arduous, as right ways are wont to be; all day long it leads through a dense forest full of brambles and thickets" (*Mimesis,* p. 112) .

The pun involving the ethical and directional meanings of "right" indicates the drift of the allegory. Place, in *Yvain,* is really only the image of an inner state, just as the "Forest of Adventure" in *Erec* is the image of a certain spiritual intention. Chrétien himself has given us a specific moralization of the direction "right" and "left" in the prologue to *Perceval.* Left signifies vainglory, right, charity:

> Le senestre, selonc l'estoire,
> Senefie la vaine gloire
> Qui vient de fausse ypocrisie.
> Et la destre que senefie?
> Carité, qui de sa bone oevre
> Pas ne se vante, ançois se coevre,
> Si que ne le set se cil non
> Qui Diex et caritez a non.
> Diex est caritez, et qui vit
> En carité selonc l'escrit,
> Sainz Pols le dist et je le lui,
> Il maint en Dieu, et Diex en lui. (*Perceval,* ll. 39–50)

Calogrenant, then, turns in the direction of charity, or love, moreover in the direction of the *right kind* of love, and away from the wrong kind.

The turn to the "right," however, is not taken once and for all; the choice between the "right" and "wrong" roads is before us continually. Thus, even though Calogrenant has turned initially in the right direction, he arrives at the end of that day at the castle of the Hospitable Host, an earthly paradise where his commitment to his quest for adventure is tested.

As the host receives Calogrenant, he holds a hawk on his wrist. We have noted that the hawk commonly signifies the pursuit of love in medieval iconography, and this meaning is borne out by Calogrenant's experience at the castle. The building itself reveals its nature symbolically; everything in it is of copper:

> " . . . Il n'i avoit ne fer ne fust
> Ne rien, qui de cuivre ne fust." (ll. 215–16)

Copper is the metal of Venus, and a house of copper is one dedicated to her service. The host calls his servants by striking three times on a copper gong. Perhaps we are meant to think of St. Paul's simile for the tongue that speaks without charity: "sounding brass," "a tinkling cymbal." It is also possible that a pun is intended on *cuivre,* which means "torment, suffering," as well as "copper." The pleasure of the Hospitable Host, that is, tastes sweet in the mouth, but it is bitter in the stomach.

Actually, both loves, earthly and heavenly, cupidity and charity, share this dual nature, indicated in the prologue by the contrast between the *angoisses* and *dolors* of love on one hand and its *granz biens* on the other. In the love of Christ, the Christian suffers anguish in this world for the sake of everlasting joy in the next; the worldly man, however, buys at the price of damnation the ephemeral delights of the flesh.

Calogrenant is led by the host's daughter into an enclosed garden:

> "El plus bel praelet del monde,
> Clos de bas mur a la reonde." (ll. 239–40)

In this garden of earthly delights, the charming young lady
tempts Calogrenant to abandon his quest—an imitation of
the temptation of Adam, whose fall transmitted his weakness to all men. Nor is Calogrenant immune:

> "La la trovai si afeitiee,
> Si bien parlant et anseigniee,
> De tel sanblant et de tel estre,
> Que mout m'i delitoit a estre,
> Ne ja mes por nul estovoir
> Ne m'an queïsse removoir." (ll. 241–46)

The right way, as Auerbach observes, is always arduous; Calogrenant has described it to his audience:

> "Mout i ot voie felenesse,
> De ronces et d'espines plainne;
> A quelqu'enui, a quelque painne,
> Ting cele voie et cel santier." (ll. 182–85)

No wonder he is almost seduced from the rigors of adventure by easy pleasure. No wonder either that few knights who
seek adventure pass that way—there is no adventure to be
found in the delightful garden:

> " . . . Itant me dist
> Li vavassors, qu'il ne savoit
> Le terme, puis que il avoit
> Herbergié chevalier errant,
> Qui avanture alast querant." (ll. 256–60)

Nevertheless, it is still the right way for Calogrenant since,
if he is not altogether invulnerable to the temptation in the
garden, he passes through it and continues on his way. The
host's words,

> "Que beneoite fust la voie,
> Par ou leanz venuz estoie." (ll. 207–8)

accurately reflect the spiritual character of Calogrenant's
journey.

Next morning, not far from the castle of the Hospitable
Host (an indication again of moral rather than geographical
proximity), Calogrenant comes upon a hideous herdsman,
who watches over wild bulls:

> "L'ostel gueires esloignié n'oi,
> Quant je trovai an uns essarz
> Tors sauvages et espaarz,
> Qui s'antreconbatoient tuit
> Et demenoient si grant bruit
> Et tel fierté et tel orguel,
> Se le voir conter vos an vuel,
> Que de peor me tres arriere;
> Que nule beste n'est tant fiere
> Ne plus orguelleuse de tor." (ll. 278-87)

The herdsman himself, although he declares himself to be a
man, is described as a bestial figure:

> " . . . Il ot grosse la teste
> Plus que roncins ne autre beste,
> Chevos meschiez et front pelé
> S'ot plus de deus espanz de le,
> Oroilles mossues et granz,
> Autés com a uns olifanz,
> Les sorciz granz et le vis plat,
> Iauz de çuëte et nes de chat,
> Boche fandue come los,
> Dans de sangler, aguz et ros,
> Barbe noir, grenons tortiz,
> Et le manton aers au piz,
> Longe eschine, torte et boçue." (ll. 295-307)

He jumps to his feet, and seems to Calogrenant like an un-
reasoning animal:

> "Si m'esgarda et mot ne dist,
> Ne plus qu'une beste feïst;
> Et je cuidai que il n'eüst
> Reison ne parler ne seüst." (ll. 323-26)

Calogrenant asks the herdsman whether he is "a good thing
or not." His reply is equivocal:

" . . . 'Je sui uns hon,' " (l. 330)

"Whose man are you?" Calogrenant presses him.

" . . . 'Tes con tu voiz.
Je ne sui autre nule foiz.' " (ll. 331–32)

The knight has set out in search of adventure—in knightly terms, election; in spiritual terms, salvation. He has begun his journey on the right, arduous road, but has had to
pass through what we saw was a type of the garden in which
man fell from grace. The herdsman and his wild bulls show
us unregenerate man, bestial and ugly in his stiff-necked
pride. The herdsman is no one's man; he is the Adam who
has broken faith with God, who hides from him among the
trees in Eden, and then is exiled from paradise. He is the
alienated Israelites, wandering in the wilderness. He corresponds by the same token to what is merely worldly, carnal,
literal: he is, he declares, *no more* than he *appears* to be.

Moreover, the herdsman's role is figurative of the Old
Law, which was instituted to maintain righteousness through
fear of punishment, but which was devoid of grace. Only
his own bestial strength is law to the savage bulls, who would
otherwise be uncontrollable, and would kill anyone who came
near them:

" 'Je gart si cestes et justis
Que ja n'istront de cest porpris.' " (ll. 341–42)

Justisier (<L. *justitia*) is a peculiar word to apply to the
control of wild bulls, except as the herdsman's function reflects this deeper meaning of the Law. Because he represents
the letter of the Old Law unfulfilled by the spirit of the
New, the herdsman knows nothing about adventure:

" 'D' 'avanture' ne sai je rien,
N'onques mes n'an oï parler.' " (ll. 368–69)

Nevertheless, just as the Old Law, itself lacking grace,

looks forward to the New Law of grace, the herdsman, though he knows nothing about "adventure," is able to direct Calogrenant to the magic fountain of storms. This may explain an otherwise confusing detail, which leads Foerster to choose what I think is an incorrect reading—the discrepancy between the herdsman's description of the basin that hangs by the fountain, and the one Calogrenant actually finds. The herdsman tells him that the basin is made of iron, but in fact Calogrenant discovers it to be of gold. The herdsman does not understand the storm-fountain's true value, which is the grace received in baptism. Thus, like Arthur, the herdsman " 'Qui bien m'ot la voie mostree' " (l. 409), "teaches" in spite of himself. He cautions Calogrenant to stay on the "right way," for there are many other (i.e., wrong) ways by which he may be led astray:

> " 'Tote la droite voie va,
> Se bien viaus tes pas anploiier;
> Que tost porroies desvoiier,
> Qu'il i a d'autres voies mout.' " (ll. 376–79)

Chrétien's source for the fountain of storms is St. Brendan's "paradise of birds," an island where the Saint and his companions on the penitential voyage celebrate Easter (after commemorating the Harrowing of Hell, the evening of Holy Saturday, on the back of a whale, symbol of the devil). Near a spring grows a wonderfully tall tree, in which a great multitude of birds chants the service of the divine hours. Chrétien's fountain is situated in the shade of a tree whose leaves never wither. We recall from the discussion of the *Joie de la Cort* (chapter 5) that this is the right kind of tree to seek shade under, anti-type of the tree whose leaves wither and fall. In patristic commentary, this Old Testament figure of the evergreen leaf is commonly associated with the word of God. Birds flock to the branches of the tree after the clearing of the storm to sing their "service." The fountain of storms is a type, then, of the true paradise, and stands in opposition to the garden of the Hospitable Host. Jean Daniélou tells us that from very early on, the Church regarded the preparation for baptism as the anti-type of the temptation in the garden of Eden, and that the Fathers comment frequently on the analogy between Adam and the catechumen. Thus baptism, the first sacrament, the "door" to the Church, is spiritually the return to paradise.[3]

Maxwell Luria, in a study of the medieval iconography of storms, has pointed out the sacramental character of Chrétien's storm-fountain.[4] The fountain, he shows, is a type of the scriptural *fons vitae,* the evergreen of incomparable beauty, a type of the *arbor vitae,* associated by medieval exegetes with Christ and the Church. The scene as a whole represents the paradise of redemption.

The storm itself is a figure of baptism, related typologically to the Pentecostal descent of the Holy Spirit in tongues of flame on the gathered apostles. Calogrenant's adventure at the fountain of storms, and Yvain's after him, occurs at Pentecost for good reason. First, we have seen that the journey from the Hospitable Host and the wild herdsman to the fountain of storms is spiritually a passage from the Old Law of righteousness to the New Law of grace. The Jewish Pentecost, although it was originally a harvest festival, the offering of first fruits, came to commemorate the giving of the Law to Moses on Mount Sinai, and this meaning was retained by the Church. But the Christian Pentecost celebrated specifically the advent of the *New* Law in the

---

3. Jean Daniélou, "The Sacraments and the History of Salvation," *The Liturgy and the Word of God* (Collegeville, Minn., 1959), p. 23. For the figure of baptism as the "door" to the Church, see also the article on "baptism" in *The Catholic Encyclopaedia.*
4. Maxwell S. Luria, "The Christian Tempest" (Princeton Ph.D. dissertation, 1965); Luria's chapter on *Yvain* has been revised and published as "The Storm-making Spring and the Meaning of Chrétien's *Yvain,*" *Studies in Philology* 64 (1967): 564–85.

Holy Spirit's descent, related in the second chapter of Acts.[5]

Second, Pentecost was especially associated with baptism. In the early church, it was the day on which were baptized all those who had not been baptized on the Easter vigil. In later times, although the sacrament could be administered on other days throughout the year, at least the water of baptism had to be consecrated on Holy Saturday or Pentecost. Tertullian says that Pentecost is peculiarly appropriate for baptism because on that day "the grace of the Holy Spirit [was] first given, and the hope of our Lord's coming [*adventus*] made evident: because it was at that time, when he had been received back into heaven, that angels said to the apostles that he would so come in like manner as he had also gone up into heaven, namely, at Pentecost."[6] Moreover, the descent of the Holy Spirit on the apostles was itself considered a baptism—the baptism of the spirit, which completed the baptism of water, fulfilling the prophecy of John the Baptist: "I indeed baptize you in water unto penance, but he that shall come after me, is mightier than I, whose shoes I am not worthy to bear; he shall baptize you in the Holy Spirit and fire" (Matthew 3:11).

Here John indicates the dual nature of baptism. John's baptism, of water only, is the baptism of penance; water shows outwardly the spiritual cleansing of the contrite heart. But although penance is the first step, it is not in itself sufficient for salvation. It is completed in the mission of Christ by the second baptism, of fire, that is, of the Holy Spirit, in which the grace of salvation is bestowed. These two aspects reflect the distinction (and ultimately the unity) between the Old Law and the New. Under the Old Law, man's sins are punished; under the New, they are forgiven. The duality also underlies the ambiguous nature of the ad-

---

5. Gregory Dix, *The Shape of the Liturgy* (Glasgow, 1945), p. 341; see also articles on "Pentecost" in *The Jewish Encyclopaedia* (New York, 1901), and *The Catholic Encyclopaedia*.

6. Tertullian, *De Baptismo*, trans. E. Evans (London, 1964), p. 41.

venture. On the one hand, the setting is a paradise, graced with the joy of the birds' song and the beauty of the tree in which they perch.[7] On the other hand, the storm that is aroused when water is poured on the stone by the fountain is so terrible an ordeal that a man can barely pass through it with his life. The stormy, terrible aspect of baptism is reflected in the substantial extra-scriptural tradition in which fire is said to have burst from the waters of the Jordan at the baptism of Jesus.[8] No sooner has the storm abated (through the grace of God)[9] than Esclados, the Red Knight, challenges the stranger to combat. The ordeal is a type of penance; joy, a type of grace.

The same duality is expressed in the figure of the Deluge, identified already in the New Testament as a type of baptism,[10] and consistently so interpreted throughout patristic literature. Its function was at once destruction of the evil into which man had fallen, and salvation of the good that was nevertheless inherent in him. The waters of the Deluge cleansed the earth of the wicked giants, but on the same waters, Noah was saved.

The wood of the Ark is seen to prefigure the wood of the Cross on which the world was saved a second time. As we saw in the discussion of the sacrament in chapter 2, the association of baptism with the Crucifixion is not a casual one, for St. Paul affirms baptism to be sacramental participation in the death and Resurrection of Christ. It is that transcendent sacrifice, the axis on which all Christian history turns, to which true spiritual ordeal refers, and in terms

---

7. Luria, "The Storm-making Spring," p. 581, associates the tree with that which springs from the mustard seed in Christ's parable, Matthew 13: 31–32: "the birds of the air come and dwell in the branches thereof."

8. J. Kosnetter, *Die Taufe Jesu* (Vienna, 1936), pp. 223–27.

9. "Mes Des tant me rasseüra,/Que li tans gueires ne dura/ Et tuit li vant se reposerent: /Quant De ne plot, vanter n'oserent" (ll. 451–54). When in his turn Yvain is at the fountain, Chrétien repeats the idea that God has abated the storm: "Et quant Des redona le bel,/Sor le pin vindrent li oisel/Et firent joie merveilleuse/Sor la fontainne perilleuse" (ll. 807–10).

10. 1 Peter 3:21.

of which we are finally to understand the ambivalent "angoisses et dolors et granz biens" that are the ordeal and the joy of true lovers.

The duality of baptism—the water of penance, the fire of grace—is reflected figuratively in the nature of the storm itself. Calogrenant is pelted with precipitation of all sorts (i. e., water in various forms) and is threatened with lightning and thunder (fire):

> "Me feroit es iauz li esparz,
> Et les nues tot pesle mesle
> Gitoient noif et pluie et gresle." (ll. 442–44)

But Calogrenant, although he survives the adventure, does not fulfill it. He appears clearly as a virtuous knight, and he is the source of moral wisdom in telling his tale; but he is defeated by Esclados, whereas Yvain, who follows him seven years later, is successful against the Red Knight. It is as though his function were to prepare the way for Yvain, as John's baptism prepared the way for the baptism given through Christ. On this point, Tertullian distinguishes carefully between the earthly baptism of repentance and the heavenly baptism of remission and sanctification. John, he writes,

discharged no heavenly function, but did service prepratory to heavenly things: he was set in authority over repentance, and this is in man's power. . . . But if repentance is a human act, then the baptism of repentance must have been of the same sort: else, if it had been heavenly, it would also have given the Holy Spirit, and the remission of sins. But sins are not forgiven, or the Spirit granted, except by God alone. . . . For that which we read, *He preached a baptism of repentance for the remission of sins,* was an announcement made in view of a remission which was to be: for repentance comes first, and remission follows, and this is the meaning of preparing the way. But one who prepares a thing does not himself perform it, but provides for its performance by someone else. (*De Baptismo,* pp. 23–25)

If the pattern of John's relation to Christ does indeed underlie Calogrenant's relation to Yvain, then Calogrenant in preparing the way of adventure for Yvain does not so much fail as simply experience the incomplete, penitential promise of the sacrament, whereas Yvain's victory over Esclados (who charges at him like *fire,* "plus ardanz que brese," l. 812) indicates his reception of the sacrament fulfilled by grace. Calogrenant is introduced to us as,

> Uns chevaliers mout avenanz,
> Qui lor ot comancié un conte,
> Non de s'enor, mes de sa honte. (ll. 58–60)

Calogrenant is a valiant knight, but he tells a story "not to his honor but to his shame." But the shame that attaches to his tale does not discredit him; it is rather part of the purifying ordeal figurative of penance that the true knight must undergo for election. Perhaps Chrétien's words are intended to echo John's declaration, "Illum oportet crescere, me autem minui" ("He must increase, but I must decrease," John 3:30), when he insists that he is not himself the Messiah, but has been sent only to prepare his way.

In the continuation of the passage from Tertullian quoted above, we find a rationale also for Kay's defeat at the hands of the figuratively "baptized" Yvain: ". . . A true and steadfast faith is baptized with the Spirit unto salvation, but a feigned and feeble faith is baptized with fire unto judgment" (p. 25). The incurably foolish and meddlesome seneschal is judged and condemned by the same winnowing combat whereby Yvain (and Calogrenant, whose initial defeat Yvain has avenged) is figuratively saved.

It disturbs Loomis that Chrétien should have introduced a chapel into the landscape at the fountain of storms; that it is "alien" and "intrusive," he maintains, is proven by the absurdity of its use as Lunete's prison.[11] With this last ob-

---

11. *Arthurian Tradition and Chrétien de Troyes,* p. 291.

jection I will deal further on. At this point, however, the thematic relevance of the chapel in the context provided by the baptismal iconography of the fountain of storms is obvious. If the fountain and the tree serve to identify the landscape as a type of the Church (the earthly paradise), we understand at least the rationale for the inclusion of an actual church building. Moreover, E. Baldwin Smith explains that the font house was conventionally visualized as a shelter in a sylvan paradise, and that this is the symbolism intended by the inclusion of a woodsman's hut in the depiction of paradise in the martyrium at Seleucia Pieria.[12] Thus, the image of a baptismal paradise that includes the fountain of life, the tree of life, and a symbolic font house would be based on traditional iconography.

Chrétien's landscape was influenced by the *Voyage of St. Brendan,* but he makes it perfectly clear through an unmistakable verbal echo that he knew also the description of the legendary fountain of storms in the forest of Broceliande given by Wace in his *Roman de Rou.* Wace seems to have taken the stories about the marvelous fountain at face value, and claims to have gone in search of it, only to be painfully disabused of his gullible folly. According to legend, hunters, heated by the chase, would fill their horns with the water from the fountain and pour it on the stone. Cooling rain would then fall throughout the forest:

> Une forest mult longe e lee,
> Que en Bretaigne est mult loee.
> La fontaine de Berenton
> Sort d'une part lez un perron.
> Aler soloient veneor
> A Berenton par grant chalor,
> E a lor cors l'eve espuisier
> E le perron desus moillier.
> Por co soleient pluie aveir:
> Issi soleit jadis ploveir

---

12. E. Baldwin Smith, *The Dome* (Princeton, N. J., 1950), p. 56, quoted below, chap. 8.

En la forest e environ,
Mais jo ne sai par quel raison.
. . . .
La alai jo merveilles querre,
Vi la forest e vi la terre.
Merveilles quis, mais nes trovai;
Fol m'en revinc, fol i alai.[13]

"A fool I returned, a fool I set out," Wace admits. Calogrenant echoes these words when he finishes telling his tale of adventure to the assembled knights and ladies, but his meaning is very different from Wace's. It is in fact the opposite:

"Einsi alai, einsi reving,
Au revenir por fol me ting;
Si vos ai conté come fos
Ce qu'onques mes conter ne vos." (ll. 577–80)

"Like a fool, I have told you what I never wished to tell." Calogrenant is wary of casting his pearls before swine, and rightly so, as we see at once from Kay's stupid attack on Yvain. But Chrétien invests Calogrenant's words with special irony by echoing Wace, and inverting his meaning. Wace calls himself a fool for believing the stories about the fountain of storms; they are, he implies, nothing but empty fables. Calogrenant, on the other hand, calls himself a fool rather for *telling* the story of the fountain to men who do not understand with their hearts its spiritual meaning, who having eyes see not, having ears hear not. He is a fool for telling a story whose meaning is spiritual to those who are like the literal-minded Wace, for instance. Chrétien must have understood the story Wace relates figuratively, as an allegory of salvation. The hunters (*veneor*) are those who, heated and thirsting in their pursuit of love in this world, seek refreshment like the hart of Psalm 41 at the cold waters

---

13. Wace, *Roman de Rou*, ed. Hugo Andresen (Heilbronn, 1879), ll. 6397–420.

of the Living Fountain, the true love of God. In his commentary on Psalm 41, Peter Lombard expresses succinctly what is in essence the same figure: "I thirst in my wandering, I thirst in my journey, but I shall be filled in His Advent" (*PL,* vol. 191, col. 416).

But Wace, like the thick-headed Kay, failed to understand the baptismal meaning of the fountain in the story. IIis understanding could not pass beyond visible things. Claude Tresmontant explains that in Pauline thought, the failure to understand spiritual things is not merely passive weakness, but is willful turning away from the light:

> Always has it been taught in the Church that God is knowable from his creation, and St. Paul here takes up a theme that is equally constant in the Bible: understanding appertains to man's will and his freedom. The contrary of understanding is not misunderstanding or error; it is man's sin when he refuses to see something which he would be able to see did he not prefer darkness to light. . . . It follows that not to understand—what the prophets call "foolishness"—is the fundamental sin. Foolishness comes from a choice made in the secrecy of the heart; man's heart is darkened by his own hidden will.[14]

This philosophical attitude toward "foolishness" explains why Chrétien makes Kay's behavior appear so nasty and willful. On the other hand, it is clear that although Calogrenant calls himself a fool, he is not foolish in the same sense as Kay and Wace. Calogrenant is a "fool" rather in the paradoxical sense developed by St. Paul in 1 Corinthians:

> Seeing that . . . the world, by wisdom, knew not God, it
> 14. Claude Tresmontant, *Saint Paul,* trans. Donald Attwater, Men of
> pleased God, by the foolishness of our preaching, to save them
> that believe. For both the Jews require signs, and the Greeks
> seek after wisdom: But we preach Christ crucified, unto the
> Jews indeed a stumbling-block, and unto the Gentiles foolishness: But unto them that are called, both Jews and Greeks,
> Christ the power of God, and the wisdom of God. For the

Wisdom Books (New York & London, 1957), p. 124.

foolishness of God is wiser than men; and the weakness of
God is stronger than men. (1 Corinthians 1:21–25)

Yvain assures his cousin Calogrenant that he is a "fool" only
in a very particular, really a figurative sense. He has been
foolish only in hiding his adventure, for Yvain promises now
to avenge his injury:

> "Par mon chief, . . .
> Vos estes mes cosins germains,
> Si nos devons mout antramer;
> Mes de ce vos puis fol clamer,
> Quant vos le m'avez tant celé.
> Se je vos ai 'fol' apelé,
> Je vos pri qu'il ne vos an poist;
> Car, se je puis et il me loist,
> J'irai vostre honte vangier." (ll. 581–89)

Again, Kay shows himself to be the true fool by gratui-
tously taunting Yvain, whom he accuses of boasting drunk-
enly of a revenge he will never actually dare to carry out:

> "Bien pert qu'il est aprés mangier.
> . . . .
> Plus a paroles an plain pot
> De vin, qu'an un mui de cervoise." (ll. 590–94)

The source of Yvain's bold words, Kay implies, is only the
wine he has drunk at dinner. This accusation of drunken-
ness takes on particular meaning when we recall that the
disciples, inspired on that first Christian Pentecost to speak
"in tongues," were accused by scoffers of being "filled with
new wine" (Acts 2:13).

The word that Kay uses to describe the adventure he
thinks Yvain will never undertake is ironically fitting to the
spiritual character of the ordeal of the storm-fountain:

> "Feites le nos savoir, biaus sire,
> Quant vos irois a cel martire." (ll. 603–4)

Baptism is first of all penance. Chrétien quite appropriately drew his description of the fountain setting from the *Voyage of St. Brendan,* the narrative of a monk's penitential voyage in symbolic imitation of the life of Christ. And Kay's sarcastic word *martire* describes rather precisely the spiritual participation of the catechumen in the Crucifixion.

Calogrenant answers Kay with irony of his own. Kay, he says, is so clever and so worthy, " 'Qu'il n'i iert ja muëz ne sorz' " (l. 634). The irony here works in two senses. First, in asserting that Kay will never be mute, Calogrenant means that he ought to, but cannot learn to keep his mouth shut. Second, the figure of deafness returns us to the theme of spiritual understanding with which he prefaced his tale. He means just the opposite of what he says: Kay is indeed deaf. A dimension is added to this quip when we consider it in light of the baptismal liturgy. For one of the rites preparatory to baptism, called "the opening," centers around just this figurative "hearing" of the soul. St. Ambrose explains that the catechumen's ears are "opened" to the words of the priest:

> So what did we do on the sabbath? Truly, the opening: which mysteries of the opening were celebrated when the priest touched your ears and nostrils. What does it signify? In the Gospel our lord Jesus Christ, when one deaf and dumb had been brought to Him, touched his ears and his mouth, ears which were deaf, mouth which was mute, and said: *Effeta.* That is the Hebrew word which in Latin is said, "be opened." On that account, therefore, the priest touched your ears, that your ears might be opened to the words and to the exhortation of the priest.[15]

When Arthur finally wakes from his inappropriate sleep, the Queen recounts for him "Les noveles Calogrenant" (l. 658), a phrase that may (like the "noveles" of the opening lines of the romance) be evocative of the "good news" of

---

15. St. Ambrose, *De Sacramentis, PL,* vol. 16, cols. 417–18.

the Gospel. There is nothing literally "new" about Calogrenant's tale of the adventure that befell him seven years before, but because the tale reveals the way of salvation it is "news" indeed. Maxwell Luria points out the thematic significance in Arthur's vow to arrive at the fountain of storms by John the Baptist's Day, June 24. One might go further and suggest that the same spiritual sleep from which Arthur has not properly awakened is responsible for the nature of the vow itself. At baptism, the catechumen vows a triple renunciation: of the devil, of his works, and of his pomps. Then he is baptized "in the name of the Father, and of the Son, and of the Holy Spirit." Arthur, however,

> . . . fist trois seiremanz antiers
> L'ame Uterpandragon son pere,
> Et la son fil et la sa mere,
> Qu'il iroit veoir la fontainne. (ll. 662–65)

Arthur's parody of the triple baptismal vow is strictly in keeping with his role as earthly king. For he swears in the name of an earthly, rather than the heavenly Trinity.

Arthur's worldliness notwithstanding, his decision to seek the fountain is right (as the road leads to the right), but Yvain does not like it. He wants to arrive first, for he is afraid the honor of the adventure will fall to Kay, of all people, or Gawain. In subsequent chapters we shall see more particular reasons for suspecting the virtue of Yvain's motives; let his obvious pride suffice here, and perhaps the recollection of Christ's admonition about the first and the last.

Abstractly described, Chrétien's characteristic irony seems confusing, but in actual experience of the text it is never inconsistent with the overall spirit of the work. Arthur "instructs" by his own bad example; Yvain schemes secretively not to be outdone in an adventure whose true nature is sacramental. Chrétien keeps a straight face, but his meaning is both comic and severe. No character is immune from his irony, which arises from a deep sense of the frailty of flesh, but also from the sense of paradox that this same flesh houses the soul. Chrétien is always prepared to see his characters as exemplary of either virtue or folly (not to say vice), and he often surprises us by switching the moral valence of a character when we least expect it. Yvain remains to the end of the romance characterized by both inner light and foolishness, even madness. What we come to see is that they are the two sides of a single coin, and there is nothing inappropriate in this: we are not here dealing with psychologically developed characters, but neither are we dealing with simplistic, pasteboard allegories.

If Yvain sets out for the fountain of storms for the wrong reasons, he nevertheless finds the "right" road, the

> . . . santier tot droit,
> Plain de ronces et d'oscurté,
> Et lors fu il a seürté;
> Qu'il ne pooit mes esgarer. (ll. 768–71)

It is ambiguous whether the last two lines indicate Yvain's self-assurance, or the omniscient perspective of the narrator. Hindsight in any event shows us that everything does come out in the end. All the same, Yvain is not to be taken as an allegorical figure of the soul in the state of grace. One moment Chrétien employs him quite seriously as a Christian hero, the next, as a foil for his moral irony. Luria summarizes *Yvain* thus:

> . . . The adventure of the fountain is . . . a symbolic baptism followed by a beatific vision of salvation. Yvain's career can be summarized as follows: after successfully sustaining the trial of the fountain and acquiring the spiritual or moral regeneration of its waters (a tropological equivalent of the anagogical vision of salvation which seems to be represented by the serene harmony that follows the storm), there is a backsliding, then a recovery of spiritual status through the purgative adventures which constitute the body of the romance, and finally the reconciliation with Laudine, which signalizes and caps that recovery. ("The Storm-making Spring," p. 581)

This is a good statement of the overall scheme of the romance, but it leaves out of account the texture of irony that is itself a reflection of this same scheme, so to speak writ small. The signification of the narrative fluctuates constantly between seriousness and irony. It is this vision of man, so utterly vain and foolish, and so blessed, which is the really "marvelous" matter of Chrétien's romances.

8
Hellgate

Yvain's adventure at the fountain of storms is almost identical to Calogrenant's, and Chrétien gives only a brief summary of it. The chief point of difference is Yvain's victory over the knight who "defends" the fountain, Esclados. We saw that the Fathers extend the idea of sacramental participation in the Passion to include the struggle with the devil "under the waters" in baptism in imitation of the Harrowing. Baptism and the descent into hell are typologically related also in that they are both prefigured in the Deluge. Jean Daniélou explains how the waters that destroyed the earth and spared Noah were understood as a type of the water of the sacrament, which destroys sin and saves the soul of the catechumen. The same relation between cleansing and salvation pertains to the Harrowing: "In all three cases, there exists a sinful world which is to be annihilated by the punishment, and in all three cases a just man is spared: this man, in the Deluge, is Noe; in the Descent into hell, Jesus Christ; in Baptism, the Christian by conformation to Jesus Christ" (*Bible and the Liturgy*, p. 78).

This paradox, inherent in the fountain-adventure by virtue of its typological relation to baptism, accounts for the fact that even though he is defeated by Esclados, Calogrenant is spared, to the amazement of the Hospitable Host. The Host comforts him with the knowledge that no knight before him has ever so much as returned from the adventure.

Esclados represents the power of the devil with which Yvain must struggle. He charges, burning with wrath like an inferno: ". . . d'ire plus ardanz que brese" (l. 812). Chrétien links Esclados with the figure conventionally associated with baptism, the stag-hunt:

> Li chevaliers [vint] a si grant bruit,
> Con s'il chaçast un cerf de ruit. (ll. 813–14)

This analogy, apparently only a casual descriptive detail, actually works an ironic inversion of a major theme of the romance. The stag-hunt to which Esclados's charge is likened is not the baptismal hunt—the catechumen's thirst for salvation, or Christ's pursuit of the soul. It belongs rather to the type of hunt whose iconographical significance is expressed in the double meaning of "venery." The stag in the figure is *rutting;* Esclados, then, charges as though he were pursuing lust. The figure gives us the anti-type of the love that pervades the sacrament of baptism.[1]

Baptism as spiritual descent into hell and struggle with the forces of darkness is more clearly—at least more systematically—the subject of Huon de Mery's poem *Li Tornoiemenz Antecrit.*[2] Huon composed the *Tornoiemenz* sometime after 1234, explicitly on the model of Chrétien's *Yvain.*

1. In *Beowulf* Grendel's mere is so horrible that a hart would sooner give up its life to pursuing hounds than save its head, "hafelan beorgan," by entering the water. As Robertson points out in "The Doctrine of Charity in Medieval Literary Gardens," Grendel's mere and the surrounding landscape are an anti-type of paradise. The hart of Psalm 41 thirsts for the living waters of the *fons vitae,* but these are the waters of death, anti-type of baptism.
2. Huon de Mery, *Li Tornoiemenz Antecrit,* ed. Georg Wimmer, *Ausgaben und Abhandlungen aus dem Gebiete der romanischen Philologie* 76 (Marburg, 1888).

He admired the elder poet so much that he would gladly, he says, glean whatever "ears of grain" (ll. 3542–44) he has left behind. Huon's use of the figure of grain for poetic wisdom recalls the theme of Christ's parable, and Chrétien's uses of the same figure. The *Tornoiemenz* is not an impressive poem in its own right, but it is valuable to us because as an emulation of the earlier poem, it hints at the reading of *Yvain* of a poet who was nearly Chrétien's contemporary.

Like Calogrenant and Yvain, the speaker of the *Tornoiemenz* finds the fountain of storms in the forest of Broceliande. He pours water from the fountain on the stone, and experiences the fury of the storm that follows. When the storm has abated, a huge and terrifying Moor, Bras-de-Fer, comes to challenge him, but the poet is so terrified of the knight that he surrenders at once without a struggle, and is taken captive to the city *Desesperance*. There he dines sumptuously at the court of the lord of the city, Anti-Christ. Next morning, the forces of Anti-Christ meet the assembled forces of Christ. The poet, watching the ensuing battle, is wounded by a stray dart from the bow of Venus, one of the adversaries of Christ. After "suffering" from the wound, he repents. The forces of Christ finally overcome the forces of Anti-Christ, and take the poet to their city, *Esperance*. At last, he is returned to earth, and is left at the Church of St. Germain des Prés in Paris by a lady whose name is "Religion."

Huon clearly understood the fountain of storms in *Yvain* as an allegory. He seeks the fountain to discover the truth about it:

> Car la verte voloie aprendre
> De la perilleuse fonteine. (ll. 62–63)

His meaning is intentionally double. Spiritually, the poet wishes to learn the truth *from* the fountain, and this meaning conforms with Alexander Neckam's exposition of the fountain of storms in the *De Naturis Rerum* as an allegory of Christian instruction or conversion.[3]

Huon indicates the baptismal character of the fountain more explicitly than Chrétien:

> En plus clere eve Crestiens[4]
> Ne recut onques bautesme. (ll. 104–5)

The landscape of the fountain is also explicitly identified as the earthly paradise. After the storm, the birds gather from all over the forest to settle in the tree beside the fountain and sing,

> Une si douce melodi
> Que a ma mort ne a ma vie[5]
> Ne queïsse avoir autre gloire.
> Encore quant me vient en memoire
> M'est-il veraiement avis
> Que c'est terrïens paradis.[6] (ll. 197–202)

Figuratively baptized by the storm at the fountain, the poet is led by death, the knight Bras-de-Fer[7], to the place where the spiritual struggle of the sacrament must take

---

3. Luria, "The Storm-making Spring," surveys the various appearances of the storm-making spring in medieval literature, including Neckam's allegorization.

4. *Crestiens* here involves a pun on Chrétien's name.

5. Baptism is death and new life, in that order; Huon's phrase has the appearance of a colloquial expression, but it actually pertains to the sacrament to which the allegory pertains.

6. Huon even retains Chrétien's play on Wace's characterization of himself as a fool for having sought what was not to be found. Thinking to abate the storm elicited by the first basin-full of water, he pours another on the stone: "Or escoutez com je fui fous/ Et esperduz et entrepris,/Qu'encor plein bacin d'eve pris/Et sour le perron le flati./ . . . /Ce fu folie, ce me samble, /De .ii. foiz le bacin voidier;/Mes jel fis par mon fol cuidier,/Car le tens apeser cuidai,/Quant le segont bacin widai. /Mes lors apercui que, qui cuide,/Qu'il a de sens la teste wide,/Car en .C. muis ne puet avoir/De cuidier plein poing de savoir" (ll. 132–152) .

7. R. S. Loomis, *Arthurian Tradition and Chrétien de Troyes*, (New York, 1949) , p. 168, notes that Huon indicates this meaning by referring to the Moor regularly as "Li Mors." Whether Huon had in mind Oringle of Limors in *Erec* is not clear, but the symbolic meaning of the name is apparently similar.

place. The battle between the forces of Christ and Anti-Christ, then, is the allegorical objectification of the battle within the soul of the catechumen, the struggle "under the waters." Just as the snare of lust lies at the center of the baptismal adventure in *Erec,* and as Esclados in *Yvain* is associated with lust, so the poet in the *Tornoiemenz* is struck by a dart from the bow of Venus, who represents the love that stands in the same relation to grace as Anti-Christ to Christ. But why do these "romantic" elements intrude in a scheme that I have analyzed in sacramental terms? Because for the medieval catechumen the baptismal struggle is not merely a formula attached to an empty ritual. The soul's adversaries are not abstractions or naïve devils, but are the real weaknesses experienced in the flesh, which continually threaten to turn the soul away from God. The soul's adversaries are within it. Thus, the entire *Tornoiemenz,* though it employs apocalyptic imagery from Revelation extensively, is not a prophetic vision of the last days, but is rather a mystical allegory *in those terms* of the Christian soul's passage through baptism. The sacrament, however, is received in a particular context: the actual life of the catechumen. The "darts of Venus" reveal the particular devils with which the poet struggles; his repentance after he suffers the wound *is* the victory of the forces of Christ. When the poet "arrives" at the Church of St. Germain des Prés, where the actual baptism would have been administered, we realize that only figuratively has he been anywhere else. The "lady" Religion has brought him to the "door" of the Church. The fountain of storms is in the baptistery; the cities "Hope" and "Despair" lie in his own soul.

Yvain, unlike Calogrenant, strikes Esclados a mortal blow, and pursues the wounded knight back toward his castle through the outer gate of the city. But hard as he presses Esclados, Yvain remains always just out of reach of him. He is afraid that unless he is able to capture his adversary and return to Arthur's court with some true sign of his victory, some "ansaingne veraie" (l. 899), his testimony of vengeance will not be believed. Yvain has set out on his adventure in pride; he is concerned now not with the spiritual achievement of the adventure, but with worldly praise, for which he has had to scheme by stealing away from the court. Since Yvain is motivated by the vain desire for worldly praise, he has no faith in the integrity of his own word, and is able to trust his reputation only to tangible, "literal" evidence. He remembers the taunts of the vicious Kay, and they rankle.

Inside the city walls, Esclados leads Yvain to the gate of the castle:

> La porte fu mout haute et lee,
> Si avoit si estroite antree,
> Que dui home ne dui cheval
> Sanz anconbrier et sanz grant mal
> N'i poïssent ansanble antrer. (ll. 907–11)

This narrow gate is a passage of the same symbolic order as the arduous "right" road. It is a type of the way to salvation, of which Christ admonishes, "Enter ye in at the narrow gate. . . . How narrow is the gate, and strait is the way that leadeth to life: and few there are that find it!" (Matthew 7:13–14).

The gate of Esclados's castle is a marvelous portcullis, so contrived that only one horseman may pass through before a spring slams it shut. Yvain is "foolishly" (l. 934) in hot pursuit of Esclados, who manages to stay just beyond his reach. Esclados passes through the automatic gate, tripping the mechanism. Luckily, Yvain is leaning forward in his saddle so that the falling portcullis only grazes his back as it cuts his horse in two, and slices the spurs from his feet. This scene has been carved onto misericords in no fewer than five English churches, indicating the spiritual meaning (not necessarily a solemn one) that the medieval artist found appropriate to church decoration.[8] Yvain's narrow escape is given a providential character by Chrétien's puns on the knight's "advent" to the castle:

Et de ce mout bien li *avint*
Qu'il se fu *avant* estanduz.
Toz eüst esté porfanduz,
Se ceste *avanture* ne fust. (ll. 938–41; emphasis mine)

The real "adventure" by which Yvain is saved is not that he happens to be leaning forward in his saddle; Yvain is protected by the advent of grace in his symbolic baptism.

The horse and rider were commonly emblematic of the flesh governed by reason; the picture of the portcullis cutting Yvain's horse and the spurs that incite the horse (the picture we see as emblem on the misericords) shows us the mortification of the flesh and the passions that incite the flesh. More specifically, it represents a type of circumcision.

Circumcision and baptism, both initiatory rites, were naturally associated with each other, even in pre-Christian times. St. Paul distinguishes between the fleshly circumcision of the Old Law and the spiritual "circumcision" of the New. In Christ, he says, "You are circumcised with circumcision not made by hand, in despoiling of the body of the flesh, but in the circumcision of Christ: buried with him in baptism, in whom also you are risen again" (Colossians 2: 11–12). In the commentaries of the Fathers, circumcision is conventionally seen as a prefiguration of the sacrament. Specifically, circumcision, which was the sign in the flesh of Israel's covenant with God, is associated with the sealing with holy oil in the sign of the cross, the sphragis, performed immediately after the immersion of the catechumen. Through this typology, as circumcision was the sign of the Old Covenant, baptism becomes the spiritual sign of the

---

8. Three of these are reproduced in R. S. Loomis, *Arthurian Legend in Medieval Art* (New York, 1938), Plates 168–70.

New Covenant. Circumcision, the laver of blood, is replaced by baptism, the laver of water. Under the Old Law there could be no remission of sin without the shedding of blood. But Christ's blood, shed for all in the crucifixion, remits the sins of the faithful through baptism with water alone.[9]

It is tempting to speculate on the connection between St. Paul's description of baptism as a "circumcision not made by hand," and the elaborate machinery of the automatic portcullis. In any case, Chrétien now makes the portcullis clearly suggest the gates of hell:

> Aussi con deables d'anfer
> Desçant la porte contre val. (ll. 944–45)

Yvain's "foolish" descent into this figurative hell represents, like the fury of the storm, the penitential aspect of baptism.

Baptism is not only a spiritual descent, but, as we have seen, the door of the Church, too. This paradox is reflected in the iconography of the castle, for no sooner has Yvain narrowly escaped death by the falling portcullis than he finds himself in the great hall, whose ceiling, studded with gilded nails, looks like the ceiling of a church painted to represent a starry heaven:

> Einsi fu mes sire Yvains pris:
> Mout angoisseus et antrepris
> Remest dedanz la sale anclos,
> Qui tote estoit celee a clos
> Dorez, et paintes les meisieres
> De buene oevre et de colors chieres. (ll. 961–66)

E. Baldwin Smith has traced the history of the traditional symbolism of the architectural dome; often decorated with stars, it was thought of as the "dome of heaven."[10] Such sym-

9. See Jean Daniélou, "Circoncision et Baptême," in *Theologie in Geschichte und Gegenwart* (Festschrift für Michael Schmaus), (Munich, 1957), pp. 755–76.
10. E. Baldwin Smith, *The Dome* (Princeton, N. J., 1950).

bolism was not likely, in the Middle Ages, to be ignored. Richard Krautheimer observes that no medieval source discusses the design or construction of buildings except insofar as they reflect their practical or liturgical functions. "The 'content' of architecture," he writes, "seems to have been among the more important problems of medieval architectural theory; perhaps indeed it was its most important problem."[11]

Smith shows how the symbolism of the starry dome came to be associated particularly with the baptistery, which, in the fourth century in Italy began to adopt the form of the domical mausoleum, where "a starry dome over a tomb was visible proof that all who were purified and faithful unto death were assured of an ideal and heavenly home" (*The Dome*, p. 55). This historical relationship between the tomb and the baptistery reflects precisely the paradoxical relation of death and rebirth that pervades the meaning of the sacrament, as well as the character of Yvain's adventure.

> Because the Christians had been in the habit of using their burial places as baptisteries and their baptisteries as martyria, they transferred the imagery of the tomb, or martyrium, as a heavenly tegurium to the font house, which they then visualized as a symbolic, cosmic shelter in a sylvan paradise where animals drank at the Fountain of Life. In the Lateran baptistery, which was perhaps the first to be constructed like a martyrium with a celestial dome, golden harts stood around the edge of the font for the same reason that animals were pictured in the manuscripts about the tempietto over the sacred waters and that harts and trees were combined with a woodsman's hut to denote paradise in the martyrium at Seleucia Pieria. (*The Dome*, pp. 55–56)

In keeping with the symbolism of the starry dome, Chrétien uses the word *celee,* which denotes the ornamentation of the ceiling, and whose obvious derivation from *ciel* sug-

---

11. Richard Krautheimer, "Introduction to an Iconography of Medieval Architecture," *Journal of the Warburg and Courtauld Institutes* 5 (1942) : 1.

gests that such an ornamented ceiling was thought of as representing a sky. The walls are painted "de buene oevre"; a double meaning would indicate not only the quality of workmanship, but the subject of the painting as well, "good works," the visible manifestation of faith. Episodes from the lives of saints, exemplary of good works, typically formed a substantial part of the decoration of a church.

In this hall (whose symbolic resemblance to the Church reflects not the sanctity of the place itself, but Yvain's newly achieved spiritual state) Yvain is saved from discovery and vengeance at the hands of Esclados's men by Lunete. She reminds him of the courtesy he paid her when she appeared some time earlier at Arthur's court; she has not forgotten him. In St. Augustine's terms, Yvain has sown the seed of a work of mercy; in the protection Lunete now offers him, he is reaping a work of mercy in return.

Lunete's description of the peculiar virtue of the magic ring she gives Yvain reveals the connection between his salvation in the perilous castle and the theme of spirituality and carnality. The ring makes its wearer invisible, she explains, so long as he keeps the stone turned inward.

> "Or soiiez seürs et certains,
> Que ja, se croire me volez,
> Ne seroiz pris ne afolez." (ll. 1020–22)

Chrétien's turn of phrase hints that it is *belief* (that is, faith) that makes the ring work.

When the stone is turned into the palm, the wearer of the ring is hidden like wood under bark:

> . . . il avoit tel force,
> Come a dessor le fust l'escorce
> Que le cuevre, qu'an n'an voit point. (ll. 1026–29)

This figure is closely related to one of the many common variations on the shell-kernel analogy used to describe allegory. The "bark" is the outer covering of fiction, which hides the "wood," the true inner meaning. The motif of spirituality—of "inwardness"—is continued in Lunete's instructions to hold the stone inside the fist:

> . . . Il covient que l'an l'anpoint,
> Si qu'el poing soit la pierre anclose,
> Puis n'a garde de nule chose
> Cil, qui l'anel an son doi a. (ll. 1030–33)

The stone is the part of the ring in which the precious virtue of concealment resides, but the stone must itself be concealed in the fist of the wearer. The image we have is of the stone *enclosed* in the hand, exactly as the wood is enclosed by the bark, or the kernel by the shell. What is *within* is spiritual; thus, the wearer need fear no thing (*chose*). With this ring, Yvain is hidden from those who, having eyes, see not:

> . . . Ja veoir ne le porra
> Nus hon, tant et les iauz overz,
> Ne que le fust, qui est coverz
> De l'escorce, qui sor lui nest. (ll. 1034–37)

We think of Christ's explanation that the parables hide the truth from the ungodly. Esclados's men cannot "see" Yvain to wreak their revenge because they cannot comprehend the power of grace by which he is protected.

St. Ambrose makes a distinction between the eyes of the body and "eyes of the heart" in explaining the spiritual blindness of the unbaptized: "Consider also the eyes of your heart. You saw those things which are of the body with bodily eyes: but those things which are of the sacraments, you could not hitherto see with the eyes of the heart" (*De Sacramentis, PL,* vol. 16, col. 435). St. Paul refers to the same blindness of superficial, carnal vision when he interprets the veil over the face of Moses as the allegorical surface of the Old Testament, a mystery to the unconverted Jews, but revealed in Christ: "Even unto this day, when Moses is read, the veil is upon their heart. Nevertheless when it shall turn to the Lord, the veil shall be taken away" (2 Corinthians 3:15–16). As the retainers of Esclados, these blinded men, whom Lunete characterizes as "jant mout enuieuse et male" (l. 1068), are spiritually servants of the devil, and it is thus with typical irony that, when they fail to find Yvain between the two gates, they conjecture:

> "Qu'ancore est il ceanz, ce cuit,
> Ou nos some anchanté tuit,
> Ou tolu le nos ont maufé." (ll. 1129–31)

Devils have "stolen" Yvain, perhaps only in the sense that, in being themselves frustrated by the power of grace, Esclados's men have played their fitting role in Yvain's salvation. They have stolen him from themselves. St. Paul continues the passage quoted above: "Where the spirit of the Lord is, there is liberty" (2 Corinthians 3:17). The spirit of the Lord is what gives Yvain his invulnerability; though physically he is imprisoned, he is nevertheless, through the power of the ring, which is faith, free.

When the corpse of the slain Esclados begins to bleed in witness to the presence of his killer, the men of the castle repeat their ironic conjecture:

> "Antre nos est cil, qui l'ocist,
> Ne nos ne le veomes mie.
> Ce est mervoille et deablie." (ll. 1200–1202)

The phrase *mervoille et deablie* expresses the paradox of the baptismal ordeal—the descent into hell by which the catechumen is saved.

Yvain, we recall, has set out from Arthur's court in quest of honor. Of course, like his cousin Calogrenant, he has set out in quest of adventure for its own sake; and he seeks vengeance for the shame of Calogrenant's defeat. But his main concern has been to arrive first at the fountain of storms, lest Kay or Gawain should snatch the honor of the adventure that he desires. Now, dealing the defending knight a mortal blow is not enough; he has followed Esclados into his castle, which has turned out to be a trap, for he is desperate for some piece of evidence to bear witness of his victory at court, to silence the scoffing of Kay, and to elicit honor from his fellow knights and his king. Even after he has escaped discovery in the great hall and almost certain death, he is obsessed with the shame he will suffer if he does not return with "ansaingnes veraies" (1. 899).

Arthur's is the worldly court; the honor Yvain desires there is the honor of the world. If he has figuratively passed through baptism and has received the Holy Spirit in the ordeal of his adventure, it is inappropriate for him to pursue as he does the honor of this world for its own sake. Beside the salvation to which he is eligible, worldly honor ought to seem a paltry thing. But Yvain's faith is far from perfect. Kay's rudeness festers in his heart:

> Celes ranposnes a sejor
> Li sont el cuer batanz et fresches. (ll. 1354–55)

Suddenly, quite unexpectedly, Love appears to banish these thoughts:

> Mes de son çucre et de ses bresches
> Li radoucist novele Amors,
> Qui par sa terre a fet son cors,
> S'a tote sa proie acoillie. (ll. 1356–59)

We know from the prologue what kind of love *novele Amors* is—it is modern love, worldly and passionate. Yvain apparently turns abruptly from his anxiety over worldly honor to the "sweetness" of worldly love. In fact, they are the same thing.

Novele Amors strikes Yvain with desire for the beautiful widow of the very knight he has slain; if the corpse would prove his victory, how much more impressive would the knight's own widow seem! She is Laudine, daughter of the late duke of Landuc, Laudunet. Etymologically (medieval writers were particularly fond of fanciful as well as what we would consider sound etymology) his name suggests the Latin *laus* (Old French *los*), "praise," or "glory," and the past participle of the French verb *donner* "give," hence, "praise given." *Laudine* is then a compound of the Latin stem *laud-* plus suffix *-ine,* with the sense "pertaining to," or "of the nature of."[12]

The pursuit of personal fame and glory was a central and institutionalized aspect of chivalry.[13] As we noted in the discussion of *Erec,* without fame and glory a knight was unable to perform his legitimate function in feudal and courtly society, even in its most spiritual aspects. But chivalry is not served by the pursuit of glory for its own sake—only pride and vanity are.

St. Paul develops a theological conception of glory, in contradistinction to the glory of this world. It is a coincidence not without meaning that, in Romans, we find the praise of God in association with Paul's distinction between physical and spiritual circumcision. Chrétien plays continually with the parallelism of the two kinds of understanding, the two loves, the two Laws, and now the two kinds of glory. Paul evokes in this connection once more the distinction between letter and spirit: "Truly, not he who is so visibly is a Jew: nor is circumcision that which is visible, in the flesh: but he is a Jew who is so in concealment: whose circumcision is of the heart, in the spirit, not in the letter: whose praise is not of men, but of God" (Romans 2:28–29). Perhaps Chrétien is playing specifically with Paul's idea of genuine circumcision as that which is concealed. Yvain's protection, after all, is his invisibility. His horse, cut in half by the portcullis, remains visible to the men of the castle because

---

12. Cf. *Inferno,* II, 103: Beatrice is called "loda di Dio vera," "true praise of God."

13. See Sidney Painter, *French Chivalry* (Baltimore, Md., 1940), pp. 34–37, 44–64, 152–54.

it remains only flesh cut away, while Yvain is concealed in the spirituality, the circumcision of the heart, which he has assumed in baptism. The horse is equivalent to the Old Man, which Paul advises the Christian elsewhere in Romans to crucify and destroy (Romans 6:6). In 1 Corinthians Paul returns to the theme of the praise of God for that which now is concealed: "Do not wish to judge before the time, until the Lord shall come: who will illuminate the concealed things of darkness, and reveal the counsels of hearts: and then shall praise be to each man from God" (1 Corinthians 4:5).

Laudine represents the honor to which Yvain wishes to be "wed," but just as the word *laus* itself may mean both kinds of honor, of men as well as of God, we find that the figure of Laudine reflects now one sort, now the other. She is the widow of Esclados, whom we have identified with the devil, and Yvain's love for her, in the beginning at least, is stirred by a foolhardy passion. Yvain's reconciliation with her at the end of the romance, however, is the culmination of his quest for spiritual perfection. What sort of honor she represents, then, depends on the heart of her lover; as Yvain's love is converted from the foolish passion to the love that is the earthly image of God's love, the meaning of his marriage changes. Just as *laus* must derive its meaning from its verbal context, Laudine takes her "meaning" from the context of the narrative.

Yvain bemoans the loss of the "testimony" with which to prove his victory. Laudine and her men have just the opposite problem. Threefold testimony of the slayer's presence is all too evident: their land has been deluged by the adventure at the fountain; they have found the bloody corpse of his horse; and now the victim's body, as it is borne past the room in which Yvain hides, begins to bleed.

> Et ce fu provance veraie,
> Qu'ancore estoit leanz sanz faille
> Cil, qui feite avoit la bataille,
> Et qui l'avoit mort et conquis. (ll. 1182–85)

Laudine is a beautiful Christian, but at this moment she is not a wise one. Chrétien describes her as,

> . . . Une des plus beles dames,
> Qu'onques veïst riens terriiene.
> De si tres bele crestiiene
> Ne fu onques plez ne parole,
> Mes de duel feire estoit si fole,
> Qu'a po qu'ele ne s'ocioit. (ll. 1146–51)

Her grief leads her to folly. What follows is a conventional representation of despair; we see her cry out, faint repeatedly, rend her garments, tear her hair. She is inconsolable. Chrétien wishes us to see Laudine's behavior in the context of Christian consolation, for he reminds us of its promise of eternal life in describing the funeral procession:

> L'iaue beneoite et la croiz
> Et li cierge aloient devant
> Avuec les dames d'un covant,
> Et li texte et li ançansier
> Et li clerc, qui sont despansier
> De feire la haute despanse,
> A quoi la cheitive ame panse. (ll. 1166–72)

In light of salvation, death is no tragedy, and excessive grief is a waste. Despair, moreover, is a sin against the Holy Spirit—the unforgivable sin, in fact. Even after the burial, Laudine is inconsolable, and Chrétien ironically shows her reading the Psalter, which if she were reading with the "eyes of the heart," would give her the consolation she seeks. The others have gone,

> Mes cele i remaint tote sole,
> Qui sovant se prant a la gole
> Et tort ses poinz et bat ses paumes
> Et list en un sautier ses saumes,
> Anluminé a letres d'or. (ll. 1411–15)

That the Psalter is "illuminated" with letters of gold is a

symbolic commentary on the wisdom—the spiritual illumination—to be found there, and not merely a reflection of
twelfth-century bookmaking. But Laudine chooses the darkness of despair to the light of the Psalms. As her behavior
betrays, she does not read according to Calogrenant's admonition to let words pass through the ears to the heart.

The same lack of wisdom is evident in the long speech
in which she blames God for the death of her husband, as
well as for allowing his murderer to escape. Esclados was
the best of the best, she declares:

> "Voirs Des, li torz an sera tuens,
> S'einsi le leisses eschaper.
> Autrui que toi n'an sai blasmer;
> Que tu le m'anbles a veüe.
> Ainz tes force ne fu veüe
> Ne si lez torz, con tu me fes,
> Que nes veoir tu ne me les
> Celui, qui est si pres de moi." (ll. 1210–17)

Laudine, too, has eyes but sees not. We know from our discussion of Mark and Paul that it is not God who blinds
man, but man himself who chooses to be blind rather than
to see the light. Laudine takes Yvain to be a spirit, a phantom or demon:

> "Bien puis dire, quant je nel voi,
> Que antre nos s'est ceanz mis
> Ou fantosmes ou anemis,
> S'an sui anfantosmee tote." (ll. 1218–21)

Chrétien plays ironically with Laudine's conception of invisibility; but beneath the play lies his own notion of the relationship between spirituality and corporeality. Laudine
accuses the phantom of cowardice. Only because he could not
see his adversary was Esclados defeated, she declares, and
she suggests that Yvain's tactic of invisibility has been highly
unethical.

"Ha! fantosmes, coarde chose!

. . . .

Chose vainne, chose faillie,

. . . .

Mes ce comant pot avenir,
Que tu mon seignor oceïs,
S'an traïson ne le feïs?
Ja voir par toi conquis ne fust
Mes sire, se veü t'eüst." (ll. 1226–37)

Yvain's invisibility is no mere trick. Laudine, unaware of course that she is touching on the truth of the matter, declares that Yvain must be immortal:

"Certes, se tu fusses mortés,
N'osasses mon seignor atandre;
Qu'a lui ne se pooit nus prandre." (ll. 1240–42) .

Whether the insult Laudine intends is justified or not, the real point is that Yvain has indeed shed his mortality. Since Laudine is seeking a mortal, corporeal enemy, she is incapable of "seeing" Yvain, who is protected by grace.

There are three aspects to Laudine's knowledge of Yvain's presence in the castle: the water of the storm, the blood of Yvain's horse and of Esclados, and Yvain's invisibility. Yvain has come in search of testimony ("tesmoing"). In the First Letter, John distinguishes the testimony of God from the testimony of men. The passage affirms the triple testimony whereby the Christian may have faith in Christ:

This is he who comes by water and by blood, Jesus Christ: not in water only, but in water and blood. And it is the Spirit which testifies, for Christ is truth. For they are three which give testimony on earth: the Spirit, and water, and blood: and these three are one. If we accept the testimony of men, the testimony of God is greater: for this is the testimony of God, which is greater, for he testified of his own son. Whoever believes not in the son, he makes a liar: because he believes not in the testimony which God testified of his son. And this is the testimony that God gave us eternal life. And this life is in his son. (1 John 5:6–11)

The *Glossa Ordinaria* explains that John refers, in the first sentence of the passage, to the water and blood mixed that flowed from Christ's pierced side. The testimony of the Spirit is the descent of the dove on Christ at his baptism (*PL*, vol. 114). Tertullian interprets the water and blood mixed as itself a figure of baptism, the water, specifically, the catechumen's vocation, the blood, his election (*De Baptismo*, XVI). In keeping with this symbolism too is the Pauline association of the blood of circumcision with the water of baptism.

These three aspects of the evidence—Yvain's invisibility, both as the protection of the Holy Spirit and as it renders *him* a phantom, or spirit, the water, and the blood—involve a parody of the triple testimony of Christ's divinity, which in turn is testimony to Christians of eternal life. Laudine suspects Yvain of immortality. Naturally, a great deal of irony is involved in this parallelism. While Yvain's invisibility is the sign of grace, salvation is never deserved, and we have good reason to suspect his motives. He chooses for no spiritual reasons to give up the protection of invisibility. In doing so, he forgets about the testimony he has wanted, which is, it is true, the "testimony of men." But his new pursuit is no less worldly.

The spiritual dangers of Yvain's new interest are indicated by the figure of the little window through which he watches the funeral. He asks Lunete if there is a window through which to watch the procession,

> Mes il n'avoit antancion
> N'au cors n'a la procession. (ll. 1275–76)

It is really Laudine he wants to watch:

> Mes por la dame de la vile,
> Que il voloit veoir, le dist.
> Et la dameisele le mist
> A une fenestre petite. (ll. 1280–83)

Chrétien wants us to notice the window, for he repeats:

> Parmi cele fenestre agueite
> Mes sire Yvains la bele dame. (ll. 1286–87)

At this window, Love attacks and captures him. After the funeral,

> . . . Mes sire Yvains est ancor
> A la fenestre, ou il l'esgarde,
> Et come il plus s'an done garde,
> Plus l'aimme et plus li abelist.
> Ce qu'ele plore et qu'ele list,
> Vossist qu'ele leissié eüst,
> Et qu'a li parler li leüst.
> An cest voloir l'a Amors mist,
> Qui a la fenestre l'a pris. (ll. 1416–24)

The plot makes it clear enough that Yvain must watch Laudine from a position of secrecy. But Chrétien draws particular attention to the window by mentioning it six times.

Before discussing the figurative meaning of the window, however, it is best to consider the allegorical context in which it appears. Lunete has left Yvain at the window in order to rejoin the crowd, lest she be missed. Yvain begins again to regret his failure to secure some piece of evidence of victory. He thinks ruefully of the new jibes Kay will bait him with, when suddenly, *novele Amors* conquers him and takes away the bitterness of his thoughts.

There are actually two separate figures in the allegory of love that Chrétien inserts at this point. First is the figure of love as a wound, which grows worse the nearer the "doctor" approaches the "patient." The theme of love as martyrdom has been introduced in the prologue, and pertains, we have seen, to both worldly and spiritual love. In keeping with this thematic ambivalence, when Chrétien says that

> Son cuer an mainne s'anemie,
> S'aimme la rien, qui plus le het, (ll. 1360–61)

we may be struck by the ironic parallel with Christ's commandment: "Love your enemies; do good unto them that hate you" (Matthew 5:44). Chrétien returns to this theme a hundred lines later. Yvain, who is struggling with despair over his present situation as the hated slayer of Laudine's husband, reasons that if he is to be true to Love, he must love his enemy:

> "Ançois aimerai m'anemie;
> Que je ne la doi pas haïr,
> Se je ne vuel Amor traïr.
> Ce qu'Amors viaut doi je amer." (ll. 1450–53)

"Love" wishes him to love his enemy, as Christ wishes him to. As though to underscore the parallel, Chrétien continues the play on this idea:

> "Et moi doit ele ami clamer?
> Oïl voir, por ce que je l'aim.
> Et je m'anemie la claim,
> Qu'ele me het, si n'a pas tort;
> Que ce, qu'ele amoit, li ai mort.
> Et donc sui je ses anemis?
> Nenil certes, mes ses amis;
> Qu'onques rien tant amer ne vos." (ll. 1454–61)

One edge of this paradoxical equivalence of lover and enemy suggests the spiritual dangers with which Yvain is flirting, while the other edge suggests how worldly passions are transcended.

At the same time, Chrétien has shifted the figure of his little allegory, from the "wound" of love to the personified divine "guest" who has found lodging in the body of the lover. The allegorization of love in the form of a classical divinity is, like the figure of the wound, a medieval commonplace. But Chrétien uses this allegory in a highly ironic way. The prologue to *Perceval,* in which he paraphrases John's idea that God *is* love, indicates in what sense he was likely to take such a personification as a god of love. The true god of love is Christ. In the same epistle, John develops the idea that God dwells in the persons of the faithful; for example: "If we love one another, God dwelleth in us, and his love is perfected in us. Hereby know we that we dwell in him, and he in us, because he hath given us of his Spirit. . . . Whosoever shall confess that Jesus is the Son of God, God dwelleth in him, and he in God. And we have known and believed the love that God hath to us. God is love; and he that dwelleth in love dwelleth in God, and God in him" (1 John 4:12–16). The courtly convention in which the "god of love" dwells in the body of the lover corresponds, then, to this Christian concept of God's immanence in his faithful.

Chrétien's allegory is intended as a parody of these serious religious ideas, and it is by such ironical parallels that he suggests the correct perspective from which to view Yvain's behavior and the passions that inspire it. When the poet "complains" that Love lodges in humble places, unworthy of her dignity, he really means that there is no respect of persons where lust is concerned, but there is none where charity is concerned either:

> C'est granz honte, qu'Amors est tes,
> Et quant ele si mal se prueve,
> Que el plus vil leu, qu'ele trueve,
> Se herberge tot aussi tost,
> Come an tot le meillor de l'ost. (ll. 1386–90)

Read through the glass of irony, this fact is not love's shame, but its glory.

Chrétien evokes the Incarnation when he continues his complaint against

> Amors, qui si est haute chose,
> Que mervoille est, comant ele ose
> De honte an si vil leu desçandre. (ll. 1395–97)

We think of the stable of the Nativity as the "vile place" into which God was moved by love to descend, but also of the body of man. The mortality of flesh is suggested by the ashes and dust of the next sentence:

> Celui sanble, qui an la çandre
> Et an la poudre espant son basme,
> Et het enor et aimme blasme,
> Et destanpre çucre de fiel,
> Et mesle suie avueques miel. (ll. 1398–1402)

Grace is balm spread among the ashes and dust of mortality. And Christ willingly drank the chalice that his father had prepared for him in love, although it was bitter; to those who witnessed the Crucifixion, it may have seemed that he "hated honor and loved blame." Central to Chrétien's concept of love, here as in the prologue, is its dual nature. Love entails both *dolors* and *biens,* sugar and gall, honey and soot, as charity entails martyrdom and grace. We note the irony, too, of Love's "hatred" of honor in light of Yvain's love of it.

That curiously insistent image of the knight at the window fairly begs notice, and notice in allegory begs interpretation. The last occurrence of the image shows Yvain taken captive:

> An cest voloir l'a Amors mis,
> Qui a la fenestre l'a pris. (ll. 1423–24)

St. Ambrose gives us a remarkably similar image in commenting on the window of Jeremiah 9:21, through which death is said to enter:

> If you looked on a woman to lust after her, death entered through the window. . . . Therefore, close this window, through which you could see the beauty of strange women, so that death may not enter; that your eyes may not see the strange woman, nor your tongue speak perverse things. Close therefore your window, that it be not open for death to enter. But be-

ware also of a strange window; for the whore enters by the window of her house. She enters by her window, and when she enters, the lasciviousness of a sensual eye tempts someone. (*PL,* vol. 15, col. 1261)

Whether Chrétien knew Ambrose's commentary or some commentary derived from it, the spirit of his image—Yvain captured at the window by the sight of a beautiful woman—is the same. What Yvain sees through the window, what he desires, what he is "taken" with love for, is vanity: it is the praise of this world expressed in the figure of a woman. As in Ambrose's figure, death enters through the window together with lust; pursuit of praise leads Yvain to the madness that culminates in a death-like coma.

In this light, we can interpret Chrétien's statement that Love and Shame move Yvain to remain in the castle at the risk of his life:

> . . . Amors et Honte le detienent,
> Qui de deus parz devant li vienent. (ll. 1531–32)

Love and shame are two sides of one coin. His love for Laudine is his desire for glory; thus, the shame of giving up his pursuit of evidence is equivalent to losing his chance for Laudine's love. We shall see how this equivalence continues to operate in the romance:

> Il est honiz, se il s'an va;
> Que ce ne crerroit nus hon ja,
> Qu'il eüst einsi esploitié.
> D'autre part a tel coveitié
> De la bele dame veoir
> Au mains, se plus n'an puet avoir,
> Que de la prison ne li chaut;
> Morir viaut ainz que il s'an aut. (ll. 1533–40)

In Ambrose's commentary death enters the window in the form of lust. The same idea underlies the irony of Yvain's love for his "enemy." Lunete is amazed that Yvain, in mor-

tal danger, can have had a pleasant time watching the
woman who hates him:

> "Comant? Puet donc buen siecle avoir,
> Qui voit qu'an le quiert por ocirre,
> S'il ne viaut sa mort ou desirre?" (ll. 1552–54)

Lunete's question touches the perverse nature of lust, which
blindly seeks its own death. Yvain denies that he wishes
to die, but in the very words of his reply reveals that he
does not understand mortality.

> "Certes," fet il, "ma douce amie,
> Morir ne voldroie je mie,
> Et si me plot mout tote voie
> Ce que je vi, se Des me voie,
> Et plest et pleira toz jorz mes." (ll. 1555–59)

Ambrose underscores the mortal danger of that which is seductively pleasurable to look at. And because Yvain, like all
mortal men, *will* die, the sight that now so pleases his eyes
will not be able to please them forever, as he imagines.
Ambrose bids us "close the window" in order that our
thoughts may not be diverted by passing pleasures from that
which is truly immortal.

The windows of Ambrose's figure are the eyes; the context is a commentary on verse 37 of Psalm 118: "Turn away
my eyes, that they may see no vain thing." In deceiving himself about the ephemeral nature of what now pleases his
eyes, Yvain takes the path that leads (as Ambrose warns) to
death—to the semblance of it, in any case, which we take
as the sign of spiritual death. At the meeting with Laudine
that Lunete arranges for him, Yvain explains in terms of
the classical golden arrow of Cupid, which "wounds" the
lover with affection, that he has been conquered by the force
of his heart's desire. His heart, in turn, has been conquered
by Laudine's beauty, which has reached his heart through
the passage of his eyes:

"Dame!" fet il, "la force vient
De mon cuer, qui a vos se tient;
An cest voloir m'a mes cuers mis."
"Et qui le cuer, biaus douz amis?"
"Dame! mi oel."—"Et les iauz qui?"
"La granz biautez, que an vos vi."
"Et la biautez qu'i a forfet?"
"Dame, tant que amer me fet."   (ll. 2015–22)

We recognize this figurative scheme as conventional in courtly literature. But Robertson has demonstrated the connection between this originally classical scheme and the Christian aesthetics developed first by St. Augustine, then elaborated by John the Scot.[14] The first principle of this aesthetic is that the function of earthly beauty is to lead the mind to contemplation of the Creator of beauty, and thus to incite the soul to charity. If this function is perverted, the mind dwells in contemplation of beauty for its own sake, and the soul falls instead into cupidity, passionate desire of the beautiful object. "Whosoever looketh on a woman to lust after her hath committed adultery with her already in his heart." The spiritual adultery of Matthew 5:28 is for John the Scot the type of passionate abuse of beauty. The woman lusted after represents all sensible beauty, just as adultery represents all vices to which the seductions of sensible pleasure can lead. First the image of the woman is perceived by the senses; then, the image itself (not the divine beauty that it reflects) becomes the object of delightful contemplation and cupiditous desire; finally, the corrupted reason abdicates its proper sovereignty in favor of the concupiscent desires that enflame the soul.[15]

Three steps are involved, then, in the soul's pursuit of sensual pleasure: suggestion, delightful thought, and consent of the reason. Robertson shows how clearly these three steps govern the progress of love in *Cligés*. We can see them op-

14. D. W. Robertson, Jr., *Preface to Chaucer* (Princeton, N. J., 1964) pp. 83–88.
15. John the Scot, *De divisione naturae, PL*, vol. 122, cols. 825–29.

erating just as clearly in *Yvain*. First, Yvain stands at the window to look at Laudine. Then he discovers and indulges in the great pleasure the looking gives him. Finally, with the very word *consantir*, Chrétien indicates the consent of reason whereby Yvain unmanfully places himself entirely at Laudine's mercy:

> "Dame! nule force si forz
> N'est come cele sanz mantir,
> Qui me comande a consantir
> Vostre voloir del tot an tot." (ll. 1986–89)

The force that compels Yvain is the passion of love. For emphasis, Chrétien has Laudine repeat the word *consantir* in her somewhat incredulous reply:

> " . . . Ce mout volantiers savroie,
> Don cele force puet venir,
> Qui vos comande a consantir
> Tot mon voloir sanz contredit." (ll. 2008–11)

The effect of this consent to the will of the woman is, as we saw in Erec's case, to upset the natural hierarchical order, and to invite spiritual and social chaos.

The passionate and unreasonable love that thus arises between Yvain and Laudine is reflected in Chrétien's use of the conventional figure of love as a fire. Laudine in her own "delightful thought" about Yvain suddenly bursts into the flames of passion:

> . . . Par li meïsmes s'alume
> Aussi con la busche qui fume,
> Tant que la flame s'il est mise,
> Que nus ne sofle ne atise. (ll. 1777–80)

This same figure appears later in the speech in which Gawain persuades Yvain to leave Laudine to seek adventure at the tournaments. Gawain argues that Yvain ought to postpone the joys of love, whose anticipation will make them all the keener when he returns:

"Joie d'amor, qui vient a tart,
Sanble la vert busche qui art,
Qui tant rant plus grant chalor
Et plus se tient an sa valor,
Con plus se tient a alumer." (ll. 2519–23)

Still another figure for Yvain's passion, which arises out of the narrative itself, indicates Chrétien's critical attitude toward his hero's folly. Yvain is literally a prisoner in Laudine's castle through his own free choice, and in the same way he is a "prisoner" of love. Lunete employs this figure when she explains that Laudine wants Yvain in her prison, not his body only, but his heart as well:

"Avoir vos viaut an sa prison,
Et s'i viaut si avoir le cors,
Que nes li cuers n'an soit defors,"
"Certes," fet il, "ce vuel je bien,
Ce ne me grevera ja rien.
An sa prison vuel je bien estre." (ll. 1922–27)

Yvain's reply reveals the consent of reason to passion's folly. Chrétien intrudes momentarily at this point to say that not only Yvain, but all lovers are "prisoners." Lunete, he explains with a certain degree of condescension, has been speaking figuratively:

La dameisele . . .
. . . .
. . . parole par coverture
De la prison, ou il iert mis;
Que sanz prison n'est nus amis.
Ele a droit, se prison le claimme;
Que bien est an prison, qui aimme. (ll. 1936–42)

St. Paul is also talking about love when he repeatedly calls himself a "prisoner" for Christ.[16] It may be relevant that as Chrétien explains that Lunete is speaking figuratively of the "prison" of love, St. Paul explains elsewhere that

_____
16. Acts 23:18; Ephesians 3:1, 4:1; 2 Timothy 1:8.

he speaks of sin figuratively as slavery ("after the manner of men," as he puts it) so that we may understand a thing that otherwise would be obscure (Romans 6:19). Perhaps Chrétien's is an ironic echo of Paul's condescension.

Yvain the prisoner of love is also conventionally fearful, like Mabonagrain, whose fearful worship imprisons him within a wall of air. Lunete brings him to Laudine,

> Si crient il estre mal venuz;
> Et s'il le crient, n'est pas mervoille.
> . . . .
> Grant peor, ce vos acreant,
> Ot mes sire Yvains a l'antree
> De la chanbre, ou il a trovee
> La dame, qui ne li dist mot.
> Et por ce plus grant peor ot,
> Si fu de peor esbaïz,
> Qu'il cuida bien estre traïz. (ll. 1946–56)

As we saw in the adventure of the *Joie de la Cort*, fear in the presence of the lover is a standard feature of "courtly love." But true love, we also saw, is without fear. In this light, we understand that Chrétien is toying with Yvain's great passion. Laudine teases him:

> "Amer? Et cui?"—"Vos, dame chiere."
> "Moi?"—"Voire,"—"Voir? an quel meniere?"
> "An tel, que graindre estre ne puet,
> An tel, que de vos ne se muet
> Mes cuers, n'onques aillors nel truis,
> An tel, qu'aillors panser ne puis,
> An tel, que toz a vos m'otroi,
> An tel, que plus vos aim que moi,
> An tel, se vos plest, a delivre
> Que por vos vuel morir ou vivre." (ll. 2023–32)

Laudine, by contrast, makes no fancy speech; her concerns at this point are pragmatic. Her practical approach, in fact, has allowed her to be persuaded to take Yvain as her new husband. In doing so, she is acting in the interests of her land; if Yvain has been able to vanquish Esclados, he must be the better man. Laudine needs a powerful knight to defend her fountain. The deal is concluded in rather short order. Laudine asks the crucial question:

> "Et oseriiez vos anprandre
> Por moi ma fontainne a deffandre?" (ll. 2033–34)

Yvain replies confidently:

> "Oïl voir, dame! vers toz homes."
> "Sachiez donc, bien qu'acordé somes." (ll. 2035–36)

This courtship, which is concluded less in passion than in businesslike "accord," is no more exemplary of the ideals of "courtly love" than Erec's courtship of Enide. Nor is it an ideal relationship in terms of other kinds of love. Surely, its seriousness is undercut by Chrétien's humor. Yvain's passion appears ridiculous—effeminate, even—in light of the practical-minded response it evokes in Laudine.

When the man in a relationship behaves passionately while the woman remains clear-headed, we must suspect that a fundamental weakness undermines it, the inversion of natural order. This weakness shows itself in the breakdown of the marriage when Yvain abandons Laudine for the tournaments (inverting Erec's mistake). Thus, Chrétien's statement of the people's acceptance of their Lady's marriage is really an insinuation of fickleness, of lack of good judgment, and we would not expect more from a bunch of knights, not one of whom would dare defend the fountain himself. Earlier, Chrétien has drawn an invidious contrast between the lovers of today and those of the past:

> . . . Ancor vaut miauz, ce m'est avis,
> Uns cortois morz q'uns vilains vis. (ll. 31–32)

The lovers of the past are worth more than those of today because, although they are dead, they are saved. Now Chrétien echoes this contrast between the living and the dead, and subtly hints his distaste for the opportunism of Laudine's people:

> Mes ore est mes sire Yvains sire,
> Et li morz est toz obliëz.
> Cil, qui l'ocist, est mariëz
> An sa fame, et ansanble, gisent,
> Et les janz aimment plus et prisent
> Le vif, qu'onques le mort ne firent. (ll. 2164–69)

His people are no better than Esclados himself; Lunete characterizes them as cowards as she urges Laudine to receive Yvain:

> " . . . Certes une chanberiere
> Ne valent tuit . . .
> Li chevalier, que vos avez.
> Ja par celui, qui miauz se prise,
> N'an iert escuz ne lance prise.
> De jant mauveise avez vos mout,
> Mes ja n'i avara si estout,
> Qui sor cheval monter an ost." (ll. 1628–35)

Their cowardice and their shallow loyalty reflect the tenuous nature of Yvain's marriage, which has made him lord— but in name only—over the land that once belonged to Esclados.

9

Madness

It is characteristic of Chrétien's style that the moral "value" of a character often shifts between poles of meaning, while the meaning of the narrative as a whole remains consistent. When Arthur's court arrives at the fountain of storms on the eve of St. John the Baptist's day, Yvain, in his defense of the fountain against the fatuous Kay, becomes the representative of righteousness and charity. Esclados, fulfilling the same outward function, represented, I said, the power of the devil. The meaning of the allegory, then, lies not ultimately in the external details of the narrative (although they too are a *part* of the whole context out of which the meaning does emerge), but in the spiritual states of the characters. Thus, Chrétien's complex allegory reflects the spiritual morality of the New Law, under which the *act* of adultery is less important than the inward inclination to commit the act.

As Yvain has earlier feared, Kay requests and is granted the honor of challenging the knight of the fountain. He is so anxious to be first that he dismisses the consequences of his rashness:

> . . . Queus que fust la definaille,
> Il voloit comancier toz jorz
> Les batailles et les estorz,
> Ou il i eüst grant corroz.   (ll. 2228–33)

Now, in his role as defender of the sacramental fountain,
Yvain acts as the instrument of divine justice, striking down
him who would be first no matter what the outcome. At
the same time, though, his justice is tempered with mercy:

> "Ahi, ahi! come or gisiez
> Vos, qui les autres despisiez!
> Et neporquant s'est il bien droiz,
> Qu'an le vos pardoint ceste foiz
> Por se qu'ains mes ne vos avint."   (ll. 2263–67)

Kay's excuse is ignorance and folly, and although it will
not save him in the long run, charity nevertheless dictates
tempering his just deserts with mercy.

The reception of King Arthur and his retinue into Laudine's city is similar in form and theme to the advent of
Erec to his father's land discussed in chapter 3. As the advent of a king was normally seen as a type of Christ's advent, this elaborate episode in *Yvain* recalls the opening
description of Arthur in which he is set as the earthly king
over against Christ, the heavenly king. Again, Chrétien emphasizes the joy of the people at Arthur's approach, and he
conspicuously uses the word *noveles* to echo the annuncia-
tion of Christ's advent, the "good news." The "right" way
led Yvain to the fountain; this time it is the direct way (but
still the "right" one) that leads to the city:

> Maintenant montent, si s'an vont
> Vers le chastel la droite voie.   (ll. 2312–13)

Laudine is overjoyed at "the news of the king who comes":

> Quant la dame oï les noveles,

> Del roi, qui vient, s'an a grant joie;
> N'i a nul, qui la novele oie,
> Qui n'an soit liez et qui ne mont. (ll. 2320–23)

In preparation for Arthur's reception, the streets of the city have been covered with curtains under which the procession is to pass. Chrétien says that the curtains have been hung to protect the king and his retinue from the heat of the sun, but in fact it was conventional for a king entering a city to be received under some form of covering, often domical to symbolize the king's advent. Smith writes:

> The illustrations of the Utrecht Psalter furnish the most striking confirmation that the Middle Ages were cognizant of the antique palace tradition, thought of a *palatium* in the architectural terms which were characteristic of late Roman and Byzantine palaces, and still visualized a domical vestibule as a celestial *skene* in which a *Dominus et Deus* was received and worshipped. . . . The domical covering over a place of reception, whether a portable ciborum, or a permanent vault over a hall of state, was still considered to be a heavenly tent. (*Architectural Symbolism*, p. 161)

Laudine's men ride out to salute the king of Britain:

> "Bien vaingne," font il, "ceste rote,
> Qui de si prodomes est plainne!
> Beneoiz soit cil, qui les mainne
> Et qui si buens ostes nos done!" (ll. 2334–37)

The king is greeted by leaping dancers, by music of diverse instruments. Chrétien continually stresses the people's joy at the king's advent. When Laudine appears, it is in imperial guise, "more beautiful than any goddess" (l. 2367). The people repeat their welcome, this time revealing unequivocally the felt analogy between Arthur's coming and Christ's. They welcome him as "king of kings, and lord of lords" (1 Timothy 6:15):

> "Bien vaingne li rois et li sire
> Des rois et des seignors del monde!" (ll. 2370–71)

When Arthur greets Laudine by wishing her "Et grant joie
et buene avanture!" (l. 2384), we see unmistakably, in the
context of the king's advent, Chrétien's play on the meaning of adventure.

In the same episode, Chrétien plays with another figure,
a commonplace from the typology of patristic exegesis. He
likens the meeting of Gawain and Lunete to the meeting of
the sun and the moon. He does not want to waste words,
he says, but he must tell just this one thing more:

> . . . Solemant de l'acointance
> Vuel feire une brief remanbrance,
> Qui fu feite a privé consoil
> Antre la lune et le soloil. (ll. 2395–98)

Gawain, knight of knights, is like the sun, who illumines
all chivalry with his valor:

> Savez, de cui je vos vuel dire?
> Cil, qui des chevaliers fu sire
> Et qui sor toz fu renomez,
> Doit bien estre solauz clamez.
> Por mon seignor Gauvain le di;
> Que de lui est tot autressi
> Chevalerie anluminee,
> Con li solauz la matinee
> Oevre ses rais et clarté rant
> Par toz les leus, ou il s'espant. (ll. 2399–2408)

I have noted the etymological significance of several of the
names in *Erec* and *Yvain;* Chrétien himself supplies the "etymology" of Lunete:

> Et de celi refaz la lune,
> Dont il ne puet estre que une
> De grant san et de corteisie.
> Et neporuec je nel di mie
> Solemant por son buen renon,
> Mes por ce, que Lunete a non. (ll. 2409–14)

Hugo Rahner, surveying the figure of the moon in pa-

tristic literature, writes that there is no more consistent or
pervasive allegorization throughout the history of the early
and medieval Church than the analogy drawn between the
sun's relation to the moon and Christ's "marriage" with his
Church. Particularly is Lunete's connection with the fountain of storms illuminated by the traditional exegesis of the
figure. The moon that is the Church is mystically the source
of the water of baptism:

> Wie Selene in der Kraft der im Synodos mit Helios erlebten
> Vernichtung zur Mutter der lebendigen Dinge auf Erden,
> zur gnadenmilden Spenderin des fruchtzeugenden Mondwas-
> sers, zum nächtlichen Quell des Taues wird, so erhält die
> in Christus hineinsterbende Kirche gerade in der täglichen
> Vernichtung ihrer irdischen Sichtbarkeit, in der mystischen
> Finsternis ihrer vereinigung mit Christus die Kraft zur Zeugung
> geistlichen Lebens, wird zum Quell des geistträchtigen Tauf-
> wassers, zur Spenderin des Taues der Gnade, den sie im
> nächtlichen Schweigen dieser irdischen Leben ausgiesst. Sie
> führt so die Kinder, die sie geboren hat, hinauf zur seligen
> Freiheit in die reinen, ätherkuchtenden Gefilde, die über
> dem Mond sind, macht sie frei von aller unter dem Mond
> herrschenden dämonischen Gebundenheit.[1]

She is also, like Lunete, a protectress—figuratively the "mother" Church, who nourishes and protects the children to whom
she has given birth in the womb of the font.

The "acquaintance" of the sun, Gawain, and the moon,
Lunete, then, plays ironically on this typology. It is appropriate to conclude the long and elaborate scene of the king's
advent with this play on the marriage of Christ with his
Church. Christ comes as the bridegroom. But although the
scene between Gawain and Lunete is obviously suggestive of
marriage, the sacramental union never materializes, because
Chrétien's allegory is ironically conceived. Gawain makes
clear, first by his seduction of Yvain to the tournaments, then
by his blind defense of the unjust elder sister at the end

---

1. Hugo Rahner, "Mysterium lunae," *Zeitschrift für Katholische Theologie* (1939), pp. 313–14.

of the romance, that he is as much the worldly counterpart of the true "sun" of chivalry, Christ, as we earlier saw Arthur to be the worldly counterpart of the heavenly king. Gawain "loves" Lunete, Chrétien tells us, because she has saved his friend Yvain, and he offers her his perpetual service, and begs her to be his lady. Lunete thanks him, but coyly avoids accepting the offer, and nothing more is heard of the alliance.

Although Gawain is related to Christ most closely as his anti-type, Lunete, both in her role as protectress and in her persecution at the hands of wicked men, is truly a figure of the Church. She is the protectress not only of Yvain, but also of the other women in Laudine's service. When she is threatened with death, they lament the loss of their intercessor, who prompts their mistress to acts of charity. The women complain that God has forgotten them, and allowed them to go astray:

> "Ha Des, con nos as obliëes!
> Con remandrons ore esgarees,
> Qui perdomes si buene amie
> Et tel consoil et tel aïe,
> Qui a la cort por nos estoit!" (ll. 4361–65)

Through Lunete's offices they have been well clothed; now life will be different!

> "Par son consoil nos revestoit
> Ma dame de ses robes veires.
> Mout changera or li afeires;
> Qu'il n'iert mes, qui por nos parot." (ll. 4366–69)

They curse him for whom they suffer this loss:

> "Mal et de De, qui la nos tot!
> Mal et, par cui nos la perdrons!
> Que trop grant domage i avrons.
> N'iert mes, qui die ne qui lot:
> 'Cest mantel ver et cest sorcot

Et ceste cote, chiere dame!
Donez a cele franche fame!
Que voir, se vos li anvoiiez,
Mout i sera bien anploiiez;
Qui ele an a mout grant sofreite.' "   (ll. 4370–79)

We see a picture of the same selfless Lunete who offered protection to Yvain at great risk to herself. The women appreciate, too, how unique such charity is. They are not likely to find such again, they lament. Lunete is a paragon of good works as the lovers of old are paragons of true love. From now on, the women say, only those who have no need themselves will be generous enough to speak on behalf of the needs of others. From now on, it is everyone for himself:

"Ja de ce n'iert parole treite;
Car nus n'est mes frans ne cortois,
Ainz demande chascuns eincois
Por lui, que por autrui ne fet,
Sanz ce, que nul mestier an et."   (ll. 4380–84)

St. Ambrose, explaining how the moon's phases reveal by analogy the earthly sufferings of the Church, shows us that the persecution that Lunete comes to suffer is another important aspect of her symbolism as the Church, and is suffused with the meaning of Christian martyrdom:

The moon toils for you. . . . The moon "groans and travails in pain" in its changes. . . . The moon frequently awaits your release from sin, that it may be released from the servitude in which all creation shares. . . . He who has allotted His gifts to all things has allotted this to the moon. He has emptied it so as to replenish it. . . . Deservedly is the moon compared to the Church. . . . The Church has, like the moon, her frequent risings and settings. She has grown, however, by her settings and has by their means merited expansion at a time when she is undergoing diminution through persecution and while she is being crowned by the martyrdom of her faithful. . . . This is the real moon which from the perpetual light of her own brother has acquired the light of immortality and grace. Not from her own light does the Church gleam, but from the light of Christ. From the Sun of Justice has her brilliance been obtained, so that it is said: "It is now no longer I that live, but Christ lives in me."[2]

We can deal now more fully with Loomis's objection that the use of the chapel at the fountain of storms as Lunete's prison is "absurd." Certainly, even more absurd from that point of view is the fact that Yvain makes no attempt to release her from this prison, even though it is apparently unguarded. He does not release her because the meaning of the scene is figurative. Actually, Lunete and the chapel represent the same thing. Her captivity and persecution are the captivity and persecution of the Church, in whose defense the Christian soldier fights, armed with the arms of the spirit.

I have identified four different figures of the Church in *Yvain*: the garden of the fountain of storms, the chapel in the garden, the great hall of the castle, and Yvain's protectress, Lunete. To understand the coherence in this apparent confusion of images we must recall the principle of analogy that underlies patristic typology. The analogical relation among typologically related figures tends to be abstract, and rarely comprehensive. Thus equivalent figures often express different aspects of what they signify in common. The aspect of the Cross prefigured by the Tree of Knowledge, for instance, is different from the aspect prefigured by the wood of the Ark. Again, while the Deluge stresses the penitential aspect of baptism, the water springing from the Rock of Horeb stresses its power of salvation. Moreover, the continuity of time on which the narrative of the Old Testament depends does not impinge on its allegorical significance. It does not particularly matter that the Crossing of the Red Sea and the striking of the Rock of Horeb follow the Del-

---

2. St. Ambrose, *Hexameron*, IV, 8, trans. John J. Savage, *The Fathers of the Church*, vol. 42 (New York, 1961): 155–56.

uge but precede the Crossing of the Jordan. In the context of the exegetical conventions that serve Chrétien as models, then, there is no inconsistency in having many figures express the same thing. Each figure of the Church in *Yvain* stresses a different aspect of it, as the allegorical meaning of the romance requires. It is the emergence of this spiritual meaning that is Chrétien's concern; narrative consistency is a commodity he values less.

Gawain entices Yvain to pursue adventure at the tournaments. This pursuit, we know, leads to the crisis in his marriage when Laudine rejects him for his negligence and he himself falls into insanity. From the point of view of the poem's meaning, however, the choice that Gawain sets before Yvain is really no choice at all, just as the earlier choice between seeking a rendezvous and marriage with Laudine and seeking proof of his victory was merely a fictional choice. Since Laudine *is* honor, the choice is between worldly glory and a figure for the same thing. Again we see that meaning lies not so much in what outwardly *happens* (the form of the *adventure*), as in the spiritual orientation of the characters to what happens.

Gawain begins his plea with an extremely ambiguous appeal to Yvain's sense of honor, in which the notions of marriage and honor get mixed up, and never quite disentangled. One ought not to marry so as to lose honor, he argues, rather to gain it:

> "Qui por lor fames valent mains?
> Honiz soit de sainte Marie,
> Qui por anpirer se marie!
> Amander doit de bele dame,
> Qui l'a a amie ou a fame,
> Si n'est puis droiz, que ele l'aint,
> Que ses pris et ses los remaint." (ll. 2486–92)

Gawain unwittingly foresees the results of Yvain's negligence. His wife will reject him, but for the reason opposite what Gawain supposes. Actually, Yvain's negligence is only the working out in action of the motivation for his marriage in the first place.

> "Certes, ancor seroiz iriez
> De s'amor, se vos anpiriez;
> Que fame a tost s'amor reprise,
> Ne n'a pas tort, s'ele desprise
> Celui, qui de neant anpire,
> Quant il est del reaume sire." (ll. 2493-98)

Chrétien puns on the word *fame,* which can mean "fame" or "wife." Read in this light, the first question takes on particular significance. "Who makes himself worth less for the sake of his wife/fame?" The answer is that Yvain, for the sake of his worldly fame, makes himself worth less spiritually. Spiritually, Yvain has married "por anpirier." This is true, of course, whether he follows Gawain to the tournaments or not. Erec shows us the folly of the other alternative, as Gawain presents it. Perhaps another answer to the question is Adam, who was given Eve as helpmate and companion, whose situation God intended to improve by the gift, but who allowed his wife to seduce him into disobedience, thus losing "worth" by marriage. This is the loss we all inherit, which we must struggle all our lives to overcome.

The last four lines quoted above appear especially ironic when we recall how quickly Laudine "takes back her love" from Esclados when he has been slain by Yvain, who seems to her to be a phantasm, literally "nothing." In the aesthetics of Augustine and John the Scot, the image of beauty that is contemplated and dwelt on for its own sake becomes unreal and seductive—that is, it seems to be what it is not. In this sense, Yvain is truly "worsened by nothing," the ephemeral image of earthly beauty that he mistakenly imagines will please him forever.

Gawain skillfully presses Yvain at his weakest spot, his desire for personal glory: "Or primes doit vostre pris croistre!" (l. 2499). "Break the bridle and the halter," he continues, showing us again the conventional figure of horse and rider. Gawain's logic is characteristically askew:

> "Ronpez le frain et le chevoistre!
> S'irons tornoiier moi et vos,
> Que l'an ne vos apiaut jalos." (ll. 2500–2502)

It is precisely husbands who *fail* to "bridle" their wives who have reason to be jealous. Of course Gawain really means that the bridle is on Yvain, not his wife. But this further inversion only underscores the topsy-turvy nature of Yvain's marriage. Breaking free of "the bridle and the halter" on his own neck is only a solution to the problem of jealousy if he then assumes his proper sovereignty over his wife. But Gawain's proposal in this context is frivolous:

> "Or ne devez vos pas songier,
> Mes les tornoiemanz ongier,
> Anprandre estorz et fort joster,
> Que que il vos doie coster!" (ll. 2503–6)

We saw how Kay rashly disregarded the consequences of jousting. Gawain's bravado is equally ominous.

Like Yvain, Gawain ignores the ephemeral nature of Laudine's beauty. He argues that Yvain ought not to care about leaving a pleasure that will always be waiting for him:

> "Mervoille est, comant an a cure
> De l'eise qui toz li dure.
> Biens adoucist par delaiier,
> Et plus est buens a essaiier
> Uns petiz biens, quant il delaie,
> Qu'uns granz, qui l'an adés essaie." (ll. 2513–18)

The joys of marriage, however, will not last forever. The only joy that truly lasts forever is the bliss of salvation, but Gawain, as his ironical role of "sun" of chivalry indicates, is not the one to know it.

At this point in the speech, Chrétien drops all pretense of seriousness. He has Gawain warn against the very danger to which Yvain falls prey. Habits, he argues, are hard to break:

> "L'an puet tel chose acostumer,
> Qui mout est grevainne a retreire;
> Quant an le viaut, nel puet an feire." (ll. 2524–26)

Gawain means that Yvain, like Erec, stands in danger of giving over the glory of chivalry for the joys of the nuptial bed. But it is because he cannot draw himself away from the tournaments to which he has become habituated that he loses the favor of Laudine, and goes mad with remorse.

Finally, in pure buffoonery, Gawain completely undercuts his own advice by warning Yvain against preachers who fail to practice what they advise others to do, recalling Christ's rebuke of the Pharisees. He admits that personally he would consider himself a fool to leave such a beautiful woman:

> "Et por ce ne le di je mie,
> Se j'avoie si bele amie,
> Con vos avez, sire conpainz!
> Foi, que je doi De et ses sainz,
> Mout a anviz la leisseroie!
> Mien esciant fos an seroie.
> Mes tes consoille bien autrui,
> Qui ne savroit conseillier lui,
> Aussi con li preecheor,
> Qui sont desleal tricheor:
> Ansaignent et dïent le bien,
> Dont il ne vuelent feire rien." (ll. 2527–38)

It is a sign of Yvain's present befuddlement that he listens to all this with an apparently straight face, wide-eyed even. Whether it is wise or foolish, he is persuaded by Gawain's crazy logic:

> Ou face folie ou savoir,
> Ne leira, que congié ne praingne
> De retorner an la Bretaingne. (ll. 2544–46)

The verb *avenir* expresses the fortuitous aspect of adventure, what unforeseeably *happens* to the knight, what befalls him. But the Christian knows that what appears to be the operation of mere chance in the world is really governed by providence, although our vision may be too dim to perceive it. Laudine grants Yvain permission to accompany Gawain and Arthur's court to the tournaments on the condition that he return within one year from that day, the octave of John the Baptist's day. Yvain sighs, and answers,

> "Dame! cist termes est trop lons.
> Se je pooie estre colons
> Totes foiz, que je voldroie,
> Mout sovant avuec vos seroie." (ll. 2581–84)

Yvain's figure echoes the Psalmist's "wings of the dove": "Who will give me the wings of the dove, that I may fly away and find rest? Behold, fleeing I wandered far: and I remained in solitude" (Psalm 54:7–8). Indeed, although he cannot foresee it, Yvain will not return to Laudine before he has undergone the arduous spiritual perfection of penance, which begins for him "in solitude," having "wandered far" into the wilderness of insanity. He continues:

> "Et je pri De que, se lui plest,
> Ja tant demorer ne me lest.
> Mes tes cuide mout tost venir,
> Qui ne set, qu'est a avenir." (ll. 2585–88)

The second couplet of this passage has the ring of a proverb, and shares the theme of innumerable biblical admonitions about the insecurity of man's life on earth, and the necessity for preparing the soul for eternity. Yvain cannot know what will befall him:

> "Et je ne sai, que m'avandra,
> Se essoines me detandra
> De malage ne de prison." (ll. 2589–91)

What Yvain intends as an excuse, Chrétien undercuts with irony. He has just described the situation he is currently in. He has been "detained" at Laudine's castle by *malage* (Love's "wound") and by the imprisonment he refuses to escape when he has the chance. What we see, then, between the lines of Yvain's hedging is that the evil he fears may befall him on his journey, "l'essoine de mon cors" (l. 2594), has already befallen him because it lies in his own will. Adventure, which appears to be chance, is pervaded not only by providence, but by will. There is also the obvious double meaning of this last-quoted line that the hindrance to love *is* his body, his carnality.

At this point in the romance, Laudine begins to emerge as a figure in her own right, distinct from Yvain's desire for her. Her value, so to speak, shifts from Yvain's immediate, carnal desires to his ultimate goal of spiritual perfection, achieved at the conclusion of the romance. This new spirituality of her character is expressed in the nature of the magic ring she gives Yvain:

> "Prison ne tient ne sanc ne pert
> Nus amanz verais et leaus,
> Ne avenir ne li puet maus,
> Mes qu'il le port et chier le taingne
> Et de s'amie li sovaingne,
> Einçois devient plus durs que fers." (ll. 2604-9)

No evil, only good can befall (*avenir*) him who wears the ring and remembers his love. The ring, of course, *is* love; Laudine says, "par amor le vos doing gié" (l. 2613). She stresses the necessity of remembering her—precisely what Yvain fails to do:

> " . . . Bien vos promet,
> Que, se Des de mort vos deffant,
> Nus essoines ne vos atant
> Tant con vos sovandra de moi." (ll. 2596-99)

The spiritual character of this love is indicated by Laudine's response to Yvain's premature excuse, "l'essoine de mon cors." No corporeal hindrance can hedge the love of the spirit. In the second line above, Chrétien purposely confuses the protection of God with the protection of the ring. Moreover, the "amanz verais et leaus" is the type of true lover that Chrétien in his prologue identifies with charity. The ring is only the palpable symbol, the "letter," of the spiritual condition of holy love.

Yvain "sows" his parting kisses with tears:

> Ne sai, que vos doie conter,
> Comant mes sire Yvains s'an part,
> Et des beisiers, qu'an li depart,
> Qui furent de lermes semé. (ll. 2624–27)

In light of the poet's attitude toward the folly of Yvain's passion, the echo of Scripture seems typically ironic: "They that sow in tears shall reap in joy."[3] The paradox of the romance, however, is that the scriptural proverb proves true. Yvain must sow other tears, tears of true contrition, before he can reap true joy, but miraculously he does.

As we might expect, Yvain is unable to use the ring as Laudine has warned him he must. In spite of the heat of his passion (but in keeping with its misguided nature), he does forget her—within fewer than one hundred lines of the gift of the ring, so the irony's bite is sharp. In a long passage in which he elaborates on what was probably already a convention of courtly poetry, the conceit of the lover's heart that stays behind with his beloved,[4] Chrétien assumes a naïveté the humor of which we realize only a few lines

---

3. Psalm 125:5. I have referred earlier, in chapter 1, to Augustine's commentary on this verse.

4. See W. H. Holland, ed., *Chevalier au Lyon* (Hannover, 1862), pp. 107–8, n.; same author's *Chrestien von Troies* (Tübingen, 1854), pp. 181–82, 275; J. Morawski, "La Flours D'Amours," *Romania* 53 (1927): 187, n.; E. Mätzner, *Altfranzösische lieder* (Berlin, 1853), pp. 141–42; C. S. Lewis, *The Allegory of Love*, p. 31.

later, after the passage of more than a year, when Lunete arrives at court to upbraid Yvain for his neglect of her mistress, and to demand the return of the ring. Yvain leaves so reluctantly, the poet tells us, that his heart does not move; the king may take his body to the tournaments, but his heart so cleaves to her who stays behind that he has no power to take it with him. And this marvel raises a conundrum:

> Des que li cors est sanz le cuer,
> Donc ne puet il vivre a nul fuer;
> Et se li cors sanz le cuer vit,
> Tel mervoille nus hon ne vit.
> Ceste mervoille est avenue.   (ll. 2647–51)

This conceit means that Yvain remains with Laudine in imagination, or in spirit, as Laudine has put it in her instructions for the ring's use, by remembering her. This spiritual union, in turn, entails loving after the pattern of God's love. But Yvain's love turns out to be ephemeral. Since it is based on the physical sight of the beloved, it loses its force as soon as the lovers are separated. The truth that underlies Chrétien's ironic use of this conceit is that Yvain's body without his heart is truly without spiritual life. If we recall what the heart signified for Calogrenant, we see that the figure indicates the spiritual deadness with which Yvain pursues glory. He throws himself entirely into the tournaments, and forgets his promise to return to Laudine by the octave of John the Baptist's day.

When Lunete comes to rebuke him for his negligence, she accuses Yvain of being a false, hypocritical lover, and she reverses the earlier conceit of Yvain's heart and body. It is Laudine's heart that has gone with Yvain, or rather that he, under the pretense of love, has stolen away. If it is a miracle that Yvain's "body can live without the heart," Lunete declares simply that Laudine's body cannot live without hers. Yvain has "killed" her. True lovers do not steal hearts they care nothing for:

"Cil n'anblent pas les cuers, qui aimment,
. . . .
Et cil sont larron ipocrite
Et traïtor, qui metent luite
As cuers anbler, dont aus ne chaut." (ll. 2729–39)

In the name of her mistress, Lunete demands the return of
the ring, and when the stunned Yvain fails to react, she herself slips the ring from his finger, and leaves the court.

It is perhaps sad, but true, that the conscience functions
most effectively after the fact of sin. Even though Yvain forgets his promise to Laudine, it is principally his own conscience that tortures him:

A grant painne tenoit ses lermes,
Mes honte li feisoit tenir. (ll. 2702–3)

Although Laudine forbids him to return to her, Yvain inflicts the real penance on himself in the form of exile. His
own remorse drives him mad, and he flees into the wilderness, where no one may follow him:

Mis se voldroit estre a la fuie
Toz seus an si sauvage terre,
Que l'an ne le seüst, ou querre,
N'ome ne fame n'i eüst,
Ne nus de lui rien ne seüst
Ne plus, que s'il fust an abisme. (ll. 2784–89)

From hindsight we know that exile leads Yvain to a higher
spiritual plane than he could have attained without this crisis, just as Dante can reach paradise only through the gates
of hell. Hell in this sense is the recognition of sin, and is
the first necessary step toward salvation. Thus, Chrétien likens Yvain's exile in the "sauvage terre" to an abysm, to hell.
Laudine's rejection is insignificant compared with Yvain's
recognition and hatred of his own sin:

Ne het tant rien con lui meïsme,

Ne ne set, a cui se confort
De lui, qu'il meïsmes a mort. (ll. 2790–92)

Madness is his self-inflicted penance:

Mes ainz voldra le san changier,
Que il ne se puisse vangier
De lui, qui joie s'est tolue. (ll. 2793–95)

Remorse pulses in his head and he flees the other knights. By chance, he passes a servant who holds a bow and five sharp arrows. These, Chrétien tells us, Yvain has sense enough to grab from the boy and run off with. The five arrows, with which Yvain hunts and sustains life, are the five senses, that is, the elementary physical existence to which Yvain is now reduced. The word *san* is a pun on this meaning:

S'ot tant de san, que au garçon
Est alez tolir son arçon
Et les saietes qu'il tenoit. (ll. 2819–21)

Yvain has as much sense as the five senses, lowest common denominator of human life, but no more.

The misery to which Yvain is now reduced appears in sharp contrast to his style of life in the scene immediately preceding, in which he and his companion, Gawain, have so exalted themselves that they do not deign to visit even King Arthur's court. Rather, the king must visit theirs, for they have gathered the best knights around them. From a twelfth-century viewpoint this must appear as overweening pride, which has upset the established secular order. It is inevitable that Yvain's spiritual investment in ephemeral values leads to his present catastrophe. Fortunately, it is a purgative catastrophe.

Chrétien lays particular stress on Yvain's nourishment during his exile. At first, he is compelled to hunt deer, and to eat the meat uncooked:

>Les bestes par le bois agueite,
>Si les ocit et si manjue
>La veneison trestote crue. (ll. 2824–26)

After a time, he comes upon the cottage of a hermit, whose charity prompts him, though he is terrified of what he takes to be a naked savage, to share his coarse bread and cold water.

That this nourishment is figuratively nourishment of the spirit is indicated both by Chrétien's emphasis and by the obviously spiritual character of the hermit. His humility stands out against the background of Yvain's triumphs and his pride. Yvain lives alone in the wilderness like a savage until,

>. . . une meison a un hermite
>Trova mout basse et mout petite,
>Et li hermites essartoit. (ll. 2827–31)

In the context of the theme of Christian initiation, the venison, unleavened bread, and cold water from the fountain suggest the typology of the Paschal meal instituted at the Exodus, figurative for Christians of the Eucharist.

Like Israel, sustained and protected by the grace of God in its flight through the wildnerness, Yvain is sustained by the charity of the hermit. Exodus chronicles a series of miracles of salvation, revolving conspicuously around sacred sustenance: the Paschal meal of lamb and unleavened bread, and the blood of the lamb on the lintels and door-posts; the parting of the Red Sea; the manna; the water sprung from the Rock of Horeb.[5]

The hermit, fearing the savage, leaves bread and "pure water, for charity," outside his narrow window. Yvain's hunger drives him to the bread, but it proves hard and bitter discipline to him:

---

5. The connection already noted between the giving of the Law and the festival of Pentecost makes the parallel with Exodus particularly appropriate.

> . . . Cil vient la, qui mout covoite
> Le pain, si le prant et s'i mort.
> Ne cuit, que onques de si fort
> Ne de si aspre eüst gosté. (ll. 2842–45)

It is sharper than leaven, and dry as bark (as unleavened bread is) :

> N'avoit mie cinc souz costé
> Li sestiers, don fu fez li pains,
> Qui plus iere egres que levains,
> D'orge pestriz atot la paille,
> Et avuec ce iere il sanz faille
> Moisiz et ses come une escorce. (ll. 2846–51)

Guiot's manuscript preserves a line (Foerster favors another reading) that states explicitly that the hermit's bread is unleavened:

> Et li boens hoem estoit an painne
> de cuir vandre et d'acheter pain
> d'orge, et de soigle sanz levain.
> (ll. 2878–80, correspond to Foerster's
> ll. 2882–84)

The hermit gives Yvain "cold water from the fountain," the water of life, to drink. And although Yvain eats his venison raw when he first enters the forest, the hermit sees to it that the meat is cooked:

> Et li buens hon s'antremetoit
> De l'escorchier et si metoit
> Assez de la veneison cuire,
> Et li pains et l'eve an la buire
> Estoit toz jorz sor la fenestre
> Por l'ome forsené repestre;
> S'avoit a mangier et a boivre
> Veneison sanz sel et sanz poivre
> Et eve froide de fontainne. (ll. 2873–81)

Moses is instructed by God not to eat the flesh of the Paschal lamb uncooked: "Eat not of it raw, nor sodden at all with water, but roast it with fire" (Exodus 12:9).

St. Paul was the first commentator to allegorize the unleavened bread of the Paschal meal, and his symbolism is retained by the later exegetes. Daniélou explains that because leaven was made from some of the old dough fermented, the azyme, or the first bread from the wheat of the new harvest, was made when there was as yet no leaven. Thus, unleavened bread was seen as a symbol of newness of life. "Eaten after the Pasch, the azymes signify that after the immolation of Christ, of which Christians have been made participants by Baptism, they are dead to the old life and live with a new. . . . The azymes . . . are the figure of the time that follows the baptismal initiation, and, more generally, of Christian life" (*Bible and the Liturgy*, pp. 173–74). Yvain's nourishment in the forest, then, is figurative of the sacramental meal that follows baptism, the Eucharist.

The spiritual renewal that is thus signified allegorically by Yvain's food is further reflected in the story. Yvain is revived from his death-like faint or coma, the culmination of his madness, by the magic salve of the Dame de Noroison (whose name, which sounds like *norrissance,* echoes the function she serves), nursed by her to good health, given new clothes and arms, made literally a new man. In his new character, Yvain regains the love of Laudine through a progressively more demanding series of good works. The crux of his spiritual renewal is that the motivation of these deeds has been converted from pride to charity.

Yvain's miraculous recovery has a specifically sacramental character as well. The abrupt transition from his life in the woods with the hermit to his discovery by the damsels occurs by a logic that implies a connection closer than a merely narrative one:

> S'ot puis tote sa livreison,
> Pain a planté et veneison,

Qui li dura tant longuement,
Qu'un jor le troverent dormant
An la forest deus dameiseles
Et une lor dame avuec eles,
De cui mesniee eles estoient. (ll. 2885-91)

Indeed, we must consider these two episodes, together with the episode at the fountain of storms, as a group infused with the meaning of the three sacraments of Christian initiation: baptism, Eucharist, and confirmation.

The rite of confirmation, the sacrament that perfects the already baptized Christian, and enlists and arms him as a soldier of Christ, centers around the anointing of the catechumen's forehead with holy oil. Daniélou explains that confirmation "is the sacrament of the perfecting of the soul, as Baptism is that of its generation. It has for object the development of the spiritual energies infused in the baptismal water. It corresponds to the progressive setting to work of these energies, by which the baptised person, a child in Christ, becomes an adult, until he becomes a perfect man" (*Bible and the Liturgy*, p. 126). Grace is given in "seedform" in baptism; in confirmation, the plant bears fruit.

In this light, we see why Yvain, in spite of his successful passage through the sacramental adventure at the fountain of storms, can have come to such a desperate pass. Although baptism cleanses the soul of sin already committed, it does not equip the initiate to resist sin in the future. But the perfecting rite of confirmation, with its rite of chrism, is suggested in the damsels' healing of Yvain with the precious ointment. Typically, Chrétien leaves ambiguous whether it is actually the ointment, or simply "the aid of God" that effects the cure:

La dame dist: "Or n'aiiez soing!
Que certes, se il ne s'an fuit,
A l'aïe de De, ce cuit,
Li osterons nos de la teste
Tote la rage et la tanpeste.

Mes tost aler nos an covient;
Car d'un oignemant me sovient,
Que me dona Morgue, la sage,
Et si me dist, que nule rage
N'est an teste, que il n'an oste." (ll. 2946–55)

If these three episodes, the adventure at the fountain, exile and madness, and his discovery and cure by the damsels,
are indeed sacramental in character and represent the three
parts of Christian initiation, then we must understand
Yvain's lapse into madness and his return to sanity as typologically imitative of Christ's death and resurrection. That
baptism is participation in the Passion is, as we saw, a Pauline notion, but it is extended by the Fathers to include the
whole of Christian initiation. "One could say that the whole
Christian initiation is a participation in Christ dead and
risen again," Daniélou asserts (p. 128). And each of the sacraments repeats this typology. Thus, Daniélou says of the
Eucharist that "this spiritual nourishment is not to be
thought of apart from the sacrifice of Christ. It is only a
participation in this sacrifice, that is, in the Death and Resurrection of Christ" (p. 139). Confirmation involves the
same typology. It is, "a real participation in the grace of
Christ, by a sacramental imitation of His life. . . . In the
same way as Baptism configures us to Christ dead and risen
again, so Confirmation configures us to Christ anointed by
the Holy Spirit. The Baptism of Christ, followed by the descent of the Spirit, is thus seen to be a prefiguration of
His death followed by His royal enthronement, of which the
Christian in turn partakes by means of the two sacraments
of water and of the anointing" (p. 118).

Yvain's cure by anointing takes on special meaning in
light of the fact that the seven gifts of the Spirit, in sum,
spiritual wisdom, are conferred in confirmation. Thus, Chrétien emphasizes that the cure may be effected only by
anointing the head of the deranged, and that the damsel's
liberal application of the ointment over the rest of Yvain's
body may be well-intentioned, but is superfluous nonethe-

less. Her mistress instructs her specifically not to be overly generous with the precious ointment:

> . . . Trop large
> Li prie, que ele n'an soit;
> Les tanples et le front l'an froit,
> Qu'aillors point metre n'an besoingne.
> Les tanples solement l'an oingne
> Et le remenant bien li gart;
> Qu'il n'a point de mal autre part
> Fors que solemant el cervel. (ll. 2964–73)

But the damsel is carried away by her charitable mission, and anoints his entire body, "down to the toe," using up all the ointment in the box. When she realizes what she has inadvertently done, she is terrified at the thought of confronting her mistress with the empty box. On the way back to the castle, she throws it into a stream, and fabricates a story to explain the loss of the ointment. Her mistress believes the fabrication, but is angry over the loss nevertheless, which she describes as the loss of her best and dearest possession. Chrétien's insistence on this apparently insignificant narrative detail may be intended to recall the disciples' rebuke of the woman who anointed Christ's head with precious ointment, and Christ's defense of this act of charity.

> There came unto him a woman having an alabaster box of very precious ointment, and poured it on his head, as he sat at meat. But when his disciples saw it, they had indignation, saying, To what purpose is this waste? For this ointment might have been sold for much, and given to the poor. When Jesus understood it, he said unto them, Why trouble ye the woman? for she hath wrought a good work upon me. For ye have the poor always with you; but me ye have not always." (Matthew 26:6–11)

The niggardliness of the Dame de Noroison is shown to be foolish when Yvain, restored to sanity and health, repays her by saving her from the attacks of the Count Aliers.

Yvain's madness is figurative. According to the logic of the narrative, it is the result of the shock and shame of re-

jection. But in terms of the narrative's meaning, it expresses
the folly of the behavior for which he has been shamed.
Yvain's prideful pursuit of glory and his madness are the
same. Confirmation, as the sacrament of perfection, of mat-
uration, of wisdom, illuminates for us Yvain's moral position. Chrétien's description of Yvain's awakening from madness is reminiscent of Adam's discovery of his nakedness.
Yvain, too, is shamed to discover himself naked:

> . . . Cil ot dormi assez,
> Qui fu gariz et respassez,
> Et rot son san et son memoire.
> Mes nuz se voit come un ivoire,
> S'a grant honte . . .
> . . . .
> . . . que nuz se trueve. (ll. 3017–23)

He sees the clothes that the damsels have left nearby, a *new*
robe.

> Devant lui voit la robe nueve,
> Si se mervoille a desmesure,
> Comant et par quel avanture
> Cele robe estoit la venue;
> Mes de sa char, que il voit nue,
> Est trespansez et esbaïz,
> Et dit, que morz est et traïz,
> S'einsi l'a trové ne veü
> Riens nule, qui l'et coneü. (ll. 3024–32)

His eyes have been opened to his condition, and like Adam
he clothes himself at once: "Et tote voie si se vest" (l. 3033).

Adam's sense of his nakedness is symbolic of his recognition of sin. Yvain has come to the point of maturity at which
this recognition leads not merely to self-hatred and despair
(exile from paradise), but to good works and faith, through
which the soul regains its lost innocence. The second half
of the romance shows us Yvain's gradual spiritual perfection
through a sequence of struggles with creatures who represent the dangers presented by the world to the Christian
soul in this life.

10

The Knight of the Lion

Near the middle of the romance, the first of these struggles takes place. Yvain, in gratitude for his recovery, defends la Dame de Noroison against Count Aliers. He is not yet accompanied and aided by the lion, the figure that otherwise pervades the second half of the romance, and which becomes Yvain's emblem, but as if in anticipation of this alliance, la Dame de Noroison's people admiringly liken Yvain's prowess to a lion's:

> "Ahi! con vaillant sodoiier!
> . . . .
> Tot autressie antre aus se fiert,
> Con li lions antre les dains,
> Quant l'angoisse et chace la fains." (ll. 3199–204)

Here again we find the sacramental motif of the deer hunt.

Yvain is the spiritually initiated Christian now, and it is in that character that he fights so valiantly. Chrétien puns on "virtue," for example, when he describes Yvain's prowess:

Si feri de si grant vertu
Un chevalier . . .
Qu' . . .
. . . .
. . . Onques puis cil ne releva. (ll. 3155–59)

Yvain's motives have become spiritual; he fights no longer
for the joy of fighting or the vain desire for glory that it
brings, but for charity. But he receives glory even though it
is unsought. The people lavish apparently excessive praise on
him, and as in the ironical comparison of Gawain with the
sun, Chrétien hints with his extravagant escalation of similes that Yvain is like Christ. In fact, he uses the figure of
the sun again. The people

> . . . dïent, que buer seroit nee,
> Cui il avroit s'amor donee,
> Qui si est as armes puissanz
> Et dessor toz reconoissanz,
> Si con cierges antre chandoiles
> Et la lune antre les estoiles
> Et li solauz dessor la lune. (ll. 3243–49)

The application of this figure, so closely associated with the
symbolism of Christ and his Church, is now as appropriate
to Yvain's new spiritual strength as it was inappropriate to
Gawain's worldliness. The poet pursues this meaning when
he likens Yvain's valor to a stone wall. Yvain rides out after the fleeing Aliers,

> Mes il chace mout de pres
> Et tuit si conpaignon aprés;
> Que lez lui sont aussi seür,
> Con s'il fussent anclos de mur
> Haut et espés de pierre dure. (ll. 3259–63)

The protection that Yvain affords those who are near him
is the spiritual strength that he radiates. The figure of the
wall, high and thick, built of "pierre dure," applies to Yvain

the strength on which Christ established his Church, Peter, the "rock."[1]

At the exact center of the romance occurs the episode in which Yvain rescues the lion that comes to assume such importance, both as his defense and as his symbolic device. Riding through a thick forest absorbed in thought, Yvain comes on a lion and a serpent locked in mortal combat. The serpent holds the lion fast by the tail, burning it about the loins with its fiery breath. Yvain deliberates over which of the beasts he should help, and decides finally to rescue the lion. His choice is clearly a moral one, and Chrétien makes it perfectly clear that Yvain chooses correctly. Yvain reasons,

> Qu'a venimeus et a felon
> Ne doit an feire se mal non.
> Et li serpanz est venimeus,
> Si li saut par la boche feus,
> Tant est de felenie plains. (ll. 3357–61)

Julian Harris has investigated the role of Yvain's lion in the light of the animal's traditional associations, particularly the Bestiary tradition, and has shown that Chrétien's intention was to present in the lion the emblem of Christ.[2] The serpent is thus representative of the devil.

The curious detail that the grip of the serpent's jaws is so powerful even in death that Yvain must cut off that part of the lion's tail in order to free him is intelligible as the symbol of martyrdom, and reflects the parallel incident when Yvain's horse is cut in two by the falling gate. We may note in connection with this parallel the Pauline and patristic identification of circumcision as prefiguration of the Crucifixion.[3] The image of the serpent burning the lion about its loins ("li ardoit trestoz les rains de flame ardant," ll.

---

1. Cf. passage quoted from *La Queste del Saint Graal*, below, where the phrase *pierre dure* is used explicitly of the Church.

2. Julian Harris, "The Role of the Lion in Chretien de Troyes' *Yvain*," *PMLA* 64 (1949) : 1143–63.

3. See Daniélou, *Bible and the Liturgy*, pp. 64–67.

3350–51) evokes the familiar scriptural admonition, "Gird up the loins of your mind" (1 Peter 1:13),[4] as a figure of preparation for spiritual struggle.

Not only gratitude, but love moves the lion to pledge fealty to Yvain in a pantomime of the ritual by which a vassal binds himself to his lord. He hunts deer to feed Yvain (the sacramental motif again); he guards Yvain at night by watching while he sleeps; he saves Yvain's life by aiding him in battle. The "great love" that binds him to Yvain "all the days of his life" (l. 3454), is informed by the love that moved God to assume a mortal body in order to save man.

The Bestiary tells us that lion cubs are born dead, and remain lifeless three days, after which time their father breathes in their faces, making them alive. In the same way, the Bestiarist reminds us, Our Heavenly Father restored His Son to life after three days in the tomb. Thus the lion symbolizes the Resurrection. Like Erec, Yvain is raised from the semblance of death. The physical semblance, however, expresses rather the failure of carnal love. Thus, the lion is the emblem of the resurrection of true love within Yvain, the spiritual love of which he is now capable and which leads to his reconciliation with Laudine.

We have a picture of what such an emblematic episode could mean to a medieval audience in the thirteenth-century *Queste Del Saint Graal*. There the same adventure is adapted and transferred to Perceval. It is furnished with an exegesis that confirms my interpretation of the episode in *Yvain*. Perceval, alone on an island where he is to be tested by God, sees a dragon fly away with a lion cub that it has captured. The parent of the cub, roaring pitiably, chases the dragon and engages it in combat. Like Yvain, Perceval rea-

---

4. This is one of any number of examples of the figure; e. g., Isaiah 11:5: "And righteousness shall be the girdle of his loins and faithfulness the girdle of his reins"; Ephesians 6:14: "Stand therefore, having your loins girt about with truth, and having on the breastplate of righteousness."

sons with himself to aid the lion because it is the nobler of the two beasts, and because, on the other hand, the dragon is the more malevolent. When Perceval has slain the dragon, the lion does not attack him, as he fears it may, but fawns and allows him to stroke its bowed head. So long as Perceval remains on the island, the lion is his companion.

That night, Perceval has a marvelous dream. Two women appear to him, one young, riding a lion, the other old, astride a dragon. The young woman speaks first, charging him in her lord's name to arm himself for battle the next day with "the champion of the world who is most to be feared." She warns that if he is defeated he will be shamed forever; but if he is victorious he will have honor.

Next, the old woman on the dragon reprimands him for having slain her dragon the day before. She demands that Perceval become her man by way of atonement. When he refuses, she argues that before he gave homage to his present lord he was already her man. She will not release him, she says, from that precedent bond.

Perceval is deeply troubled by his dream, which he does not understand. When he wakes the next morning he prays God to send him some counsel that will be of profit to his soul. In answer to his prayer, an old man in the guise of a priest, wearing a crown with the name of "Our Lord" inscribed on it, arrives on a marvelous ship to expound his vision. The young woman, he explains, signifies the New Law, mounted on the lion, that is, Christ. The old woman signifies the Old Law, mounted on the serpent, the devil. Note incidentally the use of the phrase "pierre dure" here to signify the Church, the same phrase that Chrétien uses, only somewhat more covertly, in the episode of Yvain's battle with Aliers:

Cele qui sor le lyon estoit montee senefie la Novele Loi, qui sor le lyon est, ce est sor Jhesucrist, qui par lui prist pié et fondement et qui par lui fu edifiee et montee en la veue et en l'esgart de toute crestienté, et por ce qu'ele fust mireors et veraie lumiere a toz çax qui metent lor cuers en la Trinité. Et cele dame siet sor le lyon, ce est sor Jhesucrist, et cele dame si est Foi et Esperance et creance et baptesmes. Cele dame est la pierre dure et ferme sor quoi Jhesucrist dist qu'il fermeroit Sainte Eglyse.[5]

The young lady has appeared to Perceval, the old man assures him, out of love, to tell him from "her lord" that he must fight against the most feared champion of this world, the enemy, the devil, who is at pains to ensnare man in mortal sin and take him to hell. The woman whom Perceval saw riding the serpent "est la Synagogue, la premiere Loi, qui fu ariere mise, si tost come Jhesucrist ot aporté avant la Novele Loi (*Queste*, 102–3) ."

The exegesis of Perceval's dream is detailed and exhaustive, but it is neither mechanical nor literal-minded. Each figure is given a number of related significations, according to the spirit of the dream's whole meaning, rather than to the letter of the fictional exigencies. Thus, the young lady is the figure of the Church, the meaning of which is in turn expressed by two other figures, the mirror and the light. Moreover, if she is the Church, she is faith and hope and belief and baptism. She is the "firm rock." Likewise, the meaning of the serpent is a complex of related meanings. The serpent, who the ancient exegete affirms is the same as that which tempted Adam and Eve, is also "l'Escriture mauvesement entendue et mauvesement esponse, ce est ypocrisie et heresie et iniquitez et pechié mortel (*Queste*, 103) ."

We require a similar exegetical agility to read Chrétien's allegory. An interpretation based on rigidly conceived meanings simply will not remain consistent. For example, the old woman on the dragon mourned the dragon that Perceval had slain the day before. Yet the exegete says otherwise:

---

5. *La Queste Del Saint Graal,* ed. Albert Pauphilet, *Classiques Français du Moyen Age* (Paris, 1923) , p. 101. The same episode with virtually the same exegesis appears in Malory's version.

she mourned not the dragon slain the day before, but the dragon she was riding, which is to say, he adds, the devil. Like Christ's explanation of parables, this explanation cannot be taken at face value. The old woman mourns in reality neither dragon; "she" mourns what the "dragons" both signify. The narrative inconsistency that the exegete thus introduces is of no consequence once we understand the narrative's meaning.

The episode of the grateful lion in the *Queste* does not, of course, prove that its meaning in *Yvain* is similar. But it does demonstrate that such an allegorical interpretation presented itself naturally to the mind of the medieval writer and his audience. It is true that we need to understand why the later author of the *Queste* provides the exegesis that Chrétien leaves to the intelligence of his audience. Presumably, the more popular Arthurian romance became, the more its form was taken for granted, the less extraordinary its marvelous adventures must have seemed. Once form becomes conventional and provides its own *raison d'être,* it no longer automatically raises the questions of meaning that exegesis must then point out and answer. The author of the *Queste* apparently felt it necessary to explain narrative elements that Chrétien was confident would, if not speak for themselves, at least present themselves as problems requiring a solution.

When Yvain, who has returned ("by adventure" as the poet puts it) to the fountain of storms, faints of despair and unwittingly cuts himself on his own sword, the lion responds in keeping with his symbolic role. He wishes to accept the same death that he believes has killed Yvain:

> Il . . .
> . . . a talant, que il s'ocie
> De l'espee, don li est vis,
> Qu'ele et son buen seignor ocis. (ll. 3511–14)

In the same manner Christ, in taking on the Incarnation,

accepted the death that had killed Adam, the mortality of the flesh. This is the theological doctrine that underlies the figurative tradition according to which the wood of the cross comes from the tree of knowledge. The lion carefully lays the sword across a fallen log, buttressing its pommel against the trunk of a tree in order to run himself through. The sword across the fallen log forms a cross, as the act itself is filled with the meaning of Christ's sacrifice. Of course, suicide is the ultimate manifestation of despair, the unforgivable sin. If the lion embodies the attributes of Christ, how can he be guilty of despair? Two things can be said in this connection. First, the lion does not commit suicide, but only suffers the temptation. Even Christ, at the penultimate moment on the cross, cried out in despair. The miracle of the Crucifixion is that, in tasting the last dregs of mortality, even despair, Christ transcends it. Second, we must remember that we are dealing with a figurative narrative. Suicide here, then, is figurative too, and represents self-sacrifice. We should heed Augustine's warning not to judge according to the letter that which is to be understood according to the spirit.

Yvain's remorse when he wakes to find the lion on the brink of suicide is appropriate. Why should his own soul remain in his body to suffer the "martyrdom" of separation from his beloved, when he sees this other prepared to die for love of him? Whoever loses bliss through his own fault, he reasons, has only himself to blame: " 'Mout se doit bien haïr de mort' " (l. 3544). He deserves not even grace:

" . . . Qui ce pert par son mesfet,
N'est droiz, que buene avanture et." (ll. 3561–62)

Yvain's self-reproach accords with justice. He has failed to keep his promise to return to Laudine within the year. By the letter of their agreement, his banishment from her court is exactly just. Ideally, however, their agreement is not a contract of law, but a covenant of love, under which Yvain might hope not only for justice, but for mercy. Thus, even as Yvain judges himself guilty, the lion's selfless gesture is an emblem of the rule of mercy under the New Law of love. The Christian doctrine that provides the background against which we must read Yvain's soliloquy of remorse is the Pauline conception of the inadequacy of the Old Law. If man may be saved only through righteousness, by fulfilling the letter of the Law, then no one, not even Paul himself (he confesses modestly), is worthy of salvation. Only the miracle of grace can wipe away the inevitable stain of original sin, and make him eligible for salvation in spite of his innate unworthiness. Yvain's judgment of himself is shortsighted. Only so far as the Old Law is concerned is he correct that he who loses happiness ("buene avanture") through his own fault should not find it again. Christ's advent fulfilled the Law, saving man from the death that had been the just wages of sin, which Yvain contemplates as just self-punishment in this passage.

Yvain's discovery of Lunete imprisoned in the chapel at the fountain is not a new episode, but rather a thematic continuation of this last. Lunete (whose symbolic meaning here as the Church was discussed above) has been condemned to death. Yvain, whom Lunete accuses as the cause of her predicament, assures her that he will defend and save her from this judgment. We may read the episode of Lunete's redemption abstractly thus: the Church, that is to say man, is condemned to death on account of the sin of Adam (as Lunete suffers innocently for Yvain). Christ, the New Adam (like the spiritually renewed Yvain), redeems his Church from this mortal judgment by assuming the physical struggle through which its fate is determined. Significantly, as Lunete's champion, Yvain faces not one adversary, but three. If Lunete's sentence of death signifies the mortality of man, then her three adversaries must be the scripturally conventional triple enemy of man, the world, the flesh, and the devil.

That Yvain's sequence of combats in the second half of the romance represents his progressive achievement of spiritual as opposed to worldly honor, and thus his growing worthiness of Laudine's forgiveness and love, has been generally recognized by critics of the poem. It is more difficult to associate a precise moral value with each of the victories. Julian Harris suggests that the giant Harpin de la Montaingne is to be identified with pride ("The Role of the Lion," p. 1151). This seems correct. It is the first combat after Yvain's alliance with the lion, and indicates the knight's victory over pride not only because this was conventionally the first and root of the sins, but also because pride is obviously Yvain's principal weakness. Yvain in turn calls the giant's behavior pride (l. 4137), and vows to *humble* him (l. 4152). At the same time, Yvain has exhibited the contrary of pride in his demeanor at the castle. When the lord's wife and daughter try to fall at his feet, he prays that pride not rule him (ll. 3983–85). That the giant's threat is spiritual rather than physical is indicated by the numerological detail that Yvain is met at the castle by seven pages, and that the giant's outrages endanger the lord's seven children.

The spiritual character of Yvain's alliance with the lion is also underscored in this episode, in which for the first time he takes the name "li Chevaliers au Lion." Yvain gives the people of the castle hope, particularly because of the marvelous lion which lies at his feet like a lamb:

> . . . An buene esperance les met.
> Et tuit et totes l'an mercïent;
> Qu'an sa proesce mout se fïent
> Et mout cuident, qu'il soit prodon,
> Por la conpaignie au lion,
> Qui aussi doucement se gist
> Lez lui, come uns aigniaus feïst. (ll. 4006–12)

The faith and hope that they place in him suggest his role as their redeemer:

Por l'esperance, qu'an lui ont,
Se confortent et joie font,
N'onques puis duel ne demenerent. (ll. 4013–15)

Chrétien compares the lion to a lamb; both animals are conventional symbols of Christ, and they express in their different natures the duality of his mission, judgment and grace. When the lord of the castle presents Yvain to his wife and daughter, he indicates that the knight has been sent by God and "buene avanture" (l. 3973). Chrétien remarks that they would value Yvain a thousand times more if they knew his true worth. We understand that he is referring to the new worth of his spiritual knighthood, symbolized by the watchful lion. Thus, the prayer of the people that God defend Yvain in battle is answered through the agency of the lion, who comes to his rescue and makes it possible for him to deal the mortal blow to the giant, "li maufez, li anemis" (l. 4173).

Yvain's rescue of Lunete is also pervaded by the intimation that his is a divinely appointed mission. The change in his character from the beginning of the romance is exemplified in the restraint he shows when he sees Lunete bound before the pyre on which she is to be burned. Yvain "reins in" his heart, Chrétien tells us,

Si con l'an retient a grant painne
Au fort frain le cheval tirant. (ll. 4350–51)

Reason has assumed its rightful sovereignty over passion in his soul. By the same token, after the battle Yvain is concerned not about his own serious wounds, but only about his wounded companion, the lion. Chrétien, quite playfully, relates the lion to God as one of a trinity. Yvain puts "good faith" in two companions who are on his side, God and the Right, "Et son lion ne rehet mie" (l. 4336). Yvain repeats the idea that God and the Right are his allies in response to the seneschal's boastful warning to leave the field:

"Des se retient devers le droit,
Et Des et droiz a un se tienent;
Et quant il devers moi s'an vienent,
Donc ai je meillor conpaignie,
Que tu n'as, et meillor aïe." (ll. 4444–48)

To the seneschal's second warning that he leave Lunete to her fate, he replies that God would not let him abandon her:

"Ne place le saint Esperite!
. . . .
Ja Des ne m'an lest removoir,
Tant que je delivree l'aie!" (ll. 4468–71)

On his own, Yvain fights bravely and well, but he is about to be overcome by his triple adversary's superior strength when the lion rushes into the battle to aid him. Thus, the lion is the actual form in which the aid of God and the Right manifests itself, as Christ, whom the lion represents, is the actual manifestation in the world of the Trinity.

11
Redemption

In contrast to the spiritually renewed character of Yvain in the second half of the romance stands the figure of Gawain. Although he remains in the background throughout most of the poem, his presence is nonetheless pervasive, and turns out to be thematically more important than at first appears. He is seen first among the group of knights who have gathered to hear Calogrenant's marvelous tale of adventure. Yvain worries that Gawain will be given precedence over him in avenging Calogrenant's defeat. From the outset, then, Yvain and Gawain appear in competition for knightly honor. The nature of the honor they both pursue becomes clear when Gawain persuades his companion in arms to abandon his new wife to seek the worldly honor of the tournaments. We recall the ironical scene between the "sun" and the "moon" in which Gawain dedicates himself to Lunete's service. Both in his defense of Lunete and in his victory over the giant Harpin, Yvain has been doing Gawain's work for him. Lunete tells the unknown Knight of the Lion that only two men would dare challenge these three adversaries. One is Gawain, who has pledged himself to her defense, but is unfortunately busy chasing the Queen, who has been abducted through the bungling of Arthur and Kay. He allows the business of the worldly court to divert him from his knightly duty to charity—figuratively, the defense of the Church. The other knight who can defend Lunete—who *does* defend her though she does not recognize him—is Yvain. Gawain's pursuit of Guenivere and Meleagant prevents him also from defending his own kin, the family of his sister, from the outrageous predations of Harpin, and again Yvain's fortuitous arrival covers for Gawain's absence.

Yvain still seeks honor; his quest is to be restored to the graces of his wife, who *is* honor. But it is no longer the honor he sought with Gawain at the tournaments. First, it is the honor without which the knight cannot properly function. Thus, Yvain directs Gawain's nephews and niece to take the vanquished Harpin's dwarf prisoner to their uncle Gawain, and report to him how the Knight of the Lion has borne himself. Good works should be seen,

> Car por neant fet la bonté,
> Qui ne viaut qu'ele soit seüe. (ll. 4280–81)

Good works are shown abroad not to increase the glory of the doer, but to propagate charity and faith. Yvain does not want glory for himself. He tells them to call him simply "li Chevaliers au Lion," and to tell Gawain,

> "Qu'il me conoist bien et je lui,
> Et si ne set, qui je me sui." (ll. 4295–96)

The name he assumes acknowledges the aid of the lion (i. e., Christ), but Yvain takes no personal glory for himself. It is the honor of God he seeks.

Chrétien sets up Gawain as foil for Yvain; taken together, they represent opposing, although complementary ideals. That is, in the context of chivalry, worldly and spiritual glory are antagonistic ideals only so long as they are separate. In Yvain, as in Erec, we see these ideals reconciled. The romance climaxes logically with the combat between the two great knights, Gawain, knight of this world, and Yvain, knight of Christ. Just as Gawain has been too occupied with the foolish business of the worldly court to protect those for whom he is responsible, so he rashly agrees to defend the unjust elder daughter of Noire Espine in her attempt to disinherit the younger.

The younger daughter, too, asks Gawain to defend her. His equivocating rejection of her suit, however, has the ring of hypocrisy:

> . . . "Amie! an vain
> M'an priiez; car je nel puis feire;
> Que j'ai anpris un autre afeire,
> Que je ne leisseroie pas." (ll. 4768–71)

Arthur, according (as he says) to the law recognized in all courts, gives the younger sister forty days to seek a champion to defend her claim to her part of the inheritance. The elder sister is forced to acquiesce to the king's law.

The younger sister sets out in search of the Knight of the Lion, but she wanders through many lands without success. When she falls ill with sorrow, the servant girl of a friend takes up the quest. In the thematic context that centers around the meaning of Pentecost, commemoration of the giving of the Law, the hardships she endures in her wanderings take on the spiritual likeness of those endured by Israel in her wandering in the wilderness. During those forty years of exile, Moses was forty days on Mount Sinai to receive the Law from God. The servant wanders through dense forests, through nights so dark she cannot see the horse she rides on, through rain as heavy "as God can make it." The roads are so bad that often her horse is up to its saddle girth in mud (ll. 4839–54). The dispute, we must remember, is not between the two knights, but between the sisters. As the combat between Yvain and Gawain comes as the logical climax of Yvain's spiritual initiation and his perfection as a Christian knight, so does the dispute between the sisters come as the logical climax to the theme of Pentecost as the fullfillment of the Old Law by the grace of the New.

From the ninth century, the motif of the dispute between Church and Synagogue, or Old Law and New, appears with great frequency in both visual and literary art. Typically, this dispute is represented figuratively by two women. I have discussed the example from the *Queste del Saint Graal*. The earliest extant instance of the motif in literature, the *De Altercatione Ecclesiae et Synagogae Dialogus*, (*PL*, vol. 42, cols. 1131–40), attributed in the Middle Ages to St. Augustine, represents the dispute as precisely over the right to an inheritance, although between the two spouses of a rich lord, not his two daughters. The elder spouse, Synagogue, has been disinherited because she is charged with adultery, but she has usurped the inheritance of dominion over the gentiles from the younger spouse, Church. The tradition that proceeds from the *Altercatio* offers countless variations on this theme. For example, Pflaum cites the oldest French paraphrase of the Song of Songs, from the end of the eleventh century, in which Synagogue is a false pretender for the hand of the spouse, who is set aside in favor of Church, true bride of Christ.[1]

In visual art, we frequently find this motif represented by the juxtaposed figures of Church, crowned and holding a scepter, and Synagogue, whose crown and scepter are broken and falling. Margaret Schlauch asserts that there is no more conspicuous or consistently applied trait of the figure of Synagogue than blindness, usually represented by a blindfold.[2]

---

1. H. Pflaum, "Der allegorische Streit zwischen Synagoge und Kirche in der europäischen Dichtung des Mittelalters," *Archivum Romanicum* 18 (Florence, 1934) : 294ff.

2. Margaret Schlauch, "The Allegory of Church and Synagogue," *Speculum* 14 (1939) : 448–64.

This motif has its source in the commonplace figure of blindness or deafness applied to the refusal of the Jews to accept Christ as the Messiah. I have discussed this doctrinal theme in some detail above. In the present context, blindness indicates lifeless adherence to the letter of the law in contradiction of its spirit.

When the servant finally finds Yvain, he promises to aid the younger daughter of Noire Espine. He prays,

> "Or me doint Des eür et grace,
> Que je par sa buene avanture
> Puisse desresnier sa droiture!" (ll. 5104–6)

The double meaning of *avanture* is unmistakable. Happiness and grace indeed come to man through God's advent in the flesh, as Christ. Moreover, the advent of grace is precisely what is represented by the younger sister's victory over the elder, the victory of the New Law over the Old.

The phrase "buene avanture" is especially underscored by its juxtaposition with the castle of Pesme Avanture of the intervening episode. We have noted many pairs of antitypes in connection with the romances; here is another. It is generally recognized in the source studies that the setting of this episode, the castle of Pesme Avanture, derives from the Celtic land of the dead, associated with the Christian hell. A. C. L. Brown conjectures that "Nothing is easier than the transition from the Celtic Other World to the Christian Purgatory and Paradise. . . . The Happy Other World became confused with the Christian Earthly Paradise. This identification once under way, a connection with Purgatory, a place of punishment, would not be difficult" (*Iwain*, p. 122). Nor, we might add, would the further identification of the Other World with hell—given the proper context—be any more difficult.

Yvain sought honor at the fountain of storms, type of paradise. At Pesme Avanture, antitype of paradise, type of hell, he is warned by the people (whom he calls appropriately

"Janz sanz enor," l. 5136) that he can only find shame here:

> "Cist ostés vos fu anseigniez
> Por mal et por honte andurer." (ll. 5116–187)

That the shame and the evil of which they warn pertain rather to the soul than the body is hinted by the curiously gratuitous remark they add: " 'Ce porroit uns abes jurer' " (l. 5118).

In general, we observe a close relationship between type and antitype. Baptism is the door to the Church, the earthly paradise, but it involves a descent into hell; by the same token, the descent into hell is the only way to paradise. To the lady who warns him of the dangers of the castle, Yvain apologizes with irony for his "foolish heart."

> " . . . Mes fos cuers leanz me tire,
> Si ferai ce, que mes cuers viaut." (ll. 5176–77)

His heart's folly, however is the wisdom of God, for he undertakes this "heavy adventure" for love. The lady has explained that the warnings are for his own good, " 'Se tu le savoies antandre' " (l. 5147). Her admonishment is reminiscent of Calogrenant's, to listen and understand with the heart, and of the scriptural figure behind it of those "who have ears to hear." We may also be reminded of Calogrenant's tale "Non de s'enor, mes de sa honte," when the people tell Yvain that he will suffer such shame that he will never tell of it:

> "Hu! hu! maleüreus, ou vas?
> S'onques an ta vie trovas,
> Qui te feïst honte ne let,
> La, ou tu vas, t'an iert tant fet,
> Que ja par toi n'iert reconté." (ll. 5131–35)

When Yvain responds that his "foolish heart" leads him into this figurative hell, he indicates the Pauline paradox that love leads him there not to be shamed, but in imitation of Christ's "folly," as a redeemer.

As the castle is the antitype of the fountain of storms, so Yvain's arrival there evokes a response that presents itself as the antitype of the joy that attends the advent of a king to his city. The time of day adds to the ominous warning of those who watch his approach:

> . . . Li jorz aloit declinant.
> Au chastel vienent cheminant,
> Et les janz, qui venir les voient,
> Trestuit au chevalier disoient:
> "Mal veigniez, sire, mal veigniez!" (ll. 5111–15)

Yvain enters the castle to the ironic words of the porter:

> . . . "Venez tost, venez!
> An tel leu estes arivez,
> Ou vos seroiz bien retenuz,
> Et mal i soiiez vos venuz!" (ll. 5181–84)

Yvain's liberation of the three hundred maidens held as slaves in the castle of Pesme Avanture is properly seen as a type of Christ's liberation of Adam and his descendants from hell. Several details suggest that the maidens represent the inheritors of original sin. For the folly of another, they suffer exile from a land of innocence, the "Isle as Puceles." Their king, seeking "news" at various courts, has foolishly fallen into the power of the two demons of the castle, and has ransomed himself by pledging to send thirty maidens a year as slaves. His coming to this place was an unhappy one, exclaims the maiden to Yvain:

> "An mal eür i venist il!
> Que nos cheitives, qui ci somes,
> La honte et le mal an avomes,
> Qui onques ne le desservimes." (ll. 5262–65)

The maidens are employed weaving silk, and embroidering it with golden thread, although they themselves are given only rags to wear. Perhaps Chrétien intends to represent the connection I have discussed above between clothes and the Fall of Adam. On the one hand, clothes of gold-embroidered silk produced by slaves suggest the pride through which Lucifer fell, and after him Adam. On the other, the rags in which the maidens are dressed indicate the shame that original sin inflicts on its inheritors. The slavery itself represents the labor that Adam suffered as punishment for his sin, which devolves upon all his descendants.

As the sons of Adam were bound in hell until Christ subdued the power of death and Satan, so the maidens are bound in slavery "Tant con li dui maufé durroient" (l. 5287). Talk among them of liberation from their servitude is considered childish folly. But we recognize it as the "folly" that Paul preached as the Good News. Those who are "childish" enough to speak of deliverance (ll. 5295 97) have "become as little children," who shall "enter into the kingdom of heaven" (Matthew 18:3).

The relationship between the captive maidens and the lord of the castle is ambivalent. On the one hand, the lord reaps unjustly the fruits of their labor. On the other hand, he is bound to force all errant knights to fight the two demons, in whose power (although he calls them *his* men) he appears to be, and to keep his daughter unwed until they are defeated in battle. Thus, the lord of the castle is liberated by Yvain's victory too, and, together with his wife and daughter, suggests another aspect of Adam's heritage. Unredeemed man was bound in hell until he could be liberated by Christ. But in another sense, he is the promised spouse, awaiting the bridegroom, Christ. Chrétien weaves this figurative conception of salvation into his classical allegory when he returns to the figure of the god of love. His allegory is a parody of the doctrine of the Incarnation of the God who *is* love. The lord's daughter is so beautiful and graceful, he tells us, that the "God of Love" would put aside his divinity for the sake of her love. The daughter,

... estoit si bele et si jante,
Quan li servir meïst s'antante
Li Des d'Amors, s'il la veïst,
Ne ja amer ne la feïst
Autrui se lui meïsme non.
Por li servir devenist hon,
S'issist de sa deïté fors
Et ferist lui meïsme el cors
Del dart, don la plaie ne sainne.   (ll. 5375–83)

The dart with which the God of Love wounds himself for his bride's sake is the Crucifixion, which Christ took upon himself for the salvation of man. Appropriately, Yvain next morning hears mass "An l'enor del saint Esperite" (l. 5456), in honor of love itself.

The theme of Incarnation reappears after Yvain's victory; Chrétien tells us that the maidens' joy at their liberation was greater than if God should come to earth:

Je ne cuit pas, qu'eles feïssent
Tel joie, come eles li font,
De celui, qui fist tot le mont,
S'il fust venuz de ciel an terre.   (ll. 5780–83)

The ladies' enthusiasm is no sacrilege; typologically, their liberation and the liberation of man, when God, incarnate, "came from heaven to earth," are identical. Yvain's adventure at the castle of Pesme Avanture shows us the advent and Incarnation of Christ as they recur continually in the faith and works of the Christian in this life.

One other iconographic detail in this scene deserves comment. The lord and his wife lie on their sides in the castle garden as they listen to their daughter read aloud from a romance. Adam and Eve are shown in a similar reclining position in the well-known relief by Giselbertus in the horizontal panel of the lintel over the north portal at Autun.[3] That the sculptor intended the horizontality of the reclining position to express the spiritual condition of the Fall

---

3. See Denis Grivot, *Giselbertus; sculpteur d'Autun* (Paris, 1960), pp. 138–44; PLs. I (a)–I (e); Plan IX.

is suggested by the striking juxtaposition of the resurrection of Lazarus carved on the vertical column supporting the lintel. Here too, the reclining position of the lord and his wife indicates their unredeemed condition in the figurative hell of Pesme Avanture. And a garden is where we would expect Adam and Eve to be.

Yvain's victory over the two demons, typologically related to Death and Satan, shows us the freeing of the descendants of Adam from the bondage of the Old Law, that is, from justice without mercy. As in his previous battles, Yvain is not able to achieve victory without the lion, whose aid expresses figuratively that human nature is unable without the aid of grace to overcome the consequences of the Fall, sin and death. As it is grace that aids Yvain, so he himself exhibits mercy. When one of the demons, mortally wounded, begs for mercy, Yvain, who has in any case come to relieve him from further attacks by the lion, freely grants it. Likewise, when the people of the castle beg their liberator's pardon for their rude welcome, Yvain answers graciously,

> "Je ne sai," fet il, "que vos dites,
> Et si vos an claim trestoz quites;
> Qu'onques chose, que a mal taingne,
> Ne deïstes, don moi sovaigne." (ll. 5789–92)

The judicial combat between Yvain and Gawain over the claim of the younger sister to her share of the legacy of Noire Espine appropriately climaxes the development of the theme of fulfillment of the Old Law. The new spirituality that it signals, which we have seen develop in Yvain, pervades the entire court. As Yvain's quest has shifted from worldly to heavenly honor, so does Arthur seem to have grown from a foolish to a wise king. His handling of the judgment between the two sisters is strikingly reminiscent of the exemplary judgment of the paragon of wise kings, Solomon. When two women come before Solomon, both claiming the same child, he orders that the child be cut in two and divided equally between them. The incisive king knows the true mother of the child is the one who begs that it be given whole to the other woman rather than let it be slain.

The sisters agree at least to abide by Arthur's judgment. He pledges that he will decide the dispute "in good faith," but like Solomon, he settles it by means of a ruse. Nowhere does the Pauline distinction between letter and spirit more obviously underlie the story than in this episode. For the ruse works by what seems superficially to be an outrageous adherence to the letter in contradiction of what is clearly the elder sister's intention. But paradoxically, this ruse, like the apparently literal-minded judgment of Solomon, actually serves to reveal the elder sister's real motives. Arthur asks with a straight face,

> "Ou est . . . la dameisele,
> Qui sa seror a fors botee
> De sa terre et deseritee
> Par force et par male merci?" (ll. 6384–87)

Although the elder sister does not mean to condemn herself "out of her own mouth," she inadvertently takes Arthur's bait, and replies, "Sire! . . . je sui ci" (l. 6388). Arthur has tricked her into confessing her guilt, of which he has been aware all along:

> "Bien le savoie grant pieç'a,
> Que vos la deseritiiez." (ll. 6390–91)

Christ establishes the principle that whoever refuses to accept the New Law, law of spirit and forgiveness, shall be judged according to the letter of the Old Law. On this principle, Arthur is justified in holding the elder sister to the confession she has let slip in this verbal trap. But the real wisdom of Arthur's maneuver is that spirit and letter are not separate, but are unified in her confession. His judg-

242   THE ALLEGORY OF ADVENTURE

ment prohibits her from interfering with her sister's legacy
again:

> "Ses droiz ne sera mes noiiez;
> Que coneü m'avez le voir.
> Sa partie par estovoir
> Vos covient tote clamer quite." (ll. 6392–95)

The elder sister protests this judgment, of course. Arthur ought not to take literally ("prandre a parole") something whose spirit was obviously different. A king, she says,
ought to beware committing an injustice. But Arthur has
the insight to see through the captious legalism of her argument; he knows that the spirit of truth has given the lie
to her intentions.

> "Sire!," fet ele, "se j'ai dite
> Une response nice et fole,
> Ne me devez prandre a parole.
> Por De! sire, ne me grevez!
> Vos estes rois, si vos devez
> De tort garder et de mesprandre." (ll. 6396–6401)

Again her mouth betrays her intentions. Because a king
should do no wrong, Arthur judges in favor of the younger
sister:

> "Por ce," fet li rois, "vuel je randre
> A vostre seror sa droiture;
> Que je n'oi onques de tort cure." (ll. 6402–4)

Also reminiscent of Solomon's ruse is Arthur's threat to
declare Gawain vanquished in arms, thus shaming him on
the elder sister's account unless she voluntarily cedes to his
judgment. He has no intention of actually making such a
declaration (which would be "against his heart"), but he
knows that only fear (like the bulls' fear of the wild herdsman) will make her submit to his will:

> . . . Nel deïst il a nul fuer;
> Mes il le dist por essaiier,
> S'il la porroit tant esmaiier,
> Qu'ele randist a sa seror
> Son heritage par peor;
> Qu'il s'est aparceüz mout bien,
> Que ele ne l'an randist rien
> Por quanque dire li seüst,
> Se force ou crieme n'i eüst.   (ll. 6420–28)

Reluctantly, she accedes to the king's demand, not because she accepts its justice, but because she fears to do otherwise:

> Por ce qu'ele le dote et crient,
> Li dit: "Biaus sire! or me covient
> Que je face vostre talant,
> Mes mout an ai le cuer dolant."   (ll. 6429–32)

In contrast to her elder sister, who respects only the force of the letter of the Law, the younger daughter is concerned more with the spirit of her father's testament than with the actual property itself. She loves her sister in spite of the wrong she has done her, and asks no more than her just share. In fact, earlier she has even offered out of love to give her sister part of her inheritance if only she will acknowledge her right to it. But she refuses to yield to force:

> " . . . Avoir porroit ele del mien
> Par amor, s'ele an voloit rien;
> Que ja par force, que je puisse,
> Por qu'aïe ne consoil truisse,
> Ne li leirai mon heritage!"   (ll. 4781–85)

The gracious attitude of the younger sister expresses the important theological idea that the New Law does not destroy or replace the Old, but rather fulfills and continues it. Her conciliatory gesture, however, is parried with her sister's sardonic reply,

> "Maus feus et male flame m'arde,
> Se je te doing, don miauz te vives!"   (ll. 5978–79)

Of course she has it backwards. If indeed she escapes the fires of hell that she conjures so casually, it will be on account of her younger sister's graciousness, not her own deserts.

The scriptural parallel to this episode is particularly fitting because of the conventional exegesis of the story of Solomon and the two women. We may take the *Glossa Ordinaria* as exemplary of patristic tradition; there, we are shown in the wise judgment of Solomon an allegory of the victory of Church, true claimant to its child, the soul of man, over Synagogue (*PL,* vol. 113, cols. 582–83).

One of the devices on which the episode of judicial combat depends is the concealment from each knight of the other's identity. But this device has thematic implications also. The motif of concealment and discovery is closely related to the theme of vision (spiritual understanding); the concealment of the knights' identities reflects the relationship between Old Law and New. The allegorical figure of Synagogue is typically blind to express the idea that the unconverted Jews cannot (or will not) see the truth of the fulfillment of the messianic prophecies. From the Christian point of view, however, the two Laws are not in conflict. If only the Jews will see the truth, remove the veil from their eyes, they will recognize the relationship of love between "Christians" and "Jews." Because they do not recognize Christ, they mistakenly believe that there is enmity between the two Laws.

Similarly, Yvain and Gawain believe they hate each other only because they fail to recognize each other. At the beginning of the romance, Yvain finds himself enmeshed in the paradox that he loves his enemy, whom he should hate. Now Chrétien expresses the predicament of the combatant knights in terms of a similar paradox. Do these two warring knights still love each other? the poet asks. Yes and no, he answers:

> Mes ne s'antreconoissent mie
> Cil, qui conbatre se voloient,

Qui mout antramer se soloient.
Et or don ne s'antraimment il?
"Oïl" vos respong et "nenil." (ll. 5998–6002)

If they were to recognize each other, each would rejoice in the fellowship of the other, and would risk his own life for him. Not recognizing each other, however, each wishes to shame and injure the other. How, asks Chrétien, can Love and Hate be found together in a single vessel? How can two such contraries lodge in the same mansion? The answer that Chrétien works out in his whimsical allegory is that the house may have many rooms, some of them secret, where Love may conceal herself from Hate and avoid strife, while Hate, who wishes rather to be seen, shows herself from the open gallery. Chrétien challenges Love to reveal herself:

Ha! Amors, ou es tu reposte?
Car t'an is! si verras, quel oste
Ont sor toi amené et mis
Li anemi a tes amis. (ll. 6045–48)

The enemies of the friends of Love are "these same, who love each other in holy Love":

Li anemi sont cil meïsme,
Qui s'antraimment d'Amor saintisme;
Qu'amors, qui n'est fausse ne fainte,
Est precïeuse chose et sainte. (ll. 6049–52)

In an undertone, Chrétien has indicated the solution to the paradox; the real enemies of the allegory are not Love and Hate, but rather the Love that hides herself, and the Holy Love, "Amor saintisme," which makes both Yvain and Gawain the enemies of its contrary. The love that hides herself is worldly love, and in fact is more closely akin to hate than to true love. Thus, it dwells appropriately in the same mansion with hate. Both Love and Hate, the poet tells us, are blind. This attribute is doubly appropriate because of the typical blindness of Synagogue and of the classical god of love from which the figure itself derives (see Panofsky, "Blind Cupid"). Love has eyes but sees not:

> Ci est Amors avugle tote,
> Et Haïne ne revoit gote;
> Qu'Amors deffandre lor deüst,
> Se ele les reconeüst,
> Que li uns l'autre n'adesast
> Ne feïst rien, que li pesast.
> Por ce est Amors avuglee
> Et desconfite et desjuglee,
> Que çaus, qui tot sont suen a droit,
> Ne reconoist, et si les voit. (ll. 6053–62)

Chrétien would hardly call "Holy Love" "completely blind," although the strategy of his irony is to lure his audience momentarily into that trap. Actually, he is distinguishing between the love that is blind and the love that sees. True love is holy inasmuch as it reflects the love that moved God to take human form. Worldly love, on the other hand, is blinded to spiritual realities by its pursuit, for example, of worldly honor, like the knights', or its pursuit of power and wealth, like the elder sister's. The whimsical allegory of "Love" and "Hate" that Chrétien inserts in what would seem rather the most dramatic and climactic battle of the romance expresses the inadequacy of merely earthly love, whether the passionate love of a woman or the pursuit of glory or the camaraderie of knighthood. In the apparent strife of *Amor* and *Haïne,* Chrétien points to the far more significant opposition between worldly *Amor* and *Amor Saintisme;* the outcome of the judicial combat shows us the ultimate victory of Holy Love over the blind passion that would destroy both the knights.

The happy outcome stems from the love that binds Yvain and Gawain together. It is clear, however, that true love comes first to Yvain, and that Gawain is converted from his pursuit of worldly glory only after the truce. It is Yvain who asks that they rest for the night and resume fighting in the morning, and it is he who asks his adversary's name. Once their names are revealed, they recognize their true relationship. Gawain freely admits the injustice of the cause for which he has fought. Not only because of Yvain's greater prowess, but also because of the wrongness of the elder sister's claim, Gawain concedes, Yvain would have killed him had they continued the battle.

Yvain graciously argues that he has not vanquished his comrade, rather that he himself has been vanquished. But Arthur demonstrates by his subtle judgment that he is now wise enough to know that, even though the elder sister is wrong, *both* knights, in discovering their love, have really won. Thus, although he threatens to declare Gawain vanquished, it would be against his own heart's wishes, and Chrétien assures us that he has no intention of actually doing so. The elder sister accedes, and no judgment between the knights is ever made. As comrades in arms they retire from the field of battle.

The implied theme of the victory of Church over Synagogue, or of New Law over Old, has less to do with ecclesiastical history than with the spiritual development of Yvain himself. Yvain's victory expresses his new spiritual condition, and is in some sense equivalent to the whole series of acts of charity by which, throughout the second half of the romance, he has perfected himself. His perfection—the shift in values from the pursuit of worldly to the pursuit of spiritual adventure and honor—frees him from subjection to the Old Law, law of righteousness, justice, and retribution. Because he has shown mercy, he is eligible to receive mercy (not bare justice) from Laudine. He has made a covenant with her and broken it. So long as he pursued the honor of the flesh, he could expect only the letter of their agreement, banishment. Having sown mercy, he can also reap it.

Chrétien's irony in having Lunete trap Laudine with a verbal ruse similar to Arthur's is based once again on the

distinction between spirit and letter. Yvain returns to the
magic fountain and in desperation throws water on the stone
to cause a storm, since he has no better idea how to achieve
reconciliation with his lady. We know, however, that this is
not a random act at all, but is figurative of the penance
that Yvain has imposed on himself. Laudine, unaware that
it is Yvain who has caused the storm in her land, asks Lunete how she shall defend her fountain. Lunete knows at
least the true identity of the Knight of the Lion, and makes
Laudine swear an oath that she will do all in her power—
in return for the knight's defense of the fountain—to restore him to the graces of his lady, whoever she might be.
Lunete makes her mistress swear on her knees over a rel-
iquary, which sanctifies the oath,

> "Einsi m'aït Des et li sainz,
> . . . .
> L'amor li randrai et la grace,
> Que il siaut a sa dame avoir,
> Se j'an ai force ne pooir." (ll. 6653–58)

When Yvain comes before her and reveals his identity
(and thus the identity of his lady), Lunete insists that her
mistress abide by the letter of their agreement, as Laudine
has banished Yvain according to the letter of theirs. But
the *letter* of the oath is perfectly true to the *spirit* of the
Amor Saintisme that Yvain, unbeknownst to his wife, has
achieved through his trials and good works. Allegorically,
Laudine's love must be understood to represent now the
grace to which Yvain, through his conversion, has become
eligible. Lunete has assured Laudine of her ability to effect
the peace that the Knight of the Lion seeks; the peace is,
of course, her own love, which she has unwittingly promised,
"sanz guile et sanz feintise" (l. 6619). Lunete's trickery,
however, is only apparent, only literal as it were; it cannot
ultimately affect the genuine spiritual substance of Laudine's
love for her spouse, to which it is in any case true.

Laudine objects vigorously at first to the ruse, but Yvain soothes her wrath by appealing to her mercy. He is, he declares, a penitent sinner, and such ought never to be refused forgiveness:

> . . . "Dame! misericorde
> Doit an de pecheor avoir.
> Conparé ai mon fol savoir,
> Et je le doi bien conparer.
> Folie me fist demorer,
> Si m'an rant coupable et forfet.
> Et mout grant hardemant ai fet,
> Quant devant vos osai venir;
> Mes s'or me volez retenir,
> Ja mes ne vos mesferai rien." (ll. 6780–89)

Since grace descended on the first Christian Pentecost, penitence has been the only requirement for mercy, and Yvain as it were acknowledges the correct source of it, the Holy Spirit, as he thanks Laudine for relenting:

> "Dame!," fet il, "cinc çanz merciz!
> Einsi m'aït sainz Esperiz,
> Que Des an cest siecle mortel
> Ne me porroit lié feire d'el!" (ll. 6795–98)

Taken at face value—taken literally—Yvain's oath expresses the meaning of the romance. If Laudine's love is truly the greatest joy Yvain can know, it must be equivalent to grace, at once the greatest joy in this world and the transcendence of it.

Yvain's love at the end of the romance is equivalent to his quest for salvation, as his love in the beginning is equivalent to his quest for status. Love and adventure are the subject of the romance, but its development reveals the conversion of courtly to spiritual values. Yvain, proud knight of Arthur's court seeking adventure, rides into the world of the magic fountain, and can never successfully return to the world of merely courtly values. In the adventure at the fountain, he undergoes spiritual initiation, and although he is lured away from his new spouse, Yvain knows the value of what he has lost when Lunete shames him with his negligence. His lapse into despair and insanity is actually the way toward perfection. At the close of the romance Yvain, Knight of the Lion, whose desire once was merely to be the greatest knight at Arthur's court, has become the perfect knight of Christ, whose obligation is no longer to glory, but to love.

Bibliography

Alanus de Insulis. *Distinctiones Dictionum Theologicum.* Edited by J. P. Migne. *Patrologiae cursus completus, Series latina.* Paris, 1844. vol. 210. Hereafter, Migne's *Patrologiae* will be abbreviated as *PL.*

————. *De planctu naturae. PL.* vol. 210, cols. 429–82.

————. *The Complaint of Nature.* Translated by Douglas M. Moffat, Yale Studies in English. New York, 1908.

Allen, D. C. *Image and Meaning.* Baltimore, Md., 1960.

Ambrose, St. *Expositio psalmi CXVIII. PL.* vol. 15, cols. 1197–1526.

————. *Hexameron. PL.* vol. 16, cols. 123–274.

————. *De mysteriis. PL.* vol. 16, cols. 389–410.

————. *De sacramentis. PL.* vol 16, cols. 417–62.

Auerbach, Erich. *Mimesis: The Representation of Reality in Western Literature.* Translated by Willard Trask. Garden City, N. Y., 1957.

Augustine, St., *The City of God.*

————. *De doctrina christiana. PL.* vol. 34, cols. 15–122.

————. *Ennaratio in psalmum CXXV, PL.* vol. 37, cols. 1656–67.

————. *On Christian Doctrine.* Translated by D. W. Robertson, Jr. New York, 1958.

Baisier, Léon. *The Lapidaire Chrétien, Its Composition, Its Influence, Its Sources.* Washington, D. C., 1936.

Barfield, Owen. *Poetic Diction: A Study in Meaning.* New York, 1964.

Bayrav, Süheyla. *Symbolisme Médiéval. Béroul, Marie, Chrétien.* Istanbul, 1957.

Bede. Commentary on Psalm 41. *PL.* vol. 93.

————. *In Marci Evangelium Expositio,* Bedae Venerabilis Opera. Pars II Opera Exegetica 3, Corpus Christianorum, series Latina. vol. 120. Tourhout, 1960.

Beowulf. Edited by Fr. Klaeber. Boston, 1922.

Bestiary, The. Translated by T. H. White. New York. 1954.

Boethius. *The Consolation of Philosophy.* Translated by Richard Green (Indianapolis, Ind., 1963).

Bradley, C. H. M., Sister Ritamary. "Backgrounds of the Title *Speculum* in Medieval Literature." *Speculum* 29 (1954): 100–115.

Brown, Arthur C. L. *Iwain: A Study in the Origins of Arthurian Romance,* Studies and Notes in Philology and Literature. vol. 8. Boston, 1903.

Capellanus, Andreas. *The Art of Courtly Love.* Translated by John Jay Parry. New York, 1957.

Catholic Encyclopaedia. 16 vols. New York, 1908.

Chrétien de Troyes. *Arthurian Romances.* Translated by W. W. Comfort. London and New York, 1914.

————. *Erec et Enide.* Edited by Wendelin Foerster. Halle, 1934.

————. *Le Roman de Perceval* ou *Le Conte du Graal.* Edited by William Roach. Textes Littéraires Français. Geneva and Paris, 1959.

————. *Yvain.* Edited by Wendelin Foerster and T. B. W. Reid. Manchester, England, 1942.

————. *Le Chevalier au Lion* (*Yvain*). *Les Romans de Chrétien de Troyes.* vol. 4. Edited by Mario Roques. Les Classiques Français du Moyen Age. Paris, 1960.

Cigada, S. "La Legende medievale del Cervo Bianco e le origini della 'matiere de Bretagne.' " *Atti della Accademia Nazionale die Lincei.* Memorie, classe di scienze morali, storiche e filologiche. series 8, vol. 12. 1965.

Cohen, Gustave. *Un grand romancier d'amour et d'aventure au XII⁰ siècle, Chrétien de Troyes et son oeuvre.* Paris, 1948.

Curtius, Ernst Robert. *European Literature and the Latin Middle Ages.* Translated by Willard R. Trask. New York, 1963.

Daniélou. Jean. *The Bible and the Liturgy.* Notre Dame, Ind., 1956.

———. "Circoncision et Baptême." *Theologie in Geschichte und Gegenwart* (Festschrift für Michael Schmaus) . Munich, 1957.

———. *From Shadows to Reality.* London, 1960.

———. "The Sacraments and the History of Salvation." *The Liturgy and the Word of God.* Collegeville, Minn., 1959.

———. "La symbolisme des rites baptismaux." *Dieu Vivant* (1945) , p. 1.

Dante Alighieri. *A Translation of Dante's Eleven Letters.* Translated by Charles Sterrett Latham. Edited by George Rice Carpenter. Boston, 1891.

Davies, J. G. *The Architectural Setting of Baptism.* London, 1962.

De Lage, Raynaud. *Alain De Lille: Poète du XII⁰ Siècle.* Montreal and Paris, 1951.

DeWald, E. T. *The Illustrations of the Utrecht Psalter.* Princeton, N. J., London and Leipzig.

Dictionnaire D'Archéologie Chrétienne et de Liturgie. Edited by dom Fernand Cabrol. 15 vols. Paris, 1910.

Dix, Gregory. *The Shape of the Liturgy.* Glasgow, 1945.

Dodd, C. H. *The Parables of the Kingdom.* New York, 1963.

Donovan, Mortimer J. "Priscian and the Obscurity of the Ancients." Speculum 36 (1961) : 75–80.

Faral, E. *Légende Arturienne.* Paris, 1929.

Frappier, Jean. *Chrétien de Troyes, L'homme et l'oeuvre.* Paris, 1957.

Gilson, Étienne. "La cosmogonie de Bernardus Silvestris." *Archives d'histoire doctrinale et littéraire du Moyen Age 3.* Paris, 1928.

Glossa ordinaria. PL. vols. 113–14.

Godefroy, Frédéric. *Dictionnaire de L'Ancienne Langue Française.* 10 vols. Paris, 1881.

Goldin, Frederick. *The Mirror of Narcissus in the Courtly Love Lyric.* Ithaca, N. Y., 1967.

Grivot, Denis. *Giselbertus; sculpteur d'Autun.* Paris, 1960.

Guyer, Foster Erwin. *Romance in the Making.* New York, 1954.

Hall, Robert A., Jr. "The Silk Factory in Chrestien de Troyes' *Yvain.*" *Modern Language Notes* 56 (1941) : 418–22.

Harris, Julian. "The Role of the Lion in Chrétien de Troyes' *Yvain. PMLA* 66 (1949) : 1143–63.

Harris, R. "The White Stag in Chrétien's *Erec et Enide.*" *French Studies* 10 (1956) : 55–61.

Hartlaub, G. F. *Zauber des Spiegels: Geschichte und Bedeutung des Spiegels in der Kunst.* Munich, 1951.

Hauser, Arnold. *The Social History of Art.* Translated by Stanley Godman. New York, 1952.

Helsinger, Howard. *"The Book of the Duchess* and the Hunt of the Hart."* Ph.D. dissertation. Princeton, N. J., 1970.

Henry, Françoise. *Irish High Crosses.* Dublin, 1964.

Holland, W. H. *Crestien von Troies.* Tübingen, 1854.

Holmes, Urban T., Jr., and Klenke, Sister M. Amelia. *Chrètien, Troyes, and the Grail.* Chapel Hill, N. C., 1959.

Huon de Mery. *Li Tornoiemenz Antecrit.* Edited by Georg Wimmer. *Ausgaben und Abhandlungen aus dem Gebiete der romanischen Philologie* 76. Marburg, 1888.

Huppé, Bernard F., and Robertson, D. W., Jr. *Fruyt and Chaf: Studies in Chaucer's Allegories.* Princeton, N. J., 1963.

Javelet, Robert. *Image et Ressemblance au douzième siècle de Saint Anselm à Alain de Lille.* Strasbourg, 1967.

Jewish Encyclopaedia. 12 vols. New York, 1901.

Kantorowicz, Ernst H. "The King's Advent." *Art Bulletin* 26 (1944) : 207–31.

Kölbing, E. "Christian von Troyes *Yvain* und die Brandanuslegende." *Zeitschrift für vergleichende Litteraturgeschichte* 11 (1897) : 442–48.

Kosnetter, J. *Die Taufe Jesu.* Vienna, 1936.

Krautheimer, Richard. "Introduction to an 'Iconography of Medieval Architecture.'" *Journal of the Warburg and Courtauld Institutes* 5 (1942) : 1–34.

Lampe, G. W. H. *The Seal of the Spirit*. London, 1951.

Leisegang, Hans. "La connaissance de Dieu au miroir de l'âme et de le nature." *Revue d'Histoire et de Philosophie réligieuses* 17 (1937) : 145–71.

Lewis, C. S. *The Allegory of Love*. New York, 1958.

Loomis, C. Grant. "King Arthur and the Saints." *Speculum* 8 (1933) : 478–80.

Loomis, Roger Sherman. *Arthurian Legend in Medieval Art*. New York, 1938.

————. *Arthurian Tradition and Chrétien de Troyes*. New York, 1949.

————. "Calogrenanz and Chrétien's Originality." *Modern Language Notes* 43 (1928) : 215–23.

de Lubac, Henri. *Exégèse Médiévale*. Paris, 1959.

Lovejoy, Arthur O. *The Great Chain of Being*. New York, 1960.

Luria, Maxwell S. "The Christian Tempest." Ph.D. dissertation. Princeton, N. J., 1965.

————. "The Storm-making Spring and the Meaning of Chrétien's *Yvain*." *Studies in Philology* 64 (July, 1967) : 564–85.

Malory, Sir Thomas. *Works*. Edited by E. Vinaver. London, 1964.

Marie de France. *Lais*. Edited by Karl Warnke. Halle, 1885.

Morawski, Joseph, ed. *Proverbes Français Antérieurs au XVᵉ Siècle*. Les Classiques Français du Moyen Age. Paris, 1925.

Muscatine, Charles. *Chaucer and the French Tradition*. Berkeley, Calif., 1957.

Nitze, W. A. "*Sans et matière* dans les oeuvres de Chrétien de Troyes." *Romania* 44 (1915–17) : 14–36.

————. "Yvain and the Myth of the Fountain." *Speculum* 30 (1955) : 170–79.

O'Connell, J. *Church Building and Furnishing: The Church's Way*. London, 1955.

Painter, Sidney. *French Chivalry*. Baltimore, Md. 1940.

Panofsky, Erwin. *Studies in Iconology*. New York, 1939.

Peter Lombard. *Commentarium in psalmum XLI. PL.* vol. 191, cols. 413–24.

Pflaum, H. "Der allegorische Streit zwischen Synogoge und Kirche in der europäischen Dichtung des Mittelalters." *Archivum Romanicum* 18 (Florence, 1934) : 243–340.

Plato. *Timaeus.* Edited and translated by Francis M. Cornford. Indianapolis, Ind., 1959.

Pschmadt, Carl. *Die Sage von der verfolgten Hinde.* Greifswald, 1911.

La Queste Del Saint Graal. Edited by Albert Pauphilet. Classiques Français du Moyen Age. Paris, 1923.

Rahner, Hugo. "Mysterium lunae." *Zeitschrift für Katholische Theologie.* 1939, pp. 311–49, 428–42; 1940, pp. 61–80, 121–31.

Reason, Joseph H. *An Inquiry into the Structural Style and Originality of Chrestien's Yvain.* Studies in Romance Languages and Literature. vol. 57. Washington, 1958.

Robertson, D. W., Jr. "The Doctrine of Charity in Medieval Literary Gardens." *Speculum* 26 (1951) : 24–49.

———. "Marie de France, *Lais.* Prologue, 13–16." *Modern Language Notes* 44 (1949) : 336–38.

———. *A Preface to Chaucer.* Princeton, N. J., 1962.

———. "Some Medieval Literary Terminology with Special Reference to Chrétien de Troyes." *Studies in Philology* 48 (1951) : 669–92.

———. "Translator's Introduction." St. Augustine, *On Christian Doctrine.* New York, 1958.

Rydbeck, Monica. *Skånes Stenmästare före 1200.* Lund, 1936.

Schlauch, Margaret. "The Allegory of Church and Synagogue." *Speculum* 14 (1939) : 448–64.

Schneider, Hans. *Sir Gawain and the Green Knight.* Cooper Monographs. Bern, 1961.

Silvestris, Bernard. *De mundi universitate.* Edited by Carl Sigmund Barach and Johann Wrobel. Innsbruck, 1876.

Smith, E. Baldwin. *Architectural Symbolism of Imperial Rome and the Middle Ages.* Princeton, N. J., 1956.

———. *The Dome.* Princeton, N. J., 1950.

Spicq, C. *Esquisse d'une histoire de l'exégèse latine au moyen age.* Paris, 1944.

Spitzer, Leo. "The Prologue to the *Lais* of Marie de France and Medieval Poetics." *Modern Philology* 41 (1943-44) : 96–102.

Strunk, Oliver, ed. *Source Readings in Music History: Antiquity and the Middle Ages.* New York, 1965.

Tertullian. *De Baptismo.* Translated by E. Evans. London, 1964.

Tresmontant, Claude. *Saint Paul.* Translated by Donald Attwater. Men of Wisdom Books. New York and London, 1957.

Tuve, Rosemond. *Allegorical Imagery: Some Medieval Books and their Posterity.* Princeton, N. J., 1966.

Tynell, Lars. *Skånes Medeltida Dopfuntar.* Stockholm, 1913.

Underwood, Paul A. "The Fountain of Life in Manuscripts of the Gospels." *Dumbarton Oaks Papers,* no. 5 (Harvard, Mass., 1950) , pp. 43–138.

von Simson, Otto. *The Gothic Cathedral.* New York, 1962.

Wace, *Roman de Rou.* Edited by Hugo Andresen (Heilbronn, 1879) .

Zenker, Rudolf. *Forschungen zur Artusepik: I. Ivainstudien, Beihefte zur Zeitschrift für romanische Philologie* 70 (1921) .

Index

259

ꞋUF